MW01410086

Fly-Fishing STILLWATERS *for* TROPHY TROUT

By Denny Rickards

A Stillwater Productions Publication,
Terry W. Sheely, Editor

Forward . . .
By Lani Waller

I can still remember the first time I met Denny Rickards. He was sitting in a booth at a west coast fly-fishing show, and my eyes were drawn to a wooden tray of trout flies he had on a table in front of him.

They were some of the most beautifully tied patterns I had ever seen. Slivers of translucent dubbing were magically intertwined with traces of silk and rayon floss; silver and gold ribbing glistened from some of them, and all had an appearance which spoke of a genuine understanding and mastery of the craft.

"This guy is the real thing," I thought to myself, although neither of us said much, if anything, to one another. I simply walked away, making a note to return.

As it turned out I did return and eventually learned that this man was indeed the genuine article. His stories of legendary-sized trout and the techniques needed to successfully take such creatures were fascinating to me.

In the years since, I have always seen Denny sitting in perhaps the same booth, always smiling quietly and as always, sitting with his box of magic flies--which always include some new creation taken from yet another lesson learned on the water.

I know he is a fine angler. He is also a real gentleman. It has been an honor to know him and to have the opportunity to listen to him and to learn from him.

This book you are about to read is quite special. I know even before reading it that it comes from the heart and imagination of a poet of lakes and trout. In his words and ideas are the things that string trout fishing together like a wonderful strand of magical pearls.

All the best to Denny and the sport he loves so much.

Lani Waller

Lani Waller
Sausalito, CA

Photo: Ray Beadle

Denny Rickards

v

ACKNOWLEDGMENTS

To Mom and Dad, for allowing me to fish instead of moving the wood pile.
To Rob Steele, Gerald Steward, Dave Nolte, Tom Biscotti and Hap Scollan, for the help, laughs and sharing of ideas that were a big part of my early learning.
To Jay Fair, for dying my marabou saddle hackles and feathers colors unavailable anywhere else on this planet.

To Ray Gustad, for the many good times and big rainbows we shared together while operating Rocky Point Resort.
To Ed Rice, who provided the opportunity for exposure for me, this book and all of the other projects with which I'm associated.
And especially to my wife Gail, whose sacrifices and inspiration made this book possible.

Dedication

This book is dedicated to the memory of my close friend and fishing buddy, Hap Scollan, whose love and enthusiasm for stillwaters and big trout was contagious.

--Denny Rickards

Hap Scollan

VIII

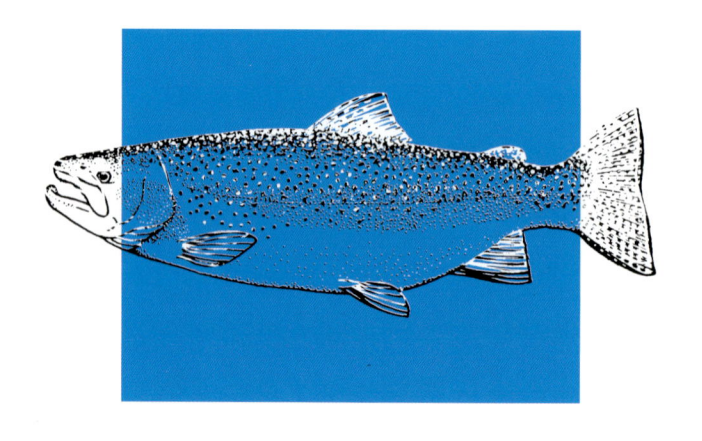

Fly-Fishing STILLWATERS *for* TROPHY TROUT

•

THE STILLWATER SYSTEM
A Fly Fisher's Comprehensive
Guide To Catching Giant Trout
In Lakes and Ponds

By
Denny Rickards

•

Edited By Terry W. Sheely
Illustrations & Original Artwork
By Dan Rickards, Clearwater Studios
Fly Plate Photos By Steve Probasco
All Uncredited Photos By Denny Rickards

A Stillwater Productions
Publication
PO Box 470
Fort Klamath, Oregon 97626

Copyright 1997 • Stillwater Productions • Denny Rickards
Printed in Hong Kong
Book Design: Nancy L. Doerrfeld-Smith
Front Cover: David Freel of Eagle Point, Oregon and the result of Denny Rickard's Stillwater System © 1997. First Edition. Stillwater Productions. All rights reserved. No part of this book may be used or reproduced in any manner without written permission, except for brief quotations utilized in review material.

Library of Congress Cataloging-In-Publication Data
ISBN 0-9656458-0-0

Author nets a bigger than average Montana brown.
[Sheely Photos]

TABLE OF CONTENTS

INTRODUCTION XII

CHAPTER 1 .... PG 1
LAKE TYPES AND THEIR DIFFERENCES
Sorting Out Trophy Waters

CHAPTER 2 .... PG 13
THE KEY FOOD SOURCES FOR TROPHY TROUT
Understanding The Feeding Habits Of Stillwater Trout

CHAPTER 3 .... PG 27
THE SUCCESSFUL PURSUIT OF TROPHY TROUT
Big Trout Demand Practice And A Plan

CHAPTER 4 .... PG 35
THE SIX KEYS TO SUCCESS ON STILLWATER
Evolution Of A Big Fish Specialist

CHAPTER 5 .... PG 37
SELECTING STILLWATER TACKLE FOR TROPHY TROUT
Rods, Reels and Lines For Big Fish

CHAPTER 6 .... PG 47
DEVELOPING STILLWATER PATTERNS
Speciality Flies That Attract Big Trout
   a. Suggestive Nymphs For Stillwater
   b. Dry Flies For Stillwater
   c. Streamer Patterns For Predatory Anglers

CHAPTER 7 .... PG 79
CASTING FOR DISTANCE
A Required Skill For A Big Trout Specialist

CHAPTER 8 .... PG 87
WHERE BIG FISH HIDE
The Ultimate Challenge: Finding Giant Trout In Stillwater

CHAPTER 9 .... PG 113
MASTERING THE PIECES OF THE TIMING PUZZLE
How To Pick The Best Hour For Big Trout

CHAPTER 10 .... PG 125
PRESENTATION
The Most Critical Skill Of Them All

CHAPTER 11 .... PG 141
STILLWATERS BY BOAT, TUBE AND WADERS
How You Get To The Trout Does Matter

CHAPTER 12 .... PG 151
FLY-FISHING THROUGH THE SEASONS
Twelve Months Of Big Trout Tactics

CHAPTER 13 .... PG 165
EXTERNAL FACTORS
Full Moons, Barometers, Storm Fronts and Fish

CHAPTER 14 .... PG 173
100 TIPS FOR FLY-FISHING STILLWATERS
The Results of 20 Years and 300 Lakes

CONCLUSION

EPILOGUE

BIBLIOGRAPHY

INTRODUCTION

Trout fishermen are in love with moving waters. We have been hooked solidly by Hemingway's *Big Two-Hearted River*, Walden's *The Last Pool*, Haig-Brown's *Return To The River*, Traver's *Trout Madness*, and hundreds of other river classics.

So strong is our commitment that we can be lost for hours leaning on guardrails staring into rivers, creeks and even drainage ditches if the water is sufficiently cool and the flow determined.

Fly-fishing for trout in moving waters is terribly addictive, in fact, it could be a near perfect religion, if catching trout was not a factor. Whenever catching exceptionally large trout becomes part of the promise, we trout fishermen prudently abandon our true love and surrender to the appeal of stillwaters.

Fly fishing lakes isn't new; it's been around since anglers began imitating insects with concoctions of fur and feathers. It is true that most fly fishermen don't share the same enthusiasm for stillwater as they do for moving water. I suspect that the reasons for our love of moving waters are because the scale of a stream is less intimidating, the holding water is easier to define, and because we can visualize the fly disappearing into the jaws of a waiting trout.

Jim Gilford, a contributing author in John Merwin's 1980 classic *"Stillwater Trout"*, wrote, *"The challenge of stillwater fishing is barely beginning to stir the interest of American trout fishermen, and is shown by the absence, in contemporary angling books, of basic information on the characteristics and ecology of stillwater habitat".*

John Merwin added an important footnote, *"The technical development of fly fishing for trout, both in England and in this country took place on streams, largely because the problems of stream fishing for trout are better defined. Thus we have no stillwater tradition, no shelves of books on stillwater technique."*

In the '70's, the belly boat burst upon the scene and suddenly, stillwater fly fishing acquired a manageable even masterful dimension. Fly-fishermen in small flotation devices began exploring lakes where previously only trollers or bait fishermen in sturdy boats had fished. No lake was beyond the reach of our float tube navy. The problem was, we were limited in knowledge and technique on how lakes should be fished. Although information on the subject was still somewhat scarce, we began to learn more about the stillwater make-up, its physical, chemical and biological characteristics.

As more and more anglers began fly fishing lakes, information about the insects that live there, the habitat that supports them along with those natural forces that influence the trout's behavior began to appear in literature throughout the country. In 1984, Ron Cordes and Randall Kaufmann's book, *"Lake Fishing with a Fly"* opened the door and shed some much needed insight on the mysteries of stillwater fly fishing. I still consider it a leading reference on the formation and chemistry of lakes and how they affect trout behavior along with the insects and habitat that make up the stillwater environment. In spite of the fact that fishing lakes with a fly is no longer the mystery it once was, many anglers are still uncomfortable on stillwater. I know some who are not only reluctant, but absolutely refuse to go near a lake. I suspect it's their lack of stillwater knowledge that intimidates them. Whatever the reason, lakes scare the hell out of them.

[Sheely photo]

XII

Most of the anglers who prefer fly fishing moving water occasionally fish lakes. Many will not do well their first time out, and often come away feeling frustrated, confused and disillusioned. But in time, lessons will be learned, confidence will grow, and they will feel less intimidated when fishing a lake for the first time.

There's another group of anglers out there, although fewer in number, who prefer the challenge of stillwater, the solitude it affords as well as the opportunity of hooking larger numbers of big trout. They share an intimate relationship with stillwater fly fishing, have honed their skills by spending long hours on the water, and have a firm understanding of what it takes to be successful.

Anglers who are uncomfortable fly fishing stillwater need to understand that lakes aren't difficult, they're just different. When compared to streams and rivers, the differences become obvious. Without current to move the fly, the retrieve becomes a critical part of presentation. Stillwater trout, instead of holding in a feeding station as they do in streams, are constantly moving in search of food and become more difficult to locate. The food sources in lakes are more varied, and the availability of that food is often at the mercy of changing weather patterns.

In rivers and streams, trout are either on the bottom, or just under the surface. In stillwaters, trout may be anywhere from the top to the bottom requiring anglers to employ a variety of fly lines and forms of presentation.

Another important difference is the need to make long casts, something that is rarely necessary on moving water.

Lakes may differ one from another much the same as streams differ from rivers. No two lakes are the same in size, shape, chemical makeup or depth. Some will be highly acidic with few nutrients while others alkaline with thick algae. An insect that is dominate in one lake may be totally absent in another. There are a number of factors that contribute to the size and numbers of trout in lakes. When beginning stillwater anglers try to sort out all of these variables, it's no wonder they feel overwhelmed.

Although there may always be some uncertainties about stillwater fly fishing, lakes are no longer the big mysteries they once were.

Just remember, there is no one fly line, pattern or retrieve that works all of the time. The fastest way to learn stillwater techniques is to spend time on the water. The more time we spend, the quicker the mysteries will unravel.

It is with that thought in mind that this book is written.

As you read, please bear in mind the focus of this book is on how to catch large trout, not necessarily numbers of trout. Some key points may seem redundant, but they are important enough to deserve repetition. Hopefully, you will come away with a better understanding of lakes, the insects and fish that live there, the fly patterns that attract big trout and those factors that influence all that live within the stillwater environment.

This Stillwater System works for me, and it will for you.

Glen Fair plays a large rainbow trout on northwestern Montana's Mission Lake.

Chapter 1

LAKE TYPES AND THEIR DIFFERENCES
Sorting Out Trophy Waters

As a youngster, I used to think that lurking beneath a lake's deep dark waters were huge trout, mysterious, shy, almost uncatchable. Now I realize that many lakes are not capable of growing large trophy-sized trout and some won't support any trout at all. On the other hand, when conditions are right some lakes can grow enormous trout. These are the lakes I choose to fish.

The size of a lake's fish, their numbers, as well as the food sources they prey upon are rooted to the physical and chemical characteristics of the water. These parts of the lakes internal system are so interrelated it's difficult to look upon them as separate entities. The influences that I refer to as external forces--wind, temperature, and light--impact both the physical and chemical characteristics, which in turn influence a lake's habitat and all living things within its boundaries. These factors, in turn, determine how you will fish that lake: the flies, the lines, the presentation.

Physical Structure

The physical structure of a lake refers to its size, depth, shorelines, bottom composition, inlets, springs, elevation, latitude and all the other physical features.

Depending on the time of year, these features, along with the chemical makeup of the water, are responsible for where we find trout, the food sources available and eventually determine if the lake is capable of growing trophy-size trout; fish in the 8-pound plus range.

Lake Types

Most of the stillwaters where we pursue trout are natural lakes, ponds or reservoirs including seepage and drainage lakes. Seepage lakes have no tributaries or outlets, but maintain year-round water through underground springs or seepage from the water table.

Trout must be stocked in these lakes since there is no moving water to provide suitable spawning habitat. *[Note, lake trout, sometimes called mackinaw, are chars and spawn naturally in lakes.]*

Trout in seepage lakes go through the motions of spawning, females depositing their eggs and the males fertilizing them, but without running well-aerated water, the spawn never develops.

Most high altitude, mountain lakes are seepage lakes and were barren unless artificially stocked. The bottoms of many higher elevation lakes are solid rock and lack the nutrients to grow plants that will produce a food chain capable of developing trout much beyond what we refer to as pan-sized, 7 to 14 inches: small trout compared to the standards of a trophy-trout specialist.

On the other hand, it's common for lowland seepage lakes to have soft, silted bottoms that are rich in nutrients with excellent habitat to support animal life and huge fast growing trout.

Drainage lakes have both inlets and outlets, are found at various elevations, support both native or planted trout and are basically self sustaining bodies of water. Depending on nutritional habitat, the latitude and elevation, these natural lakes are also capable of growing and supporting some very large trout.

Lake Types And Their Differences

Reservoirs are man-made bowls of water, efficiently designed to hold this precious commodity until it can be drained off and put to work. Until the past decade, no one gave much thought to incorporating a shoreline design that would be good for fish. As a result, most reservoirs lack the extensive shoreline shallows necessary to develop natural sustaining habitats. They can be fished

Drainage lakes have inlets where natural reproduction can take place.

out if not replenished through artificial stocking programs. Where fishing pressure is intense, few fish will survive to trophy size.

The constant water level fluctuations tend to prohibit the development of aquatic plants or weed beds necessary to produce the protein-rich food chain that can grow super trout. Reservoir trout will adjust to water level variations, but their food sources suffer, especially in late summer when reservoirs are drained down to baked, eroded mud flats for agricultural irrigation.

Summer draw down is a tough time for reservoir trout, but strangely, it can be the season of opportunity for fly fishermen. As food sources dry up and the water temperatures rise in the shallowing lakes, the seasonal draining will concentrate trout in the coolest areas of the lake. Look for these concentrations in the deepest part of the bowl, or in the fan flow of a tributary's cold-water or near an artesian spring.

If the cold-water area is large enough to give the fish a sporting chance, fishing can be terrific. If, however, the fish are concentrated in a small cold-water refuge, it is not only unsporting, but a

A seepage lake in British Columbia produced this 5-pound Kamloops rainbow.

violation of even the most liberal ethic to fish over trapped, desperate fish. Please don't.

The less fluctuation in a reservoir's water level, the more stable its fishery will become. While many of the large Western reservoirs support big trout, they are not as productive as smaller, undrained, natural lakes.

Reservoirs can support big trout but because of seasonal drawdowns are, on an average, not as productive as natural lakes

Lake Types And Their Differences

A classic big-trout pond, like this northern California water, will be well oxygenated, fed by cool-water and support a rich food base

[Sheely Photo]

Western ponds are usually wide interruptions in small narrow streams often originating in mountains. Some of the best of these ponds are crafted by beavers, which have dammed tributaries with a combination of tree limbs, sticks and mud. Most ponds are shallow, small and rich with insect life.

This combination grows trout by the basketful, some of which will fill a basket by themselves.

Most of the more productive ponds that I have fished were somewhat secluded, and were extremely productive with a mixture of brookies, rainbows and cutthroats.

Locating trout in ponds is seldom a problem. A few minutes spent watching the water will tell it all: where to fish, what insects are prevalent and what fly to use. The worse thing you can do at a small pond is to aimlessly flail away. These trout are spooky and a few minutes spent analyzing the fish and their environment will be a worthwhile investment.

I've found that the flies, lines and leaders that work well on large waters also work well on ponds--just in smaller sizes. As ponds are scaled down, so should be your tackle--especially tippet diameter.

Most ponds that support large trout cannot withstand a lot of fishing pressure, and certainly can't absorb the loss of their brood stock. I cannot imagine any reason to justify catching and keeping large beaver pond trout.

FLY-FISHING STILLWATERS

Lake Types And Their Differences

Size Of Lakes

Deep lakes are generally not as productive for fly fishermen as shallower lakes. It's a matter of sunlight, the energy source of all plant growth.

Lakes shallow enough for sunlight to penetrate to the bottom will generate and support more plant life and trout food sources than a lake with steep banks and a bottom deeper than 20 feet. This is not to say that large deep lakes don't harbor big trout. They do. They just don't fly fish well.

The amount of shallow shoreline is a clue to a lake's productivity. These areas are the first to warm in the spring, forging the links in the food chain that attract both insects and the trout that eat them. Shallow areas extend the growing season for trout. Even when summer temperatures warm the shorelines beyond a trout's comfort range, the shallows continue to produce food for trout long after they move into cooler deeper water. This is certainly in evidence when trout make those short feeding forays into the shallows to search for food.

Aquatic plant life, like this, is a sure sign that a lake is rich in nutrients and insects, two requirements for growing trophy-size trout

Lakes situated in sloping mountainous areas are generally deep with a minimum of sunlight, a short growing season and smaller trout. Food-rich shallow lakes are normally found in flat terrain at lower elevations with a longer growing season. In the West, a number of these lakes are located in remote, semi-arid sagebrush areas. These desert lakes warm quickly, are rich in nutrients, especially algae and produce large fast growing fish.

If there is a better place for a big-trout-fisherman to be at ice-out than a desert lake, I've never found it.

High desert lakes often host large, fast-growing trout such as this desert rainbow.

FOR TROPHY TROUT

Lake Types And Their Differences

Altitude

The elevation of a lake often plays a major role in how productive it will be and how large the trout can grow.

I've found that most high elevation lakes, many above 7,000 feet, tend to be acidic, short on nutrients, suffer a retarded growing season and are subject to winter kill.

Small trout, like this brookie, are typical of the trout found in high-mountain lakes.

Low elevation lakes from sea level to 3,000 feet, are just the opposite. These lakes are usually frozen for only a brief period, if at all. They are rich in plant life and nutrients, are seldom deep and can support both numbers of trout and a lot of large trout.

The biggest problem with low lakes is temperature extremes that can deplete oxygen levels and elevate water temperatures beyond a trout's tolerances. Exceptionally shallow desert lakes may be rich in the foods that grow wall-hanging fish, but suffer from infrequent summer and winter kills. [See, *Winter & Summer Kills, page 12*]

East of the coastal mountain ranges, the most productive big trout water seems to be in mid-elevation lakes between 3,000-6,000 feet. In the cooler, wet west slope of the coastal mountains mid-elevation is defined as 500 to 2,000 feet above sea level.

High elevation lakes are often spectacular places to fish, but are rarely nutritionally rich enough to produce large trout. [Sheely Photo]

The water in both of these mid-elevations has a good balance of the physical and chemical features required to support high numbers of trout, including a disproportional number of trophy-size fish.

Lake Types And Their Differences

Large, mid-elevation lakes are the most productive stillwater fisheries easily accessible to most anglers.

These lakes have shallow shorelines that are rich in aquatic plants, support well-oxygenated water, and have sufficient depth to prevent summer and winter kill by temperature extremes and oxygen depletion.

CHEMICAL BREAKDOWN

The pH Factors:

One of the most critical biochemical processes that takes place in a lake's ecosystem is the acidic and alkaline balance. Fisheries biologists rank the alkaline and acidic ratios in water by pH factors with a range of 0 to 14.

Water registering on this scale at 0 would represent an extreme acidic situation. Water that tests 14 equals a maximum alkaline condition. Neither extreme is healthy for fish.

A neutral pH balance is 7, and represents pure water. The pH ratio of quality fishing water will rank somewhere in the mid-range of 5 to 7.

Ray Beadle with a deep-bodied 10-pound rainbow caught at Sugar Creek Ranch in northern California. [Ray Beadle Photo]

Acidic conditions (with a pH of 0 to 5) are commonly found in crystal clear deep lakes that are rich in decaying organic matter, and have oxygen depletion problems. These are typical of higher elevation lakes infested with pan-size and smaller trout.

Alkaline conditions (with a pH of 8 to 14) are common to nutrient rich water where algae blooms

FOR TROPHY TROUT

Lake Types And Their Differences

are common. Alkaline water is normally cloudy, has abundant plant life and large fast-growing trout. When extreme conditions exist, a reading of 10 or higher will be present creating a negative impact on trout behavior. Trout become lethargic, inactive and often refuse to eat.

Algae bloom is a byproduct of nutritionally-rich water, and provides cover for trophy-size trout, like the rainbow being revived and released

Sunlight

Sunlight, or the lack of it, is either directly or indirectly responsible for most of what happens within a lake's ecosystem. All that lives beneath the surface, including plants, insects, fish, micro-organisms and nutrients, are influenced by the sun's rays. Yet, I'd guess that most fishermen know very little about how it affects trout behavior or the environment in which big fish live.

The sun is the energy that determines water temperature, and the quality of the food chain. Energy is delivered as light and light is affected by a myriad of factors: cloud cover, angle of the sun, time of day or year, weather, precipitation, shade and other external forces.

Trout avoid bright sunlight, yet much of what they eat, when they eat, as well as the quality of the water they live in are determined by the amount of light entering the water. From a fisherman's standpoint, this means trout will be holding in the first suitable cover near their food sources.

Temperature/Thermal Heating

Water temperature is really the heart beat of any lake's ecosystem. Most of the traumatic developments in a lake, such as turnover, stratification, nutrient growth, plant decay, algae blooms, win-

When water temperature drops below 50° (F) trout become increasingly lethargic and inactive.

FLY-FISHING STILLWATERS

Lake Types And Their Differences

ter freeze, etc. are keyed to water temperature.

A lake's water temperature is established primarily by solar radiation, not by air temperature. Water has the ability to retain the energy of the sun's rays and convert it into heat. The less water in a lake, the less solar radiation is required to heat it, which is why shallow lakes warm much quicker than deep water. Called the profundal zone, this heating process expands slowly which allows trout and the food sources they prey upon to adjust.

If the warm-water transition occurs rapidly, fish become lethargic and often refuse to feed.

Ideally, once waters begin to warm, the wind stirs a surface chop that mixes nutrients and distributes them throughout the lake. Keep in mind nutrient-rich water warms quicker than clear water because the nutrient particles absorb solar radiation.

(The effects of water temperature on trout behavior, their food and angler presentation are discussed in detail in Chapters 8 and 13.)

Photosynthesis

Photosynthesis is the process that uses radiant energy (sunlight) to produce chemical compounds such as oxygen and carbon dioxide from organic matter (plant life).

An explanation for why there is little or no oxygen near the bottom of lakes (and consequently no trout) during turnover can be found in 7th grade lessons on photosynthesis.

Live, submerged, rooted plants utilize carbon dioxide and discharge dissolved oxygen. Dead and decaying organic matter uses this dissolved oxygen and releases carbon dioxide. This you-pat-my-back, I'll-pat-your's function of the photosynthesis process directly determines the productivity of a lake.

A big fish specialist who understands this process, will be able to sort out lakes capable of producing large, fast growing trout from those with only small fish potential.

Lake Turnover

Most anglers are familiar with the term, "lake turnover", but few know what's involved or how turnover affects trout behavior.

At spring ice-out, the surface water temperature of all lakes will be 32 degrees (F). At the bottom, the lake will be 39 degrees (F).

As the warmer water rises, it brings with it nutrients that have settled on the bottom along with

This big rainbow was caught right after ice-out, a period when big trout are very susceptible.

FOR TROPHY TROUT

Lake Types And Their Differences

the oxygen depleted water stemming from winter stratification. Mixing of this mass then occurs through surface winds and currents until water temperatures become uniform top to bottom.

Turnover occurs twice a year. Once in the spring when surface water temperature finally rises above the temperature at the bottom of the lake, and in the fall when this process is reversed and the warmer water is on the bottom of the lake.

Angling opportunities are exceptional in the oxygen saturated surface waters right after ice out. During this period, trout will move into the shallows where food sources are most plentiful. There is no better time than the first few weeks after ice-out to find giant fish in shallow waters, tight to the shoreline, feeding with an abandon you won't see again the rest of the year.

Then following this period after ice-out, the bite begins to slow as trout tend to scatter, spending less time in the shallows. After spring turnover, the lake slowly warms and eventually becomes stratified into warm and cold water zones. It remains stratified until unbalanced by winter turnover. Where the two temperature zones meet in a lake is an area called the thermocline, an invisible division of temperature levels. As summer stratification sets in, trout will concentrate in the oxygen rich area just above the thermocline.

However, not all lakes are deep enough to stratify. Those that do, settle into three layers. The epilimnion (surface layer), the thermocline (a thin, cold oxygen-poor belt) and the hypolimnion, (the bottom layer) which is oxygen depleted water practically void of plant, insect and fish life.

The epilimnion layer constitutes the shallow or shoal area of a lake and is the primary target of fly-fishermen. This is where photosynthesis takes place stimulating the growth of plants creating oxygen-rich water which in turn attracts a multitude of food sources and trout.

During the warm summer months, big trout frequent these food rich areas early and late in the day when temperatures and light penetration are the most tolerable, but retreat to deeper water during mid day.

This big rainbow was hooked by the author on a Stillwater Nymph while it was feeding on scuds and dragonfly nymphs.

[Ray Beadle Photo]

Big rainbows love to cruise shallow water, especially in early spring when food sources become active, which is where this 4-pound male was hooked.

During the fall months, the upper layer begins to cool. Eventually this well-oxygenated water begins to sink through the thermocline into the hypolimnion or bottom layer. Lake temperatures will once again be a uniform 39 degrees at this point just as they were during spring turnover. The fall turnover process blends the highly-oxygenated surface waters into the rest of the water column creating excellent opportunities for anglers. This is the time for big trout specialists, a time when less dedicated fly fishermen have abandoned the water for other interests. It is also a time when big trout are caught.

Winter & Summer Kills

Lakes freeze when the surface temperature cools to maximum density and the coldest water is on the surface, an inversion that stays throughout the winter until the lake thaws in spring and turnover occurs.

Frozen, snow-blanketed shallow lakes are highly susceptible to winter kill when sunlight fails to penetrate the thick cover reducing photosynthesis. Without this process, oxygen levels are drastically reduced, carbon dioxide levels increase and fish are shut off from their oxygen supply.

Summer kills occur when the sun is blocked by cloud cover, the photosynthesis process is interrupted, oxygen is depleted, water temperatures climb and trout die of oxygen starvation.

The shallower a lake is, the more susceptible it is to winter and summer kills.

In lakes bordering on kill conditions, anglers should remember that hooked fish will be exceptionally stressed and releasing a trout unharmed isn't a guarantee it will survive.

I realize that this chapter has come dangerously close to being a science project yawner, but bear with me because a true trophy-trout specialist needs to be able to factor this information into every fishing trip.

Recognizing the features that create quality trout water, water capable of supporting larger than average trout, is a critical clue to the stillwater mystery.

Pat Hoglund with a 10-pound rainbow from Sugar Creek Ranch.

Chapter 2

KEY FOOD SOURCES FOR TROPHY TROUT

Understanding The Feeding Habits Of Stillwater Trout

Ever since I was old enough to hold a fishing rod, I wanted to catch trout, lots of trout. Like most anglers, landing a big fish was a bonus, mostly luck and never planned for. It just happened. While luck rides a roller coaster, skills only improve with age.

Over the years, as I realigned my priorities to specialize in catching difficult, trophy-size trout on flies, one of the first discoveries was that learning about trout was not nearly as important as learning about trout food.

The only inducement a trout has for eating that half-inch of bronzed hollow-point, ringed wire we call a hook, is because we dress the wire up to look like food. It would take a pretty desperate trout to inhale this impostor if it wasn't disguised as protein. In fact, anglers have become so good at imitating trout food, that it's now the only socially acceptable way to catch a trout.

So we tie a bit of hackle, muskrat or marabou on a hook until it looks like an aquatic entrée and serve it to a, hopefully, unsuspecting fish.

The way to a trophy trout really is through its stomach. If we want to catch that fish, then we need to learn what its favorite foods are, when they're available, what they look like, how they move, and where the trout will go to find it. If a trout wants a tan caddis on the surface and you offer it a black woolly bugger on the bottom--well, you see the problem.

The more we understand about the links in the food chain the better our chances are for serving up exactly what the trout is looking for.

Contrary to their common reputations for selective snobbery, most trout--especially large trout with large protein requirements--are opportunistic feeders. If it moves, doesn't require much energy to catch, and can fill a nutritional niche, it gets eaten.

Food sources that most frequently evolve toward this destiny are minnows, leeches, scuds, snails, crustaceans, fish eggs, worms, small snakes, frogs, and occasionally

The author was able to dupe this big brook trout by studying the feeding behavior in shallow water.

a small rodent and of course a zillion aquatic and terrestrial insects in all stages of development between conception and death.

Of all the entrees, aquatic insects are the bread and butter in a trout's diet.

The factors that determine which insect is available, when, where and at what stage of development are habitat, water temperature and sunlight.

When selecting fly patterns for specific lakes, I find it helps to rank stillwater food sources into categories of primary and secondary importance.

Primary food sources are those foods most often available and make up the bulk of the trout's diet throughout the year. What I consider as secondary foods, are only occasionally available and constitute less than 10 percent of what trout eat.

Where a specific food-source ranks in importance is determined by each lake's habitats and abilities to produce these food forms in great numbers. When we think in terms of what trout eat, the list is almost endless and varies not only from lake to lake, but from area to area within a lake.

I enjoy tying flies, and in fact make a fair part of my living selling flies and presenting fly-tying seminars at sports shows and fly-fishing clubs. However, when we consider how many flies it would take to imitate all the primary food sources, the "match-the-hatch" syndrome becomes overwhelming and impractical.

Fortunately, I've learned that I don't have to offer patterns that exactly duplicate the entreé of choice, but I have a lot more success with patterns that imitate a host of edible food sources.

After years of trial, error and experimentation, I've found that I can consistently appeal to a trout's opportunistic nature in any lake in North America with as few as six patterns. These flies, rather than imitate specifics, simulate a host of organisms and are easily mistaken by opportunistic fish as one of any number of different food sources.

With a little study on any lake it becomes apparent there are specific trout foods that are consistently found in stillwaters.

I separate them into four groups: aquatic insects, terrestrials, forage fish and those "other" insects that don't fit into the first three groups. The important Western aquatic insects include mayflies, caddis flies, damselflies, dragonflies and midges. Of the terrestrial insects, I consider only the ants and grasshoppers as important food sources. Forage fish are numerous and always include indigenous minnows. The forth category has three members; leeches, scuds and water boatmen. I feel leeches and scuds are the most important in this category because of their universal appeal and availability to trout.

There are many insects that make up a portion of a trout's diet that I have omitted because I find them less important to fly fishermen. These are patterns well out of the mainstream and are rarely used. When was the last time you fished a snail pattern? Even if you could tie a look-alike snail pattern, how would you retrieve it? Snails move at the same pace that grass grows and I don't know of anyone who has the patience to let their fly just rest on the bottom for very long without moving it.

Trout eat small snails, and I realize that, yet I don't own a pattern that imitates a snail. Still, I catch trout that are crammed to the gums with these marble-like organisms. Could it be that retrieve speed (presentation) is more important than pattern selection? I believe so, and I'll expand on this concept a little later.

Most fly fishermen I know are pack rats, paranoid pack rats at that. Fly fishermen, in general, are famous for carting around little boxes crammed with neat rows of fly patterns many of which we rarely recognize and almost never fish. Why? Because we don't want to be caught short during that moment when all of our old reliables fail.

The following is a list of the food sources I have found are most important to Western trout all of which can be easily imitated with only six patterns. [Refer to Chapter 6]. Keep in mind, the importance of these foods will vary seasonally and from lake to lake.

Midges

I believe midges are the most important food source for trout. This is due to their vast numbers and availability to trout on a year-round basis.

The largest midge family of interest to fly fishermen is the chironomidae. Because they reproduce in astounding numbers, chironomidae fill the food void when other insects are inactive, especially during the winter.

Midges are of the order Diptera, an order with 8,000 cousins including house flies, mosquitoes and other two-winged insects which are aquatic and terrestrial.

Midges are small, some so tiny they are impossible to match with hook and feathers. Hook sizes for midge ties can range from 12 to 22.

Midges come in a variety of colors, the most common being black, gray, tan, light orange and olive. Variations in habitat don't seem to bother the midge. They adapt to deep as well as shallow lakes, are found in all sorts of vegetation and will find a home in muck, silt or rocky bottoms.

The midge goes through a complete cycle of metamorphosis from egg to larvae, to pupae, to adult. Not all of these stages are of concern to big trout anglers although they are to the trout.

When you see trout activity on the surface, but can't make out a hatch--the odds are chironomidae are the prey. Trout feed heavily on these little insects, but do so opportunistically.

I've found that feeding trout rarely set out to look for midge larvae, but if it's available, they'll take it. Midge larvae, although not as important a stage to imitate as the pupae, are worm-like, uniform in diameter and are without legs. Most are found in deeper water beyond the shoal areas and vary in density in lakes depending on habitat needs. Larvae are high-protein food forms that are red pigmented from living in oxygen-starved bottoms and are imitated by such patterns as blood worms and the San Juan Worm. Most larvae have a wiggling motion, difficult for anglers to emulate. The pupae, on the other hand, is a different story.

Chironomid pupa, sometimes called a blood midge, is a staple in trout diets.

Fly fishermen have the most success imitating the pupae or emerging pupae. These insects vary in size but most of what I find are about a quarter to a half-inch long. Their bodies are heavily segmented with a large thorax containing the wings and legs of the adult. Pupae contort wildly as they work their way to the surface, sometimes resting while hanging stationary before hatching.

Trout find the pupae stage easy picking as the insects suspend just below the surface prior to emerging as adults. The transition is a slow process, giving trout plenty of opportunity to feed leisurely while cruising just under the surface. Adult midges are heavily preyed upon by juvenile trout, but seldom by calorie-oriented big trout. Of course, the availability of other food sources helps determine a big trout's needs for adult midges. Novice stillwater anglers often mistake surface disturbances for hatching adults when trout are actually feeding on the pupae just below the surface.

Hatching periods are most extensive during the winter months but occur all year long. Midges dislike bright sunlight. They'll hatch throughout the day but prefer low light conditions; early morning, late evening and overcast days.

Most midge fishermen select floating lines, long leaders, 12 to 15 feet greased to the tippet so they float in the film and suspend the fly subsurface. Takes are soft sips so a taut line or indicator is a must.

Midge fishing requires patience. Fishermen who understand these insects and have the willpower to fish their imitations can be very successful. Personally, I don't fish midges all that often. I find it difficult to lure a trout of 5 pounds or better to a size 18 or smaller fly attached to 6X or 7X tippets and expect to hold them.

Most stillwater big fish specialists I know don't fish this hatch very often either. Perhaps it's a flaw that keeps us fishless when trout are feeding on these insects. If you fish the high desert lakes of south-central Washington or in the Kamloops region of southern British Columbia in May-June, the chironomidae, in assorted colors, will be the fly of the hour.

One thing for sure, these little bugs are important to trout. For me it may be the most frustrating part of stillwater fly fishing. Perhaps I'll spend more time this summer improving my own "midging" techniques. We'll see.

Mayflies

Mayflies have been the centerfold for fly fishermen as long as anglers have ventured afield in pursuit of trout. Ancient angling literature leaves little doubt which insect was most important to fishermen. Sleek, delicate, intriguing, irresistible, mayflies are the heart and soul of fly fishing fantasies.

Adult mayflies, fished upstream, are the darlings of stream and river fly fishermen. Stillwater trout, however, don't rely on mayflies to the same extent as trout in moving water. Consequently, their importance to stillwater anglers is diminished as well.

What could pass for a lack of selectivity for the mayfly is probably due more to the enormous, diversified food chain in most lakes. Don't misunderstand, there should be plenty of room in the fly boxes of stillwater specialists for mayfly patterns--just don't be surprised if other available food forms sway a big trout's preference.

Mayflies are important food sources for small trout, but less important for trophy-size fish.

Without exception, the most important of all mayflies to imitate is the callibaetis. Found in almost all lakes and ponds, by sheer numbers alone they can force selective feeding.

Callibaetis supplement stillwater trout when other food sources are less available. The most important phases of callibaetis development are the nymph and dun. The spinner fall, while less reliable, can offer exciting action as big trout on occasion will take the floating flies with a showy head and tail rise.

Callibaetis hatches occur heaviest during the spring and summer months In the fall there are sporadic hatches. Callibaetis are algae feeders and the nymphs are usually found around weed beds. These nymphs are agile swimmers. and are available to trout from about mid-morning to noon. Like most aquatic insects, emergence depends on weather, water temperature and the time of day.

Mayflies prefer calm water to emerge and rarely buck windy conditions. A slightly rippled surface, however, will not necessarily diminish a hatch and may hide presentation mistakes. If the wind becomes too much of a factor, the hatch will stop until conditions improve. I have found that when wind puts down an active hatch, it often continues in protected areas with suitable habitat.

There are a number of mayfly nymph patterns that work well in stillwater. While I prefer my callibaetis nymph, perhaps the most popular is the Gold Ribbed Hare's Ear. Both patterns imitate the callibaetis nymphs in sizes 12-16.

Tan is the most common color for imitating these nymphs but on numerous occasions I've enjoyed success with dark brown, black and light olive.

Hal Janssen's method of fishing mayfly nymphs is one of the most interesting and deadly systems out there. Hal prefers a floating line with a tippet measuring one and a half times the depth he is fishing. With a small diameter tippet, yet strong enough to withstand a big fish, he can get his fly quickly to the bottom.

The fly must be weighted and retrieved slowly with a strip-pause-strip retrieve that pulls it about eight inches off the bottom. Between strips, the fly settles back just like the natural. Concentrate at the point where the line or leader enters the water.

Takes are very soft. Trout will usually suck the fly in rather than strike.

You can also fish callibaetis nymphs below the surface by using an intermediate or floating line and a leader of 12 to 15 feet. Move the fly ever so slowly with long pauses between strips. This technique will produce more aggressive strikes. The key is to keep your fly in the zone where trout are feeding. When wind is a factor, use an intermediate line and fish below the surface disruption.

The Hexagenia is the largest mayfly in the western United States, but is not common on most lakes.

The callibaetis is the most widespread species of mayfly on lakes throughout the West.

Caddis

I don't believe caddis carry the same importance in stillwaters as they do in rivers although there are some diehard caddis fishermen who disagree. In fact, I have often wondered if trout in

Key Food Sources For Trophy Trout

lakes only take caddis as a last resort. I've seen the water littered with these insects and not a single fish came to the surface to feed. Yet there are times when trout, as contrary as ever, will take the insect over all other food sources.

When trout are taking caddis flies, they don't seem to have a preference for the larvae, pupae or adult.

I assume that the availability of other insects may account for the trout's occasional interest in the caddis. We know trout feed on caddis, but to what extent appears inconsistent and is pretty much a mystery. Caddis may be a major food source for trout on one lake and barely a part of the food chain in the next.

In the larvae stage, caddis build cases from grains of sand, tiny twigs or other suitable bottom debris.

The cases are tubular, tapered and completely encase the delicate larvae. Trout will eat them case and all. If you extract the larvae from its case. you'll find it resembles a grub or a worm-like insect. This may come as a surprise, but I've found in lakes, not only does the larvae have little appeal to trout but stillwater fly fishermen aren't very interested either. Perhaps that's because we haven't found a good imitation to simulate this stage of insect.

Pupae, like the larvae, rarely shows up in stomach samples, yet I know that trout eat them. In fact, I think the pupae is the most important stage for stillwater anglers, especially big fish specialists, to imitate.

Adult caddis.

Tie caddis pupae patterns with cream, tan and olive dressings. The pupae is available primarily in spring and early summer. The hatch does not seem to be governed by the time of day.

When fishing caddis imitations, I prefer to work weedy areas with a floating or intermediate line that will hold the fly in the feeding zone throughout the retrieve.

When I compare trout reactions to caddis in stillwater with those in moving water, it's interesting to note the lack of interest stillwater trout have in the adult flies. Again, it's the availability or lack of other food forms that determines a trout's food preference.

For some reason, stillwater trout just don't share the same enthusiasm for the adult caddis as their moving water cousins. There are exceptions, of course. I've experienced a few unforgettable days using adult imitations when the trout continued feeding well into the black of night

Adult caddis are also referred to as "sedges," especially in British Columbia. It's important for anglers to remember that adult caddis, with their distinctive tent shaped wings will both flutter as though they've lost their sense of direction or lie motionless, distinctions you need to incorporate into your presentation.

Damsel Fly

Damsels excite trout as well as stillwater fly anglers. Anyone who has experienced the "bite" during a damsel hatch will most likely display symptoms of confusion, frustration, high blood pressure and occasional panic.

Damsel fly disciples are those who are conspicuously absent from work, forget their anniversaries, show signs of anxiety and suffer from insomnia before the hatch. Damsels rank high on the trout priority list because they're available and abundant throughout the stillwater environment, lakes, reservoirs, ponds even quiet areas of slow moving streams and rivers.

A damsel nymph and the author's tied Stillwater Nymph.

The most productive fishing is with damsel nymphs, not adults. Damsel nymphs vary in color with olive, brownish olive and tan being the most common. They are generally found around surface weeds and aquatic vegetation, in the shallow areas of lakes, along the bottoms and around sunken logs or other protective cover.

Most damsels live one year. At maturity, they leave their protective cover and migrate toward shore. Trout monitoring the damsels hatching schedule will then move into the shallows to intercept the migrating nymphs. Once the hatching cycle begins, the damsel nymphs will crawl out of the water and attach to solid objects such as logs, rocks or vegetation where they hatch into adults. The newly emerged adult is a light yellowish olive in color and bit awkward in flight. Within a few days the adults coloration changes to bright blue or emerald green.

Adult damsels are creatures of the sun. They only take flight during the hot sunny periods of the day and will all but disappear when the sun goes down. Any fly fisherman who has float tubed in a lake where damsels are present has probably experienced the nymphs crawling up on their tube. It's simply Mother Nature's way of telling you to switch to a damsel nymph. I'll guarantee you, the trout have.

At times, fishing the adult can offer some incredible action but I find it inconsistent on most lakes. Damsels are so widely distributed that you will rarely fish a Western lake where they are not a major protein source. My stillwater nymph has proven to be the best imitation of a damsel nymph that I've ever fished, and there are some excellent patterns out there. Perhaps, it's the suggestive nature of my nymph that has made the difference. Let me just say, it has been consistently deadly for big trout whenever these fish are feeding.

Floating lines are probably the most common choice among damselfly anglers, and I would agree, except under windy conditions when line drag nullifies an otherwise good presentation.

I prefer to use an intermediate line when fishing the nymph because these insects are best fished in the top two feet of water and retrieved in extremely slow pulls and short pauses.

Key Food Sources For Trophy Trout

Dragon Flies

Adult dragon flies have very little appeal for trout. The nymph, however, will draw the attention of trout wherever they are found.

Trout are extremely fond of these lanky worm-like insects. They just rarely get a chance to eat one. Dragon fly nymphs are elusive, well camouflaged and generally unavailable to predator fish. Dragon fly nymphs, like damsel nymphs are fierce predators, that propel themselves in rapid three-inch thrusts to attack other insects.

Trout will feed on these nymphs even when other food sources are more plentiful. From a trout's viewpoint these nymphs are a delicacy. Big trout rarely cruise lakes looking for these insects until the nymph moves into shallow water prior to emergence. The nymphs are most vulnerable now and the trout know it. It's also an ideal time for anglers. Underwater structures like dead trees, logs or aquatic vegetation are other areas that conceal these nymphs and anglers will benefit by exploring these regions.

The case of a just-emerged dragon fly.

Floating, intermediate, or sink tip lines are ideal for working the shallows with representative patterns. In deeper water, uniform sinking lines are the best choice as trout will be looking for these insects right on the bottom.

Lightly weighted Carey Specials, Randall Kaufmann's dragon, and woolly or seal buggers are excellent representatives of the nymph. Retrieves should be the slow, crawling type keeping the nymph just off the bottom with occasional twitches. It helps to raise the fly a few inches then allow it to settle back. If it's a muck or silt bottom, the debris stirred up from this retrieve catches the eye of cruising trout and often provokes strikes.

Beetle larva is a favorite trout food, but is not found in most lakes.

20

FLY-FISHING STILLWATERS

Beetle larvae, distant cousin to the dragonfly nymph in appearance only, are not well known to anglers, but wherever they exist, they are favorite foods for trout. To date, I have not been able to isolate an adult form of this insect. The larvae swims with a fast undulating movement. They are common in the tributaries of Upper Klamath Lake and I have found them in the stomachs of trout only during May and June. When trout are feeding on the fast-moving beetle larvae, I have no trouble catching them on leech and seal bugger patterns retrieved in short quick pulls.

Leeches

Leeches are ugly and intimidating, but these undulating parasites hold a high place on the food chain of giant trout. Leech patterns were practically unheard of until the early 1980s. Today, no Western fly fishermen--especially big trout specialists--would be without a comprehensive selection of leech patterns.

In my research, I've found what seems to be a direct correlation between leeches and big trout. Any lake with a concentrated population of leeches will also be a lake with a good population of trophy-size trout.

I can't imagine going fishing without a generous assortment of leech patterns in sizes 6-10 and in various colors. Most leeches I've seen are dark charcoal or reddish brown in color and range from one to six inches in length.

Although these carnivorous annelid worms are rarely seen by fishermen, they are found in nearly all lakes, reservoirs, ponds and backwaters around the world.

My home waters of Upper Klamath Lake in southern Oregon support a healthy population and make up much of our trout's diet in the spring months. The preferred habitat of leeches is tules, willows, cattails and various forms of aquatic vegetation capable of providing food and cover. They are found along the bottoms in shallow areas which is where you should be fishing your imitation.

Leeches are favorite big-trout prey, are found in all stillwaters and are best imitated by these patterns in various natural colors.

With leech patterns, I prefer an intermediate sinking fly line. There are two effective retrieves; 1) very quick one-inch pulls, 2) long slow steady strips with deliberate pauses between pulls. Leeches are flat and the most productive fly-patterns are tied with materials that are soft, breathable and maintain a wide image when wet.

I prefer to weight these flies at the head, so the fly tips down during the pause in the retrieve imitating the undulation of a natural. Most strikes will come as the fly sinks between pulls in the retrieve.

Key Food Sources For Trophy Trout

Leeches are an important and preferred food source for big trout, and I can't recommend strongly enough that you carry an assortment of sizes and colors.

In a big trout lake, you rarely get disappointed fishing this pattern, but if you do, the problem is probably not the fly, but the way you are fishing it.

Scuds

Scuds, like leeches, excite trout. Big fish will seek out these little crustaceans, sometimes called freshwater shrimp, when other food sources are readily available.

Trout love scuds. They are high energy, high calorie food, plentiful and easy to get. An example of just how much trout like these micro meals, is found in Gary Borger's book, *"Naturals,"* where he reports the Charlie Fox study of winter trout literally burrowing into bottom debris and wiggling violently, then backing out to pick off dislodged scuds.

Trout grow quickly in lakes where scuds are found. Their vast numbers, availability and nutritional value, allow trout to feed on these crustaceans all year.

These, tiny, shrimp-like creatures can transform trout into hulking proportions in only a season or two.

Scuds are of the class, Crustacea, order Amphipoda, and are a staple in the diets of trout in most trophy lakes of the West and British Columbia.

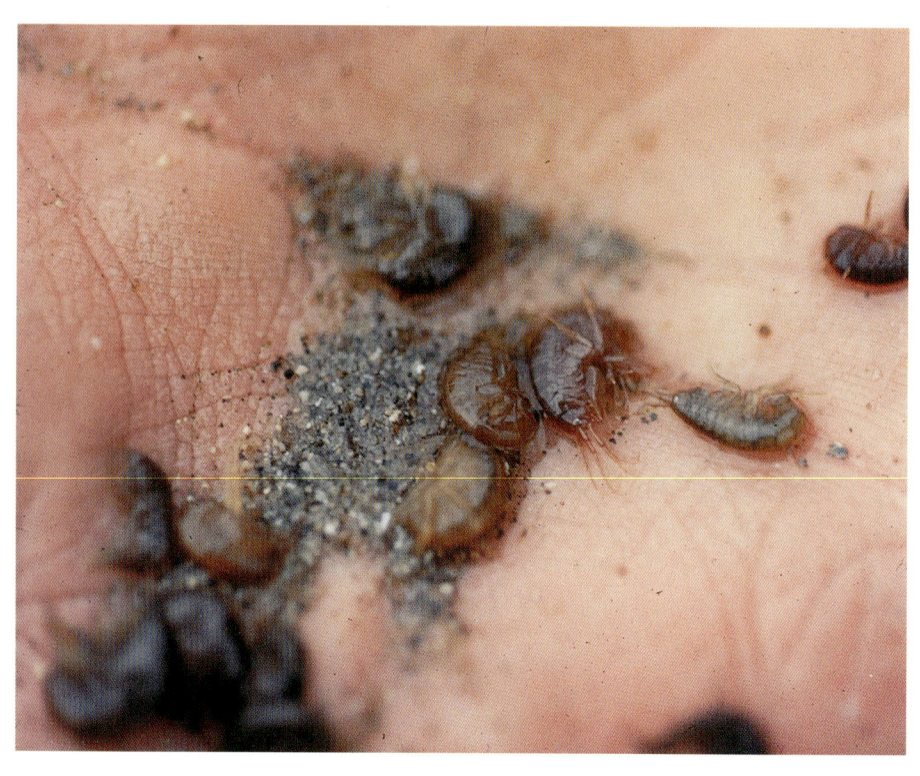

Scuds, often called freshwater shrimp, are a high protein food source highly favored by all trout.

The two most common scuds of primary importance to trout and angler are *Gammarus* and *Hyallella*. These two look-a-likes differ mostly in size with *Hyalella* being the smaller, seldom reaching more than one third of an inch in size. *Gammarus* will range from one-third to an inch in length. Both varieties are omnivorous scavengers feeding on minute animal and plant matter. Most scuds prefer shallow, highly-oxygenated water, but can be found at depths of 20 feet or more.

Preferred habitat includes not only shallow shorelines, but shoal areas where plant life is sufficient for scuds to feed with protection from predators. Scuds avoid bright sunlight and are active during early mornings, late evenings and under heavy overcast periods especially during the spring and fall months.

Trout will often feed selectively on scuds preferring the pregnant females which are identified by a bright orange colored brood pouch located beneath the thorax region. When both scuds are present in a lake, *Gammarus* is the preferred choice because of the larger size. Scuds prefer unpolluted water with *Hyallella* tolerating wider ranges of water conditions, including both alkaline and acidic lakes. Both are found in a wide range of colors usually adapting to the camouflage coloration of the habitat. The most common colors are olive, brown, cream white, gray and orange.

Feeding trout seldom refuse scuds although they may briefly abandon their interests when other food sources suddenly become available.

I prefer an intermediate line when fishing scuds, retrieving with a slow, short strip-pause-strip motion. Some anglers, however, prefer a floating line with a strike indicator. Both methods are effective.

Water Boatmen

In terms of importance, water boatmen have never been a high priority with me. However, there have been times when trout didn't share that opinion.

One early fall morning I was fishing Upper Klamath Lake near a spring almost hidden by aquatic vegetation. Trout were tailing all around my boat, completely ignoring my presence. There was an abundance of chironomids on the water and it seemed a safe assumption that trout were taking the tiny nymphs submerged in the surface film. I kept casting and they kept refusing.

In an attempt to avoid spooking fish, I inched towards the weed beds. When I peeked over the side, the reason for the chironomid refusal was obvious. Water boatmen were darting about everywhere while a school of hefty rainbows picked them off, totally oblivious to the abundant chironomids. I didn't have a good boatman pattern. The more the trout rose, the more frustrated I became. As the sun set I called it a day after failing to get a single take. That night I tied up some boatmen patterns while plotting my strategy for the next day. But, as luck would have it, the big rainbows failed to show even though water boatman were numerous and available just like the evening before.

Water boatmen are from the order *Hemiptera*, family *Coriridae*. They range in size from about a third to half an inch and are distinguished by oar-like hind legs. They are two-tone shellback in appearance with the top being a mottled dark brown to almost black while the underside abdomen is a pale yellow or cream color.

Because all lakes differ somewhat in habitat, water boatmen may be more important in one lake and less important in the next except where acidic water is a factor. Boatmen are found extensively throughout the United States in lakes and ponds below 8,000 feet elevation.

Spring and fall seem to be the preferred times for trout to feed on these insects since most species reproduce in the fall. Their numbers and availability are much greater which explains the increased interest from trout. But from my experience, trout only feed on them for short periods. For the most part, trout are not overly fond of these insects and often pass them up for other food. Only in a handful of lakes have I found a boatman pattern to be the exclusive key to catching trout.

A floating or intermediate line will cover the fishing options you will encounter when using this pattern. A short pull, slow or quick, does a good job of imitating the water boatman.

Key Food Sources For Trophy Trout

Terrestrials

Terrestrial insects are land dwellers that find their way onto lakes and ponds. Examples include ants, beetles, grasshoppers, mosquitoes, bees, wasps, tree moths and common house flies. Trout don't rely on terrestrials but if a particular juicy one is fluttering overhead, it's a very disciplined fish that will pass it up. The opportunities for big fish specialists to fish terrestrials are few.

The most popular terrestrials are ants and hoppers. When either of these insects appear on the water, it can be dry fly fishing at its best. Contrary to aquatic insects, which rely on sunlight and water temperature to hatch, terrestrials are more dependent on air temperature. As far as I know, all terrestrials become sluggish as air temperatures cool or dampness appears. I've never understood why ants are such a favorite of trout. Some fishery biologists I've known believe ants must leave them with an acidic stomach due to the numbers that could be consumed in one feeding period.

Grasshoppers are not as common on lakes as they are on rivers and streams.

When I find ants on the water they are usually the winged variety. These insects usually appear in May and June or earlier if air temperatures warm quickly. Trout are very selective when ants are on the water, rarely giving a second look at other insects. The problem is the bite may only last for a few days or as long as a week, then it's over for the year.

Grasshoppers are a favorite of trout in lakes. Mid-summer to early fall is prime hopper time and when they are abundant, it's usually around the high desert lakes or those containing grassy or weedy areas adjacent to the banks. Trout become quite selective when terrestrials are on the water, perhaps it's because they are available for such short periods.

When I fish ant or hoppers I closely match the size and colors of the dominant naturals with a floating line and a hand twist retrieve and get ready for some explosive action.

Forage Fish

I've never quite been able to understand why stillwater anglers don't fish streamer patterns more often. In lakes where big trout are plentiful, forage fish constitute a generous portion of the trout's diet.

Most anglers carry a few patterns but rarely fish them. When they do get them wet, it's only when everything else has failed to get action. If we keep in mind that the number and availability of most aquatic insects is greatest during the summer months, then it follows that during other periods trout must find substitute food.

If forage fish are available, the biggest trout are going to eat them.
Chubs, shiners, sculpins and threadfin shad are the most common varieties that trout eat. Species vary from lake to lake.

Trout can be relentless in their pursuit of forage fish until their appetites are satisfied. If you

Key Food Sources For Trophy Trout

Minnows comprise a major portion of what big trout eat.

ever witness a trout/minnow feeding frenzy, it's not a moment you'll soon forget. I'll bet you will arm yourself with some quality streamer patterns for the next time trout are chasing these little fish.

While fishing a high desert lake in eastern Oregon one fall morning, I was in the process of changing flies when I noticed a disturbance off to my left. A few inches below the surface swam a large group of shiners about an inch long. It was a shallow bay with underwater vegetation providing perfect cover as they swam along the weedy edges darting in and out as if playing follow the leader. But occasionally, they would suddenly school up and suspend almost motionless.

The reason for their erratic behavior was cruising about six feet off the weed beds. Standing perfectly still I could see several large rainbows moving back and forth seemingly uninterested in the little fish only a few feet away. For some reason the time wasn't quite right as the big trout cruised by slowly perhaps anticipating their next move.

Then suddenly and without warning, the rainbows darted into the school and the water boiled with panic-stricken little fish attempting to escape. The hungry trout moved through the school scattering the little shiners in all directions. The frantic little fish leaped into the air to evade the predators. For about 20 minutes the hungry trout cruised searching for stragglers. The more frantic and erratic the minnows movements, the more attention they drew.

Over the years I've learned that when trout are locked in a feeding frenzy they throw caution to the wind and will hit just about any minnow imitation that moves in an awkward manner.

I tied on a small Dan Byford Zonker pattern that matched the little shiners perfectly. With only six casts, I landed four rainbows ranging from 3½ to 5 pounds before the action subsided. Some of my most memorable moments on stillwater were the result of fishing streamers in front of predatory trout. I can't remember fishing a minnow pattern where the strike wasn't explosive.

Trout often display aggressive behavior when feeding on other fish and are willing to burn a few calories to satisfy their hunger. Predatory trout are relentless in their search for forage fish while cruising shallow water, along shorelines and weedy areas. When forage fish migrate, it's usually during the spring and fall, which is also when they are most vulnerable.

I use streamers when I actually see trout feeding on little fish. Only occasionally will I use streamers to prospect.

Obviously, I have omitted several popular food forms, but during 30 years of fishing lakes, I've honed my list of valued flies to match the insects described here. The others I consider surplus and expendable in the quest for big trout.

The most important thing to remember when selecting a fly for giant trout is that trout are opportunistic feeders and it is not always the fly pattern that's important, but the manner and depth at which you fish it that counts.

Big trout success is the result of a well devised fishing plan.

Chapter 3

THE SUCCESSFUL PURSUIT OF TROPHY TROUT

Big Trout Demand Practice And A Plan

Most fly fishermen, regardless of their level of casting, presentation and fishing skills, have the same dream; to hook and land a trout so large, so challenging, so exceptional that it becomes the trout of a lifetime.

For most, the pursuit never gets beyond the dream stage, and if it does it's more likely that luck, not skill determined the outcome.

To consistently catch trophy trout, plan your attack with considerations towards line options, leader lengths, tippet diameters, pattern selections, retrieval speeds, timing and locations. Save the dreams and luck for another day.

There are two reasons most fly fishermen have difficulty catching large trout. First, they lack understanding of a big trout's habits, their moods and behavior especially when influenced by external factors such as wind, water temperature and barometric pressure. Secondly, they fail to overcome flaws in their own presentation.

The majority of fly fishermen, despite popular claims have difficulty casting beyond 40 feet, and fail to fully understand the relationship between fly pattern, retrieve and line choice. With few exceptions, most fly fishermen don't fish often enough to improve their skills and judgments on the water.

For instance, who isn't guilty of fishing a fly pattern or staying with a presentation long after trout have switched to other food sources, changed locations, depth or just stopped feeding?

If I had to pick one fault that applies to all fly fishermen it would be that we fail to pay attention. We simply become insensitive to change when a shift in tactics should be obvious. We become enamored with the rhythm of casting and retrieving and drift away from our original game plan.

We are often insensitive to subtle changes and fail to make necessary corrections as these changes develop. Even experienced anglers occasionally lock onto a confidence pattern, line, or retrieve beyond the time when a change became necessary.

There is a time for loyally sticking with the comfortable success of familiar favorites. But, for big fish specialists, recognizing when to change, not as an afterthought, but when the need occurs, is what will separate their exceptional success from the pack.

A big trout specialist will learn when to change locations, switch flies and fly lines, alter retrieves and a myriad of other little mysteries that simplify stillwater fly-fishing.

Those few fly fishers who stalk lunker trout are persistent, dedicated anglers committed to hunting for trophy fish. The keys to success are their knowledge of large trout behavior. Successful big trout specialists are familiar with where big trout feed and when they're most vulnerable. They prefer to stalk big fish when conditions are favorable. They have at their disposal an arsenal of options for varying conditions. They know the limitations of their tackle, how to use it and keep it in top condition.

The Successful Pursuit of Trophy Trout

Big browns, like this 5-pounder, and Denny's AP Emerger are a deadly fall combination at Clark Canyon Reservoir, Montana. (Sheely photo)

The late Ken Miyata wrote, *"The predatory intensity that distinguishes gifted fly fishers from others can't be taught."* Whether our predatory instincts are inherited or learned is debatable. But most of the skills used when fishing must be learned, and no one skill is enough to guarantee success.

One of the first skills that any serious big trout angler needs to polish is the ability to see fish, and to see them whether they are physically visible or revealed by a nearly imperceptible stirring of the water. Experienced anglers watch for nervous water, ripples moving against a flow or wind riffle.

Jay Fair, my close friend and resident guide on California's Eagle Lake, taught me how to spot feeding fish without seeing the fish.

Mike Dehart releases a 10-pounder, a true trophy-size stillwater rainbow, taken on a Denny's Stillwater Nymph.

We were wading the shallows one fall morning as large rainbows cruised the shore linefeeding on small scuds. Because of surface distortion, spotting these fish was almost impossible. Jay had learned to spot the subtle surface disturbance that developed when trout nosed down to inhale a scud. The fanning tail would swirl the water as though it were boiling up from thebottom.

After pointing out one of these vague areas of nervous water, Jay would make his cast and repeatedly hooked trout. That lesson in watching for irregular water movement and spotting cruising fish has had an awesome impact on improving my success whether fishing fromshore, boat or float tube.

Large trout are elusive and it's no accident that few really giant trout are ever landed. If you hope to ever land one you need to understand what makes them tick. Catching these huge fish requires some unorthodox tactics, methods beyond those we use on smaller fish.

This 12-pound rainbow took a Stillwater Nymph in three feet of water.

[Gordon Honey Photo]

Big trout are moody creatures, and generally loners. They rarely school, probably because there are few other fish their size, and anything smaller than themselves will eventually become lunch.

These lunkers avoid bright sun, tiny flies and sloppy presentations. Little insects rarely interest big trout and light tippets seldom hold them.

Outlandish-size trout survive to old age by living in the most difficult places to fish. Big trout are not as difficult to catch as most anglers believe, it's just that they are few in number, nearly always live off the beaten trolling path, and have evolved an extreme wariness. They are, without exception, masters of their environments.

This large rainbow was hooked while feeding on scuds in shallow water.

FOR TROPHY TROUT

The Successful Pursuit of Trophy Trout

Trout don't think, they react. Young fish feed almost continually, but as they grow older, they abandon quantity for quality. They become more sensitive about what they eat and when they eat it. Big fish want their meals, fat, slow and easy.

There is no doubt in my mind the best time to catch a wallhanger is when big trout are the most vulnerable, and that's when they are either spawning or are in shallow water searching for something to eat.

I've learned that most fishermen leave the water before the biggest trout come out to hunt. Lunker trout of all species feed nocturnally, yet they don't feed throughout the night, as you might suspect. Instead, feeding is confined to specific nighttime periods. The most consistent of these periods, and most aggressive bite comes almost unfailingly, just before first light.

**A large rainbow chasing minnows.
Big trout want as many calories per bite as they can get.**

If you enjoy fishing with small flies and light tippets that's understandable, but you should not realistically expect to catch a 10-pound plus fish on a No. 16 midge. The odds say it won't happen.

Stomach samples taken by fish biologists suggest that big trout seldom feed on top. They prefer a diet of small fish for most of their calories. These findings explain why, more than any other style, streamer patterns are deadly for big fish. It doesn't explain why streamers are rarely a first choice pattern for most anglers.

Perhaps it's because we've been brainwashed into matching the hatch, using small flies, light tippets and light rods. Delicacy is just not consistent with hooking and holding overweight brutes. Hooking them isn't the problem, landing them is. I'm not opposed to light tackle or dry flies and let me assure you, when conditions are right, I use both. It's easy and perhaps the most enjoyable way to fish.

It's just not a good way to fish for large trout.

A few years ago on Upper Klamath Lake, the morning sun was peeking through a light cloud cover as I moved slowly along the edges of the weed beds of Pelican Bay. The shadowy form of a huge trout cruised into view no more than 30 feet away. Over the years I've caught a lot of giant trout, and it takes something really special anymore to make my blood pressure rise, and this fish was it. My heart raced with anticipation.

There was no time to change flies. Besides, any sudden movement would spook this Goliath into the weeds. A slight breeze ruffled the surface, and the huge fish slowly faded from sight. I wasn't sure if it had seen me or not. In slow motion, I dropped a cast on the water and watched the fly settle beneath the surface. A few short strips eliminated casting slack as the fly began moving in an undulating, tantalizing motion.

This is when the retrieve must be exact, making the fly behave exactly like a living insect. I was sure the big trout was lurking at the edge of the weed beds, predatory eyes fixed on each movement of my fly. I worked the fly past him nervously, anticipating the impact of a vicious strike.

It didn't happen!

The element of surprise was lost now. A second cast dropped the fly only a foot from the weeds. Where is he, I wondered, worried that maybe I had scared him after all. I had to assume he was still there. Swimming the fly past the cover once again, I pictured the monster closing in for the kill, but again nothing happened.

A Zonker streamer pattern is a favorite minnow imitation and is especially effective on big brown trout, like this northern Montana trophy caught at Battle Creek Ranch.
[Jack Salmon Photo]

The Successful Pursuit of Trophy Trout

A third cast was a bit short, but as I started moving the fly, the line tightened. For a second, I thought it was a snag--it didn't really feel like a strike. Reacting instinctively, I set the hook. Too much force would part the light leader, but instead the rod tip bowed sharply to the water. For an instant, I did nothing, waiting for the trout to move. The huge fish suddenly came to life, shaking its head side to side, thrashing near the surface. As big fish often do, there was no run, no screaming drag, just brute force and weight.

Somehow, the tippet had survived the take, but how well was it hooked? At that moment, the line started moving toward the weeds. It's a helpless feeling knowing there's nothing you can do, just keep a tight line and hope everything holds. Without warning the big fish reversed direction and headed into open water. I still couldn't see it, but I could feel the weight and it was heavy. Suddenly, it was on the surface rolling and shaking violently. Many fish pull free at this point but my luck and leader held. After a few seconds of wild thrashing, the trout began circling the boat. Like most big trout, it didn't make a streaking dash but played a powerful deliberate game.

Mistakes I had made with other big fish, started flashing through my mind. He wasn't ready and I didn't want to force the issue. Patience is a necessary skill whenever you play a fish you can't just hoist into the boat. This trout hadn't been hoist-able for years. Besides, the most critical part of the struggle was still ahead. If I lost it now, I'd never know how big it really was. No witnesses, no pictures, just the disappointment of losing a huge trout.

Losing is a part of fishing, but I don't like it. Slowly I gained a little confidence that I was wearing it down. I was wrong. He shook his head and moved off again.

Obviously this was no ordinary fish. I wondered about the limitations of my tackle, especially the tippet. If only I had checked it before casting like I usually do. Too late now. Slowly, the fish turned showing the first real signs of submission. Keep the line tight, no slack, I said to myself.

Finally, the leader came inside the rod tip. Again, the huge trout started thrashing on the surface and I just kept saying to myself, don't lose it now. But, I knew I was vulnerable. I thought about reaching for the net, but at that instant, it turned and dove again. Normally, I treasure my time alone on the water but this was one time I wished someone was here to see this magnificent fish. Every second seemed like an eternity. I could see the fish almost directly below the boat. It was bigger than I imagined, maybe 12 or 13 pounds.

As I raised the rod tip, the resistance quit. All of a sudden, the trout was lying on the surface, motionless. Lifting its head slightly, I led the fish toward the boat, my leader stretching almost to the breaking point under its massive weight.

Then, as I slipped the net into the water, I held my breath. Slowly, as the big trout slid softly over the rim. At last, the moment was mine. For an instant, I could feel my heart pounding, my fingers trembling. My God, I thought, it's huge. The massive body was overwhelming, imposing and beautiful all in one. For a moment, I just stood there, admiring the huge trout as it lay in the net, almost spent from the battle. Such a specimen was just too gorgeous to kill.

Quickly, I measured it and got it back into the water. It would be a tragedy if it died now. Grasping it by the tail, I lowered the fish into the water and gently forced water through the gills. Slowly, the big fish regained strength, and as I relaxed my grip it pulled free. With a feeling of relief, I watched it slowly disappear beneath the rippled surface.

There are no words to describe the emotions you feel after you've won this kind of battle with a big trout. There's no buddy to pound your back or holler congratulations. Besides, you don't need it anyway. You have the memory and that's enough.

It was a day I'll not soon forget, for a trout that measured 34 inches long and had an estimated weight of at least 15 pounds.

There are times when the encounter with a big trout comes down to a single moment, a brief second when all is gained or lost. Some of us have experienced that moment, others will.

The Successful Pursuit of Trophy Trout

Not every confrontation with a trophy fish has a happy ending, but the memory will last and the experience will be the foundation for new adventures. It's what fly fishing stillwaters for trophy trout is all about. It's a moment you will tell your grandkids about when the time comes that you favor a warm fire over a cold stormy day on a trout lake.

The Stillwater System *produced this thick-bodied 10-pound rainbow for Kathy Carrithers at Mission Lake, one of several trophy trout lakes on the Blackfeet Indian Reservation in northwest Montana.*

Photo: Gordon Honey

Using his Stillwater System, the author consistently catches larger than average trout even on clear, bright days in hard-fished public waters, like this Kamloops rainbow from a lake in British Columbia.

Chapter 4

SIX KEYS TO SUCCESS ON STILLWATER
Evolution Of A Big Fish Specialist

Stillwater anglers who consistently catch trout regardless of how familiar they are with the lake, succeed because they possess certain fishing skills other anglers lack.

The best have developed these skills to a level that requires constant dedication, experience and practice. Every hour spent on the water, whether watching, experimenting, perfecting casting techniques, or even fishing enhances these critical skills.

The expert stillwater angler generally has a set of priorities geared entirely toward fishing. They fish constantly, often live close to water are continuously searching for information and are always learning.

To be consistently successful catching trophy-size trout in lakes requires that you learn as much as possible about every facet of the sport. This certainly includes understanding the strengths and limitations of our equipment, *especially* rods and lines. I emphasize the adverb *especially* because of how these two tools have become so specialized in the past decade. Today's specialized rods, and specialized lines fill specific niches in the great freshwater fishing puzzle and have allowed stillwater fly-fishing to advance as far as it has.

Where your father was limited by his equipment to a couple of different rods, and a few lines to handle everything the fish, lake or weather threw at him, you have the option of selecting the best tool for each job.

After you have acquired the tools of the trade, you begin to hone the skills and unearth the information that will separate your success from the masses. This means learning to cast, especially for distance, recognizing which lines are best considering the food sources and conditions present, which fly patterns best represent the food sources available, where to find trout in lakes, the best time to fish for them and finally, to understand how those food sources move and act. These movements are the keys to pattern selection and retrieve if you hope to simulate the natural movement of the insects and minnows that trout eat.

Because trout are creatures of habit, understanding their needs, patterns of behavior, and the forces that influence that behavior gives direction to our education and that direction forms the basis for making decisions that match the constantly changing conditions on the water.

Simply stated, my stillwater fly fishing is a system that is geared to what I consider six key areas:

1. Tackle selection
2. Choice of pattern
3. Casting
4. Locating trout
5. When to fish
6. Presentation

Success is relative to how well you perform these functions. As you learn and improve in these areas, you'll not only catch more trout, but you'll become more proficient and will begin to catch bigger fish as well.

Selecting the proper tackle is a matter of exisiting conditions above and below the water.

Chapter 5

SELECTING STILLWATER TACKLE FOR TROPHY TROUT
The Rods, Reels and Lines For Big Fish

For most of us, fly fishing in lakes for exceptional-sized trout means a modification in our thinking and specialization of our tackle.

The rods, reels, lines and leaders that constitute a basic stillwater fly fishing rig are not all that different from standardized fly gear, but the differences are enough to separate those who are successful from those who want to be.

For most of the fishermen in my stillwater schools, the two biggest tackle changes have been the requirements for full sinking lines and rods with a soft tip action. Lines that sink slowly and rods that nod are a major departure from the floating or fast sinking lines and stiff rod tips that are now as common as blue heron tracks on the banks of moving water.

Believe me, I have no doubt that you can catch a large fish on any tackle combination that happens to be hanging on the rod pegs in your tackle room. Having tackle with enough oomph to land the trout of the decade is not the point.

Our challenge is to put together tackle that will *consistently* pull the pin on giant trout, one after the other, regardless of how clear the water, how hot the sun or how feather shy the fish.

The key word in that challenge is *consistently*. Any one with decent karma can occasionally luck into a giant fish.

It takes a special fisherman to do it consistently.

Rods

Selecting a rod for stillwater angling means a rod with some backbone, a long rod for power and distance, yet delicate enough to handle a big trout on light tippets. Most inexperienced anglers will use whatever rod they own and for the majority of time this works just fine, unless the pursuit is for the larger trout that inhabit our lakes and reservoirs.

Surprisingly many anglers make the mistake of matching the rod to the size of fish they hope to catch, rather than the size of tippet and fly which will balance the presentation.

Fast-action rods are simply less forgiving and much too stiff in the tip section to compensate for the power and quickness of large trout. Although they may be better suited for casting under windy conditions, fast rods fail to match up when small diameter tippets (5X-6X) are stressed to the breaking point by these bulky overweight trout.

My ideal stillwater rod is a 6-weight, 9 to 9½ foot graphite that is soft (slow) in the upper tip section, yet has sufficient butt strength to deliver 70-foot casts when necessary. This rod incorporates a compromise that may be difficult to find short of building a custom rod. For the past 15

Recognizing Fly Rod Action

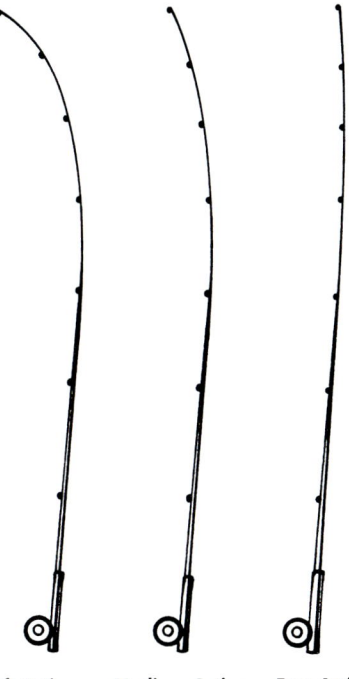

Soft Action soft tip   **Medium Action** moderate soft tip   **Fast Action** stiff tip

Selecting Stillwater Tackle For Trophy Trout

years, I've worked with the Fisher Rod Company to develop custom rods built specifically to my stillwater specifications.

Rods shorter than 9-feet lack the muscle to cast the distance needed to reach spooky fish and tend to be too stiff overall.

The key to picking a stillwater rod that is ideal for large trout is in the tip section. A soft tip rod will act like a shock absorber when the strike occurs. Some strikes are sudden and explosive causing an over-reaction on the part of the angler. Others may be almost impossible to detect, yet in our attempt to be quick, we set too hard. The end result in both instances is usually predictable: a breakoff. It's happened to me and I'll bet it's happened to you.

The soft-tip rod compensates for the solid, often aggressive strikes common with trophy-size fish. A second advantage and perhaps even more important, it allows us the option of using lighter tippets when conditions warrant.

Proof that big fish don't always require heavy tippets. This 8-pound brown was caught with a 6X tippet and a soft-tip rod.

Angler logic tells us to use the strongest possible tippet that will hold when striking a fish without sacrificing delicacy in the presentation. When a big fish breaks off, the instinctive urge is to switch to a heavier tippet.

Larger, stronger tippets, however, often compromise that free-swimming natural motion that allows the fly to look alive. You may, indeed, land a fish on a heavier tippet that you might have lost with a lighter one, but you will also hook far fewer fish. When trout are taking your fly there's no need for changes.

The problem of breakoffs can usually be traced to our own fish-playing skills or a uniformly stout rod that lacks tip-section flexibility.

Lines

This may come as a surprise, but there is no one universal fly line for lake fishing. Variety is not only the spice of life, but a definition of a lake fisherman's line locker. Still, most anglers I see fishing lakes use either floating or fast-sinking lines most of the time, which limits their options and abilities to reach big trout.

Lakes require a multitude of line styles because of the sweeping variations in depth, habitat and food sources.

Weight-forward lines in floating, sinking, sink-tips and shooting heads all have their place when exploring stillwater fisheries. There are several factors that should influence your selection of specific lines for specific purposes. Consideration must be given to the fly pattern, type of retrieve and depth of the fish.

The purpose of a fly is to match or simulate a particular insect. The retrieve brings life to the fly, but the fly line is the vehicle that makes it happen. From an angling viewpoint, the purpose of any fly line is to hold your fly at the depth fish are feeding for as long as possible.

Flies that simulate the aquatic food sources big trout eat, should be fished on slow, full-sinking sinking lines at specific depths that can range from sub-surface to the bottom. The line must present the fly at the exact depth where fish are feeding. The longer your line holds the fly at this depth through the retrieve, the greater the odds become that the fly will find a willing fish.

Consideration must also be given to the angle at which the fly is being retrieved. When trout feed on ascending insects, a floating or sinktip line is a good choice. A full-sinking line is a better choice, however, when fish are feeding on leeches, scuds, dragonfly nymphs or baitfish. These food sources are found either moving horizontally, and on or near bottom where they are most effectively imitated with retrieves possible only with full-sinking lines.

Failure to apply these principals will reflect in missed opportunities and a lack of success.

Remember, there is no single line that will perform well in all lakes or even all areas of one lake all of the time.

The effective range of any line is limited. In terms of depth, if your presentation allows the line to sink too deeply, it's time to change lines to another type with a different density that will present your fly properly. Too often we change flies assuming the fish are looking for something different, when the real problem is that we're using a line that's not presenting the fly where the fish are feeding. It's not uncommon for me to change lines more frequently than most fishermen change flies.

It's not only important, but critical that you be able to determine exactly where your line is taking the fly.

All lakes vary in structure and habitat and stillwater anglers must recognize these variances and carry an assortment of lines that match them.

Four of the best lines for fly-fishing lakes: Intermediate, Stillwater Sinking, Uniform Sink 1 and Weight Forward Ultra Floating

Floating Lines (F)

Floating lines are, in my opinion, the most versatile yet most misused of all fly lines for stillwater.

On the plus side, floating lines can be lifted gently off the water with little surface disturbance that could otherwise spook fish. They are easy to cast and the obvious choice for presenting adult fly patterns on top or emergers just below the surface. Floaters are also an excellent choice, though not an obvious one, for working weighted chironomid larvae, mayfly, or caddis nymphs up from the bottom. They are good tools for wading anglers probing shallow bays and shorelines less than two feet deep.

On the downside, floating lines are poor choices during windy conditions. A floating line, especially a double taper, lacks the density to punch through any wind that's barely more than a breeze. The motion from a rippled surface will force a bow into your line causing drag, creating an unnatural movement of your fly much the same as it does in moving water.

Selecting Stillwater Tackle For Trophy Trout

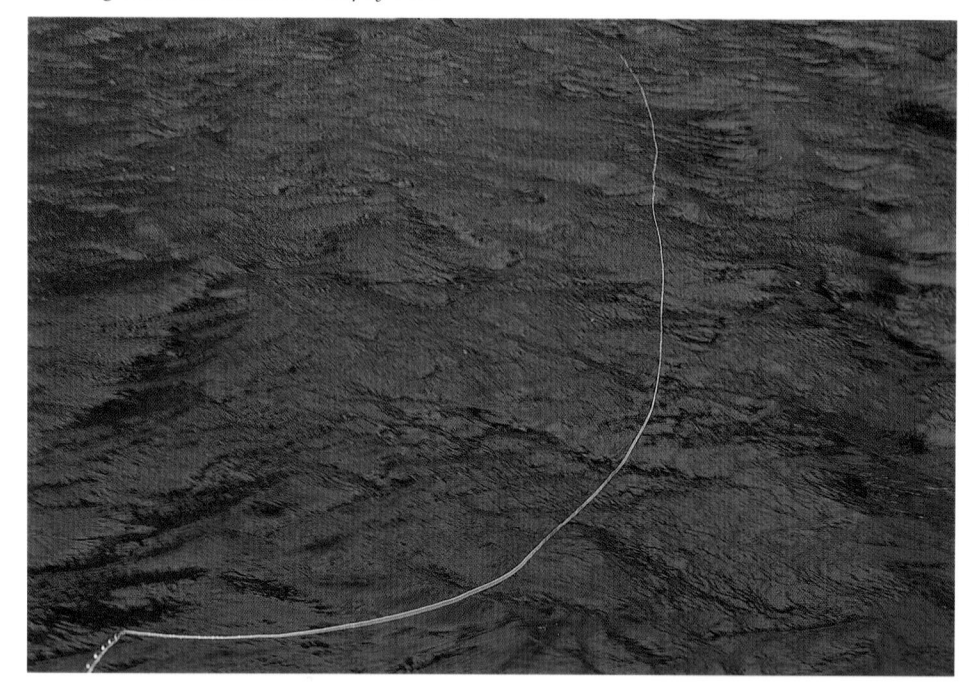

The use of floating lines under windy conditions results in line drag and a poor presentation.

Floating lines were never meant to be strip retrieved, a limitation that comes as a debatable surprise to many of the guys I fish with. Floating lines are designed to deliver a surface fly with a minimum of fuss and to keep that fly positioned on the surface until it's eaten. The only time that fly is lifted off the water, should be to reposition it for another extended float.

Because floating lines are buoyant, any effort to retrieve your fly quickly creates surface disturbance. Most fly fishers make the mistake of using floating lines during strip retrieves.

After the cast delivers the fly, even a slow pull alerts trout to the unnatural movement that results in scuffing an otherwise flat surface. All that's required is a gentle hand twist retrieve to remove slack.

Double tapered (DT) floating lines offer the advantage of a soft, delicate presentation, but these light lines can be tough to cast under windy conditions. When stiff winds blow, which often happens on big Western lakes, a weight forward (WF) floating line is a better choice. Weight forward lines turn over well, are easier to cast during windy periods and will generally cast farther than tapered lines.

Floating lines are at their best dead drifting floating flies. When fishing a dry fly, if there is so much as a breeze ruffling the surface and stalling the hatch, switch to a sinking line and a nymph pattern.

Slow Sinking Lines

Sinking lines were created with stillwater fishermen in mind. Since about 90 to 95 percent of what trout eat in a lake is consumed below the surface, a diverse inventory of sinking lines is critical for big fish arsenals. All sinking lines have two purposes. The first is to deliver a fly to the specific depth where the fish are holding. The second, and I believe most important, is to keep the fly at that depth long enough for fish to make a decision.

It does little good if your fly merely dips into the holding zone, then zips away to follow whatever depth the sinking line happens to be at. The fly and retrieve must match the natural insect's appearance and movement for as long as possible to attract the maximum amount of interest.

Selecting Stillwater Tackle For Trophy Trout

It just makes sense that the more trout that see your fly and the longer you show it to them, the better the odds of inducing a strike.

Trout are constantly on the move, changing locations, depths, feeding patterns and food preferences. To keep pace means constantly changing patterns, retrieves and often fly lines.

As I have already said, there isn't any one fly line that will match all the situations and conditions that can crop up to complicate a stillwater fisher's perfect morning.

The one line that I have found that matches most of my needs for fly-fishing lakes is the intermediate full-sinking line. This line is still either the best-kept secret in stillwater fly fishing or the most overlooked lake fishing tool on the fly-fishing market.

Most major line companies market a good intermediate line. In my estimation the Scientific Anglers intermediate line has a slightly slower sink rate than Cortland and Orvis lines, but the Cortland and Orvis products seem to sink a hair more evenly than Scientific Anglers. It's a matter of control.

The intermediate fly line is a major key to catching big trout in stillwaters.

Intermediate full-sinking lines have the uniform density it takes to carry a fly into the richest food bearing region of any lake, which is water between 1 and 6 feet deep. These lines sink at a rate of between 1 and 1½ inch per second, a rate that permits a slow retrieve through a specific water column, or a countdown depth control when required.

Even more importantly, intermediates allow you to use a retrieve that closely resembles the slow natural movements of most aquatic insects we find in lakes.

FOR TROPHY TROUT

Selecting Stillwater Tackle For Trophy Trout

A seemingly hard thing to remember, but a critical factor if you hope to consistently catch large trout, is that most aquatic insects are extremely slow moving. The majority of anglers that I watch, move their flies two to three times faster than the speed of real insects.

When trout are stratified at a particular depth, say 4 to 8 feet, over deeper water, a slow-sinking intermediate line can be controlled well enough to hold at the desired depth. Fast sinking lines get you to that depth a little quicker but generally zoom right on through the zone. (See, Chapter 7 *Presentation*)

On windy days when trout are feeding just below the surface, the intermediate has the advantage over floating lines by submerging just below the surface, ducking under potential wind drag.

I've found that between 80 and 90 percent of trout strikes occur during the first 10 feet of a retrieve and intermediate lines stay in the strike zone longer than any other line style.

Fast Sinking Lines

Fast sinking lines, while not as versatile as intermediate sinkers, are built with specific sink rates which makes it possible to select a line that most effectively explores a specific depth or gets you on the bottom more quickly.

For example, Type II lines sink at a predictable rate of between 1¾ to 2¾ inches-per second. The fastest sinking lines, Type V, plummet 4½ to 6 inches per second.

Sink rates can be matched to the depths you typically fish. If your home water has a lot of 20 foot bottom, then you'll want a different line than what you'd need in 10 feet of water. Line junkies, of course, will want them all, of course, and they should have them.

A few years ago, Scientific Anglers came out with a Uniform Sink Line which has proven to be a major improvement over earlier standard sinking lines.

The big advantage is that these new designs have eliminated the belly sag, a historically common problem with full sinking lines. By making the full line sink at a uniform rate, eliminating mid-line sag, SA has given anglers a way to fish a tight line, at a predictable depth which reduces potential for missed strikes.

The uniform sinking line works somewhat like a sink-tip line, except it's the belly of the line that's designed to sink at a slower pace than the tip section. Buoyed by the enthusiastic reception of this line among lake fishers, Scientific Angers plunged ahead on stillwater developments.

In 1994 they introduced a line specifically designed for critical, technical stillwater fishing conditions. Marketed as part of their Mastery Series, the line is appropriately named the Stillwater Line. This breakthrough line, is an improved version of Mono-core. It is a clear, single strand of dense monofilament which has proven to be ideal for working line-wary fish in clear water. The sink rate is somewhere between 1½ and 3 inches per second. The only drawback I've found is that it is difficult to remove all line coil memory especially when outside temperatures are a tad cool.

The Stillwater Line, also known as the Stillwater Taper, which is practically invisible in clear water, is simply awesome when it comes to duping hard-fished, spooky trout in clear water. After using a proto-type of this line, a prominent international fly-fisherman from Vancouver, Washington was so impressed with its covert abilities that he nicknamed it, Señor Stealth.

The single-core line is thinner than most sinking lines, enters the water smoothly with a minimum of surface disturbance, minimizes line shadow and fish don't seem to spook from the line's presence.

When you don't have any idea of what depth big trout are feeding at, a full-sinking line fished with a countdown system is the best way to prospect that I have found, especially in deep water. For example, a Type II line can be retrieved in 10-second increments such as; 10 seconds

(1 foot), then 20 seconds (3 feet), then 30 seconds etc., until the water column is systematically covered top-to-bottom.

Sink Tip Lines

Sink tips are what you get when you marry 10 feet of sinking line to the casting end of a floating line. Sink tip lines serve two basic purposes for the stillwater angler. They allow you to fish tight pockets found around weed beds and, most importantly, they lift the fly up through the water column matching the ascent of natural caddis and mayflies. I use only two sink-tip lines for stillwater angling, the intermediate and the high speed Hi-D. The intermediate sinks about an inch per second, while the Hi-D drops three to four inches per second. The sinking tip section on both lines is 10 feet long. If I have to fish deeper than 10 feet, I switch to a full-sinking line. The sink-tip has long been a favorite line for moving water, and should be just as important for stillwater fishermen who spend a fair amount of time offering ascending mayfly and caddis nymph imitations.

Leaders and Tippets

I'm not sure why, but leaders and tippets are two of the most neglected and universally misunderstood segments of our tackle systems. A well-designed leader is an integral part of a balanced system and is critical to smooth presentation. A poorly designed leader is a frustrating abomination to cast, lands in a pile, rarely turns a fly over, and is probably the single greatest puzzlement for beginners.

The key evaluations of any leader include the quality of the monofilament, taper, stretch and tippet break strength. Leaders built with poor quality monofilament break down under continued use. A high performance leader will turn over smoothly under nearly all fishing conditions. Even the best quality leader is inexpensive, and the worst possible place to try to save a few pennies. Keep in mind, the weakest part of any system is the leader. My advice is to buy the best. Personally, I avoid knotted compound leaders for stillwater fishing. They may turn over well, but the series of knots between each taper will collect algae and vegetation, putting trout on the alert.

A quality knotless leader is the best design for stillwater fishing. Leader lengths seem to always be a subject of confusion and controversy for stillwater anglers. I have a couple of standard rules that help me.

Since much of my stillwater angling is with an intermediate line in water less than 8-feet deep I use knotless leaders 12 to 15 feet long. Long leaders and small diameter tippets 5X to 6X are my rule when fishing clear, flat water and big wary fish.

When trout are feeding under cover, such as rippled water, low light, algae bloom or off-colored water, you may get by with shorter leaders and heavier tippets.

My best rule for determining leader length is to make adjustments according to conditions, with the goal of always being able to make a smooth presentation that does not spook fish. A few equipment factors to consider are retrieval speed, type of fly line and how the leader will agree with the fly pattern.

Leaders used with floating lines should be 12 to 18 feet long to minimize line disturbance near the fly. In lakes, fast sinking lines often work well with leaders as short as 7 feet.

The relationship between tippet diameter and hook size is critical to smooth turnovers. Fine tippets don't have the resistance necessary to turn a hefty hook, and a thick tippet can actually drown a light fly.

SUGGESTED TIPPET TO HOOK RATIO

Tippet Diameter	Hook Size
.011 (0X)	1/0-4
.010 (1X)	4-8
.009 (2X)	6-10
.008 (3X)	10-14
.007 (4X)	12-16
.006 (5X)	14-22
.005 (6X)	16-24
.004 (7X)	18-28
.003 (8X)	18-28

This ratio is a general guide so don't be afraid to make variations to meet specific situations to get a smooth turnover and allow the fly to act alive and natural.

With large, wind-resistant flies, a heavier butt section is often needed to turn the leader over, especially under windy conditions.

Compared to the primitive leaders of 10 years ago, today's thin diameter, reduced stretch materials are far superior. There have, however, been tradeoffs, that we have to keep in mind. Small diameter leaders lose elasticity and a small amount of stretch is necessary to absorb the shock of a strike or when a large fish suddenly reverses direction. Stretch also helps eliminate leader memory that creates those ugly coils that reduce distance and make presentation more difficult.

When tippets break at the impact of an aggressive strike from a large fish, we often blame the leader or tippet material when the real problem is more likely to be the knot or lack of rod-setting skills.

While fishing with some friends on a Montana lake one spring, one of my companions, who had fly fished for more than 30 years, broke off eight straight rainbows, each about four pounds or more. He cursed his 6x tippet and tied on a heavier tippet section. He didn't lose any fish on the stronger tippet, but then again, in two more hours of fishing he only hooked one fish on the heavier tippet.

The problem wasn't his tippet diameter, it was his fishing history. My friend had invested most of his three decades of fishing experience into small streams for pan-sized trout. He was not mentally prepared to react to the aggressive takes of these large fish. He simply set the hook too hard and the result was predictable.

The very best combination of rod, reel, line, leader, tippet and fly won't hold up when abused by bad fishing skills, but neither can polished skills make up for mismatched equipment.

Twenty years of fly fishing over 300 lakes went into development of Denny's selection of flies for his Stillwater System.

Chapter 6

DEVELOPING STILLWATER PATTERNS
Specialty Flies That Attract Big Trout

Fly fishing stillwaters for big trout is really an underwater affair and even more than that, it is primarily a nymphing affair.

The classic image of a stillwater fly-fisherman standing quietly in a small boat false casting a No. 14 Adam's on calm water dimpled with spreading rise forms--is wrong 99 percent of the time.

Trout, especially truly large trout, rarely feed on the surface. It's been estimated, reliably, that the majority of a trout's feeding efforts take place below the surface, and that's where big-trout fishermen should concentrate their efforts.

Sure, it's a lot of fun to drop small dry flies in front of rising fish, but the odds of catching a truly monstrous trout during a dry fly hatch are so remote that I won't waste time on the calculations.

If you want to offer a large trout a fly that it is likely to eat, then offer it a nymph or a minnow imitation.

Nymph fishing is often dismissed as boring--a slow hand-twist retrieve using floating lines and extra long leaders. This is one of the most popular presentation forms, but its effectiveness is highly influenced by the pattern being fished.

Because there is a close relationship between presentation technique and pattern selection, one should not be considered without the other. On many of our better stillwaters, the most commonly imitated nymphs are caddis larva, chironomidae pupae, and damsel nymphs along with

This cutthroat was sipping midges, but was caught on a damsel imitation: more evidence that trout feed opportunistically on suggestive patterns than exact imitations.

Developing Stillwater Patterns

leech and scud patterns. There is also a scattering of other nourishing food forms such as mayfly and dragonfly nymphs, water boatmen and terrestrials. These flies, while they can be productive, are less important and play a much smaller role in the diet of stillwater trout.

For years, the bread and butter nymph patterns have been the Zug Bug, Hare's Ear, Pheasant Tail and Prince. These productive stillwater patterns are not exact imitations of naturals but suggestive ties that somewhat resemble a number of different insect species.

Their success is a major contribution to the ongoing debate arguing whether the exact imitation of a natural is necessary, or merely a pleasing accomplishment for tiers. I've fished both imitators and suggestive nymphs extensively and I am convinced that suggestive patterns will consistently out-fish exact imitations.

My faith in suggestive patterns goes back to when I first started fishing lakes. At that time I took great pains to tie and fish flies that exactly mirrored resident naturals. I was convinced that cloning was better than impressionism.

I was wrong.

Fact is, my carefully-crafted imitations, that looked so good in the vise, failed miserably on the water.

It was late June 1984 when, frustrated by my own inconsistency, I began experimenting with numerous fly patterns and methods of presentation.

I was a whirling science project of fly-fishing experimentation, throwing flies into all kinds of situations and conditions, trying new patterns along with variations of established ones. I tried every accepted form of presentation, and some that were nothing more than experimental shots in the dark. I swapped a variety of fly lines and tried a variety of retrieves.

After a few months of intense comparisons, a definite trend began taking shape. Bites were becoming more and more predictable, lending credence to the change in pattern designs as well as the methods used to fish them.

By the end of the 1985 season, my thinking on how to tie and fish stillwater flies as well as how trout respond to them had changed dramatically. The changes were subtle at first. I began by incorporating materials such as seal fur that would move or breath life into my nymphs. I found that while exact imitations were not necessary, it was important to form a silhouette that was as impressionistic and life-like as possible.

The wiggling, undulating motion of a seal bugger was too much for this 8-pound Henry's Lake hybrid.

Developing Stillwater Patterns

This rainbow's mouth was packed with scuds, but it couldn't pass up this black undulating leech pattern.

    I modified the tails of some flies, substituting marabou for hair and lengthening them to create a tantalizing lifelike motion. Some fly fishermen believe that patterns with long tails result in missed strikes. It's been my experience, though, that most of these misses are because of a flaw in presentation or the hook size is wrong. Segmentation is important for impressionistic flies, and I'm convinced that segmenting a fly with saddle hackle is one of the most dependable ways to breath life into an artificial.

    By picking out the fibers between each rib of copper wire, these flies deliver exceptionally lifelike movements and offer a realistic silhouette. Finally, lead was added at the head, not just to sink the fly, but to allow the fly to rise and fall during the pause in the retrieve. This creates an undulating movement found irresistible by most big trout.

    None of these tying techniques were new, but when incorporated into a few patterns, they created life-like imitations that look and move like food.

    It was interesting to study how trout would selectively respond to certain flies and retrieves while at the same time ignoring other patterns and retrieves.

    There are many respected fly fishers who will argue that matching the hatch is absolutely critical. Where I find a problem with this devotion is trying to define exactly what "matching the hatch" means. Does it mean an exact imitation or merely suggest size, shape and color? Does it mean matching the adult stage, or the adolescent stages of the nymph as well?

    I'll agree that matching the hatch is a must when fishing dry flies on the surface, but I'll also argue that suggestive patterns are far more effective when fishing nymphs below. When the sheer volume of hatching insects is totally dominating the food chain, trout will often feed selectively. Although selective feeding only occurs about 5 percent of the time this feeding behavior is but a brief and opportunistic moment for an angler to take advantage of a trout's feeding indiscretions. It's during this feeding binge that imitating the natural is critical. But, what do you do the other 95 percent of the time when trout are feeding and there isn't a hatch? That's why nymphs take on a much greater meaning in stillwaters.

    It seems to me that we've been conditioned to match the hatch for so long that we've more or less retarded our creativity at the tying bench and on the water.

    My point is that after months of experimentation I discovered that trout are not nearly as picky as fly tiers. It's only conjecture and theory as to why a trout will select an imitation when natural insects are readily available. Again, I think we underscore the power of suggestion. But

Developing Stillwater Patterns

trout, I have found, especially those suspicious older specimens, are not fooled by patterns alone.

I'm convinced that a successful fly-pattern must be impressionistic, close to looking like a living, breathing insect, but the manner and depth in which that fly is presented must be exact.

During my trial and error period, some key observations surfaced which I now utilize in my everyday fishing. I consider these points critical to stillwater angling success.

1. When no trout are showing, fish patterns that simulate, not necessarily duplicate the food sources that inhabit lakes.

2. Flies that look and act like natural insects will be consumed faster and more often than those that don't.

3. To mimic this "natural movement" use patterns that incorporate motion.

4. Tactics used to fish a weighted nymph off the bottom are worlds apart from those used to imitate the sub-surface nymph.

5. When trout cruise, their feeding zone only extends 2 to 4 feet in front of them. It's a fly's size, shape, color and motion that will be the trout's primary focus.

6. Pattern selection is insignificant if not delivered at the depth fish are feeding.

7. Since most food forms that trout eat are not fast swimmers, the trout can afford to be cautious, rarely in a hurry to feed. Slow retrieves with lively flies are a productive combination.

My science project is a work in progress, a search for perfection that is hopelessly, and thankfully, impossible to conclude. Persistence and improvement must be ongoing.

In my opinion, the key ingredients in a successful fly pattern can be summed up in two words, *"suggestive motion"*.

SUGGESTIVE NYMPHS FOR STILLWATERS

To understand stillwater nymph fishing you need to understand motion, and to define fly motion we need to look at it from two directions.

The first is the motion derived from the materials we use to construct the fly. Materials that breath in the water have a life-like simulation of the movements of a natural insect. Since trout prefer to feed on living organisms, motion stimulates feeding instincts whether the fish is hungry or not.

The second defines the motion created by the speed, distance and length of pause between each pull during the retrieve. How you control your fly to simulate the movements of a natural is the most critical part of presentation. There are times, of course, during specific stages of insect development when the only motion necessary is a hand twist to keep the line tight.

Flies are tied either to imitate a particular stage of insect development or as suggestive patterns that could represent any number of food sources. Suggestive patterns don't match a particular insect or forage fish but catch a fish's attention because of their life-like motion.

We've all experienced those moments when fishing a pattern that doesn't match the hatch brings unexpected results. These takes are just as illogical as when trout pass up a large piece of protein for a tiny insect half the size. It's easy to justify this type of feeding behavior when we realize that trout feed opportunistically most of the time.

Decisions, decisions, decisions!

So what about all those flies in your fly box? We're all guilty of lugging around more patterns than we'll ever use. The rationalization is we don't want to be caught in that one situation when the old reliables fail.

Numerous patterns are capable of catching trout. Some flies simply work better than others, depending on the presentation used. I believe it's far more important to have a variety of sizes and colors of proven patterns than to cart around boxes of *someday* flies.

Case in point. Checking my fishing logs, for the past eight years, I found I had fished 126 dif-

Developing Stillwater Patterns

ferent lakes, reservoirs and ponds throughout the western United States, Alaska and British Columbia. During that eight year period, I averaged 810 trout of which 97 percent were hooked on only 6 patterns, all nymphs.

These six are my first six choices today. I have a variety of sizes and colors to cover selective preferences. For backup, there are six other patterns that have, at times, proven just as effective.

This deadly dozen will catch trout, if trout are there to catch--and they have caught more large trout than all the other patterns I've ever fished.

Denny's Deadly Dozen

Top 6 Nymphs Patterns
1. Denny's Seal Bugger
2. Denny's Stillwater Nymph
3. Gold Ribbed Hare's Ear
4. Denny's All Purpose (A.P.) Emerger
5. Marabou Leech
6. Pheasant Tail Nymph

Back up Nymphs Patterns
1. Denny's Callibaetis Nymph
2. Birds' Nest
3. Gordon's Chironomid Pupa
4. Zug Bug
5. Denny's Black Diamond
6. Carey Special

And One Bonus Nymph
Wheat's Fancy

The following tying instructions and tips include what I consider the best six nymph patterns for stillwater fly fishing everywhere.

Denny's Seal Bugger

This is a version of the Woolly Bugger, a popular and productive attractor pattern that doesn't match any particular insect but simulates a lot of different food sources that trout eat. I think most trout mistake it more for a leech or dragonfly nymph than for a minnow imitation.

Denny's Seal Bugger is a pattern I developed on my home waters of southern Oregon's Upper Klamath Lake. This pattern's basic appeal is its movement. It is a suggestive fly that is excellent to use when prospecting new water because it matches so many edible insects and minnows.

Denny's Seal Bugger

The body is tied with seal fur, the hackle is palmered or reversed, the tail is marabou at least as long as the body and weighted at the head. When the fly is being retrieved, all of its parts are in fluid motion, undulating up and down to simulate an insect that's either struggling, emerging or retreating from predators.

It's best fished with a slow full sinking line, retrieved in short, rapid (2-inch) or long (24-inch) slow pulls. This type of retrieve often results in soft takes as trout often inhale the whole fly.

Hook:	Size 6-10 4x long
Thread:	Black
Weight:	20 wraps of .020 wire at the head
Tail:	Black marabou (somewhat sparse)
Hackle:	Purple dyed grizzly saddle hackle palmered over the body four times
Body:	Black seal fur mixed with a pinch of red or suitable substitute, picked out after ribbing.
Rib:	Copper wire
Head:	Black

Denny's Stillwater Nymph

The Stillwater Nymph is a fly born out of frustration while fishing Oregon's Crane Prairie Reservoir. Its strength is its versatility. If I had but one fly to fish with when insects are hatching, this would be it.

In lakes where damsels and scuds are a major food source, the fly is deadly. Even when trout feed selectively or when no apparent feeding activity is taking place, the stillwater nymph draws the attention of cruising trout. I like the fly tied both weighted and unweighted and rarely fish it deeper than 8 feet.

The unweighted version should be fished in shallow water and retrieved in short, slow four-inch pulls with a definite rest between pulls. I rarely use anything but an intermediate or stillwater line when fishing this pattern.

Standard damsel patterns specify short tails, but I believe this is a major mistake. The actual damsel nymph doesn't have a short tail; it's long and with the longer tail it's easy to match this nymph's wiggling motion. When imitating a scud, the orange-tinged underbelly hackle matches the belly sack of a pregnant scud. Trout often selectively take the pregnant females, probably because of the higher protein.

Denny's Stillwater Nymph

Hook:	Size 10-14, 2x or 3x long
Thread:	Olive
Weight:	6 wraps of .013 wire at the head
Tail:	Olive marabou
Hackle:	Reddish orange dyed grizzly saddle hackle tied in tip first
Body:	Olive seal fur, marabou or ostrich herl
Rib:	Copper wire
Head:	Olive when unweighted and black when weighted
Wing Case:	Olive marabou tied down full length over the hook

Developing Stillwater Patterns

Gold Ribbed Hare's Ear

Gold Ribbed Hare's Ear

Let's just say don't go near the water without this pattern in your fly box.

The Hare's Ear is to a nymph fisherman what the Adam's is to the dry fly enthusiasts. Every serious fly fisherman has this pattern because it's so versatile. Stillwater fishermen use it to imitate nymph stages of numerous mayflies especially the callibaetis which is so prevalent on Western waters.

The Hare's Ear does such a good job of matching the naturals because it has an enormous appeal to trout. The fly can be built weighted and unweighted and fished on all types of fly lines. It should be retrieved to match emerging nymphs, either with a slow hand twist retrieve or motionless in the surface film. Tan and olive are the best colors.

Hook:	Size 10-18, 1x-2x long
Thread:	Tan
Weight:	4 turns of .012 wire for sizes 10-14 at the head
Tail:	Short hair fibers taken from inside a hare's ear
Body:	Dubbed tan hair from inside a hare's ear then picked out
Rib:	Gold wire
Wing Case:	Turkey tail or any light to dark brown tail feather
Head:	Tan

Denny's All Purpose (AP)

Denny's A.P. Emerger
(All Purpose)

This fly took two years to develop because of constant changes in materials.

I wanted to create a suggestive fly that would imitate not one, but several aquatic insects. Depending on the fly-line and retrieve used, I believe this pattern meets that requirement.

It does an excellent job of matching emerging mayfly, caddis, dragonfly nymphs, water boatmen and maybe a few others. The AP has proven its worth to me and has become one of my top go-to patterns.

I prefer to fish it with an intermediate sinking line and a short slow pull and pause retrieve or with rapid 2-inch pulls.

Hook:	Size 10-14 3x long
Thread:	Olive
Tail:	Wood duck
Body:	Hare's ear
Rib:	Copper wire
Thorax:	Peacock
Wing Case:	Wood duck
Hackle:	Partridge (tied down over the thorax)
Head:	Olive

Hal Janssen's Marabou Leech

Any angler who has spent much time fishing lakes knows the meat and potatoes value of a leech pattern.

These slinky creatures are found in all types of water, and a favorite prey of oversized trout.

A good leech imitation should have a tail at least as long as the body to give it a life-like wiggle. For me, the Hal Janssen leech pattern has been consistent in most of the lakes I fish. Although these creatures come in a variety of colors, black, brown and olive seem to be the most consistent and I never fish it unweighted.

Hal Janssen's Marabou Leech

Leech patterns should be retrieved with long, slow pulls on slow-sink lines. Pause to allow the fly to dip after each pull. This creates an undulating movement representative of the swimming motions of all leeches. Hal Janssen's Marabou Leech is dependable all season, but is most productive during April to June when leeches are most available.

Hook:	Size 6-10, 3x or 4x long
Thread:	Black
Weight:	20 wraps of .020 wire at the head
Tail:	Black marabou (sparse)
Body:	Black marabou
Wings:	Three wings of marabou tapered back toward the head
Head:	Black

Developing Stillwater Patterns

Pheasant Tail

The only change I've made in the classic standard version is in the tail where I prefer moose mane because of its durability. This pattern is normally fished with a floating line, a long 15 to 18-foot leader and a slow hand twist retrieve.

A common mistake is to move the fly too fast. Little or no movement is best with this pattern. I prefer the pheasant tail nymph unweighted to simulate an emerging mayfly nymph and rarely fish it deeper than 3 feet. Because of its versatility, it can be effective in a weighted version fished up from the bottom. The fly can be deadly all season but is most productive during the fall months when other food sources become less available.

Pheasant Tail Nymph

Hook:	Size 14-16 2x long
Thread:	Black
Tail:	Moose mane
Body:	Pheasant tail
Rib:	Copper wire
Wing Case:	Pheasant tail or turkey tail feather
Thorax:	Peacock
Throat:	Brown hackle barbules tied down under thorax
Head:	Black

SIX BACKUP PATTERNS

The next six nymphs are my backup patterns, but could easily make the first-team depending on the water fished and conditions present.

Denny's Callibaetis Nymph

This is the best fly I've ever used when callibaetis are present. Trout, when feeding on the surface, seem to take the nymph just as readily as they do the adult. Even though the pattern is tied to simulate callibaetis nymphs, its real strength may lie in its suggestive nature.

Some very good anglers have told me this fly does an excellent job of imitating a scud, while others say it resembles a water boatman. Depending on the retrieve used, it

Denny's Callibaetis Nymph

could represent all of these insects. I prefer it in size 10-14 in olive, cinnamon, black or natural hare's ear color and always unweighted. I found it best to keep the fly in the top six inches when trout are feeding near the surface.

The fly seems to be most effective when fished with a very slow four-inch pull, with short pauses or a hand twist retrieve, on floating or intermediate lines.

Hook:	Size 12-16, 2X long
Thread:	Olive
Tail:	Lemonside wood duck breast feather
Body:	Hare's ear
Rib:	Copper wire
Hackle:	Small natural grizzly wrapped 3 times and tied in tip first
Wing Case:	Same as tail tied full length of hook
Head:	Olive

Bird's Nest

Named after my close friend, Cal Bird of Reno, Nevada, this fly is another pattern that closely simulates many caddis and mayfly nymphs found around the western U.S. and British Columbia. We are never really sure what trout mistake our flies for, except when we match the hatch. But who cares, as long as they take them.

The Bird's Nest is as good in moving water as it is in stillwaters. Floating, sinking, and sink-tip lines all work with this fly. It should be retrieved with short, slow four-inch pulls allowing the fly to sink back after each pull. Don't be afraid to experiment with the speed of the retrieve when the recommended retrieve does not produce.

Bird's Nest

The most consistent colors are tan, olive and dark brown. It should be tied both weighted and unweighted.

Hook:	Size 10-16, 3x long
Thread:	Same color as body.
Weight:	6 turns of .012 wire, positioned at head
Tail:	Dyed mallard breast to match body
Body:	Dubbed natural animal fur (I prefer a mix of rabbit and otter)
Rib:	Copper or gold wire
Wings:	Mallard breast feather tied in V form on top of hook, in front of head.
Head:	Same color as body

Developing Stillwater Patterns

Gordon's Chironomid Pupa

In England, they refer to it as a buzzer. Canadian anglers call it a blood worm when tied with a red body, although this is actually the larva stage.

Chironomids are members of the midge family and found in virtually all lakes around the world. Because of its numbers and availability, it is the most important insect on the trout menu. From an angling viewpoint, the pupa is the stage fishermen should most often try to imitate.

Trout can become extremely selective when feeding on this stage and a wrong color on the fly is all that's necessary to draw a refusal. The most effective form of presentation is with a floating line, 15 to 20-foot leader, and an extremely slow hand twist retrieve. The fly should be allowed to sink naturally while you focus on the point where the line enters the water.

Takes will be subtle and any movement of the line can signal a hit. Although there are numerous versions of this fly, the one I find most consistent was shown to me by Gordon Honey of Kamloops, British Columbia.

Gordon's Chironomid Pupa

Hook:	Tiemco 2457 Size 10-16
Body:	Frostbite in Crimson, Green and Brown
Rib:	Copper or silver
Thorax:	Peacock herl (1 strand)
Gill Cover:	White ostrich
Head:	Should match body color

Zug Bug

This fly has been around a long time on both still and moving water. The Zug Bug impersonates several insects, but I'm never really sure just what the trout mistake it for. It's best fished on a floating or intermediate line with short slow pulls. A good fly to use when you're not certain what to start with.

Hook:	Size 12-16 1x long
Thread:	Black
Tail:	6-8 pieces of peacock sword
Body:	Peacock
Rib:	Gold wire
Thorax:	Peacock
Wing Case:	Wood duck
Hackle:	Brown tied under
Head:	Black

Zug Bug

Developing Stillwater Patterns

Denny's Black Diamond

While fishing Diamond Lake in southern Oregon one fall day in 1974, I was struggling for action until a fellow angler took pity on me and gave me the original form of this pattern. I have made a few changes, substituting seal fur for the body and thorax which gives the fly a more impressionistic look, and moose mane for the tail.

The fly is particularly effective when fished vertically through the water column simulating a rising mayfly nymph or near the bottom imitating the dragon fly nymph. Both a very slow four-inch pull and pause or hand twist retrieve work with a high speed HI-D sink-tip or fast sinking lines. I've also had good success experimenting with a rapid short two-inch pull on an intermediate line.

I like this pattern in size 10 to 12 and always fish it weighted.

Denny's Black Diamond

Hook:	Size 10-14, 3x long
Thread:	Black
Weight:	8-10 turns of .012 wire at the head
Tail:	Moose mane or black hackle barbules
Body:	Black seal fur or substitute
Rib:	Copper wire
Thorax:	Black seal fur or substitute
Wings Case:	Turkey tail feather
Hackle:	One or two turns of black hackle tied down over thorax
Head:	Black

Carey Special

There hasn't been a pattern over the past 50 years that imitates a dragonfly nymph any better than the Carey Special.

I'm sure trout take it for something other than a dragonfly nymph at times, which is a testament to its effectiveness. The Carey has been around for a long time, yet is not popular in the United States except among stillwater anglers.

In Canada, especially British Columbia where this fly originated, the Carey, in any of its many versions, is considered one of the primary patterns for the Kamloops rainbow.

Carey Special

FOR TROPHY TROUT

Developing Stillwater Patterns

It's a simple fly, tied with pheasant tail back feathers for the tail and hackle, chenille or natural hair for the body and silver or gold oval tinsel for a rib.

The fly is most effective when fished on the bottom. Use a slow hand twist retrieve. Line choice is based on the depth you're fishing but fast sinking lines are normally a good choice.

Hook:	Size 8-10, 2x long
Thread:	Black
Tail:	Pheasant back or rump feather
Body:	Olive or black chenille or Angora goat for more suggestive appearance
Rib:	Medium silver or gold oval tinsel
Hackle:	2 turns of pheasant rump feather tied down over body
Weight:	6 turns of .020 wire at the head
Head:	Black

BONUS NYMPH

This is my bonus nymph, given to me by my good friend, Irv Wheat, from Chester, California. It could easily fit into my top dozen and probably will by the time you read this.

Wheat's Wood Duck Nymph

Wheat's Wood Duck Nymph

Also known as Wheat's Fancy or Wheat's Bird Nest, this little mayfly pattern is deadly in stillwater.

Originator Irv Wheat uses a strike indicator with this pattern, but also finds it effective by casting and retrieving it using a floating or intermediate line. Irv ties this little critter in various sizes, but believes it is most productive in Nos. 14 and 16.

Trout will take it even when selectively feeding on midges, which is testament to its effectiveness. Olive and black are the best colors. Because of its small size the fly should be fished in very slow, short pulls. Added weight is a key for balancing the fly when using a Yakima Bait "Corkie" for a strike indicator.

This pattern has proven deadly for me and it will for you.

Hook:	Size 14-16, 2X long
Thread:	Color to match body
Weight:	6 wraps of .015 lead
Tail:	Lemonside wood duck or mallard breast feather
Body:	Sparkle blend in Hare's Ear, black or medium olive
Rib:	Fine gold wire
Wing Cases:	Wood duck tied in same length as tail, pull over thorax and tie down. Divide excess for legs.
Head:	Color to match body

Developing Stillwater Patterns

Well, those are my deadly dozen plus one. If I interviewed 100 anglers on their top dozen stillwater patterns, no list would be the same. Many flies will work, of course. Besides, we tend to fish those we have the most confidence in most of the time, anyway.

I obviously prefer suggestive flies that simulate motion, not mirror the physical features of a natural. I believe that patterns that move appeal to the predatory instincts of big trout, triggering a feeding response even when trout are not feeding or selectively taking other food sources.

I encourage experimentation, but remember: it's not always the fly that's important but how we are fishing it.

Developing Stillwater Patterns
STILLWATER DRY FLIES

Floating a dry fly over rising trout is what fly fishing is all about.

It's the height of anticipation, exciting, extremely addictive as well as frustrating. To watch a floating fly disappear in an explosive rise, or simply disappear from the surface, is what keeps us glued to the sport. Once you have experienced a full-blown, bar-the-door, dry-fly frenzy, you're never quite the same.

For most of us, fly fishing is a sport that begins with floating lines, light tippets and tiny dry flies. So, right from the beginning we are drilled on the importance of matching the hatch with small mayflies, caddis flies or some other floating insect. But, most anglers don't give a hoot if they catch big trout with dry flies or not. It's so much fun watching their fly being eaten that trout size is not a driving force. Or is it?

Large trout will rise to dries in the narrow, often food-poor environment of moving water, but getting a trophy sized lake fish to leave the bounty of the bottom and come up for a little dry fly is difficult, very difficult. On lakes, it is almost impossible, and yes, I realize there are occasional exceptions.

Frankly, I've been accused by some dry-fly purists of being about two clicks away from the twilight zone, but let's remember that I'm dealing with the trophy-size trout minority, and I don't measure success by the number of fish caught. I love catching trout on dries as much as the next guy, but it's the hardest way I know to consistently tangle with giant stillwater fish.

Art Lee, Northeast Field Editor for Fly Fisherman magazine, wrote: *"Dry fly fishing is essentially an inefficient means of catching big trout."*

According to Art, he fishes just enough, both on the surface and underwater, to disbelieve all portrayals of big trout being predominantly insect eaters.

Big fish want as much protein per bite as possible, and they get it in large chunks with leeches, fat nymphs, crayfish and slow minnows that abound in lakes.

Don't let that stop you from trying with dries. After all, it's fun, and the day you pull off the impossible and bring a 15-pound rainbow up to a No. 16 blue-wing olive, will be a day you can paint red, tear off the calendar and frame.

When fishing lakes with dry flies for the first time, it's important to understand the difference between moving water and stillwater presentations. Without a current flow to move the fly, it will just sit on the surface, looking pretty, waiting for a fish to find it. Now, I don't know about you, but I don't have the patience to watch a fly float until a hungry trout happens to cruise by. Some of us could be on life support by the time that happens.

It's been my experience throughout the West that big trout pay little attention to surface activity except for a few specific hatches during the warmer months when smaller trout are gulping (cruising and feeding).

As I've said, most fisheries biologists agree that 95 percent of what trout eat is below the surface, not on top of it. For younger trout to put on weight they must eat constantly. Anything that moves, wiggles or even looks appetizing is fair game. In most of the public lakes, small trout, from 6 to 12 inches, outnumber their larger cousins by a large ratio. That's why the majority of adult insects are consumed by small trout, not the heavyweights.

There are a couple of reasons why big trout are difficult to bring to the surface.

The predatory instincts of a trout became increasingly aggressive as it grows and trout that eat other fish rarely look to the surface for food. Leeches, scuds and crustaceans are bottom dwellers. Secondly, large trout being wary creatures, are careful about disclosing their whereabouts to predators. Surface feeding and shallow water make them nervous.

When trout with shoulders do go to the top, they either feed selectively on an insect that we must match in size, shape and color, or they feed opportunistically on anything that acts natural. Selective feeding usually occurs when sufficient numbers of a chosen insect appear on the water. Trout respond by intercepting the little duns while cruising just below the surface, but

Developing Stillwater Patterns

selective feeding binges are usually brief.

To make dry fly fishing harder, as if it needed to be, trout often switch selective preferences in the middle of a hatch. Generally, the fish don't turn from one species to another, but from one stage of development to another: nymph, to emerger, to dun. Multiple hatches occur but are usually of minor importance on lakes.

Adult insects get smaller as the season progresses, as evidenced by this mayfly imitation that matched the hatch in June, and the same insect as it appears in September.

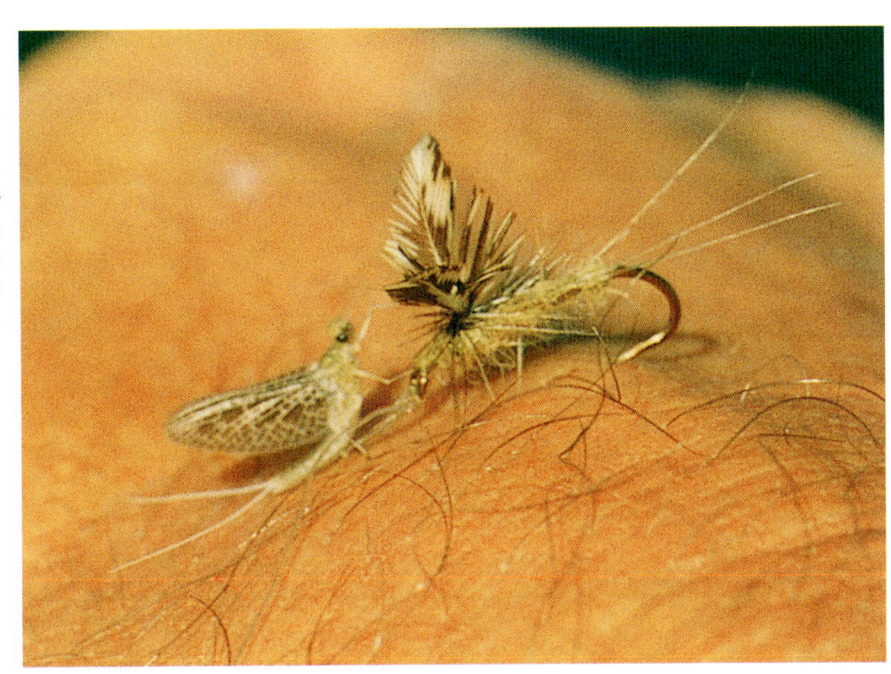

One of the funniest scenes I ever witnessed occurred on the Upper Sacramento River as this old timer struggled valiantly, but in vain, to match the hatch. Adult caddis were buzzing across the water everywhere just before dark as he urgently searched his fly box for the right fly. Trout were splashing noisily all around him as twilight slipped away.

He continued to frantically change flies as more and more trout began to show on the surface. I had just released a nice fish and was quite sure he was unaware of my presence. He crouched down apparently to pick up a fly, and by then I was close enough to hear him mutter to himself about how damn particular the trout were being.

Finally he had the fly he had been looking for. He waded further into the current, but in his haste to thread the end of the leader through the eye, he dropped the fly. Slowly, it drifted downstream while he looked frantically for it in the dim light. When he finally spotted the fly, he lurched wildly after it, stumbling through the water, the fly always just beyond his grasp. The slippery bottom eventually took its toll as he lost his balance and landed right on his wallet. Soaking wet, he barked curses at the darkness, glared at his hat floating downstream, and sloshed back to his spot at the tail of the pool.

Despite the commotion, trout continued to rise in increasing numbers which only seemed to frustrate him more. With water dripping from his chin, he grabbed his fly box, tore it open and emptied the contents on the water. As the mass of patterns drifted slowly downstream, he muttered to himself, *"that ought to confuse the little bastards:"* at which point he picked up his rod and vanished into the brush.

It took almost 5 minutes before I could regain my composure, dry my eyes and think about fishing. I guess a trout that is selectively feeding can do that to you.

You can expect some frustration trying to match the hatch at times, but I'm not sure it's worth an entire box of flies.

FOR TROPHY TROUT

Developing Stillwater Patterns

Opportunistic feeding, on the other hand, is just the opposite of selective feeding.

Trout behave like scavengers and are rarely particular about their choice of calories, only in the manner in which they are presented. Many anglers are unaware that trout feed opportunistically the majority of the time and not selectively. The reasons are obvious: lack of hatches, changing conditions, insufficient numbers of a particular insect, water temperature--the list is endless.

The point is, trout are not picky about what they eat so long as it looks and acts natural. Trout tend to cruise more when feeding in this manner and don't particularly need company when they are on the hunt.

This hefty Upper Klamath Lake rainbow left the security of deep water to eat leeches in the shallows, not an unusual occurrence.

In shallow lakes where the depth is less than 8 feet, trout normally feed either in the top two or three feet of water or near the bottom. This may come as a surprise, but I've found the depth trout feed is usually more important than what they feed on. Even when trout feed selectively, they will take other food organisms when the opportunity presents itself. It took me several seasons before I began to understand this principle. For example, once trout finally key into a surface hatch, I often fish my callibaetis or stillwater nymph in the surface film or a few inches below, a strategy that rarely fails even though trout are looking for the adult. Just remember, the key for stillwater anglers is to find the zone where trout look for food. If they are eating adults on top it's critical to keep your fly near the surface, retrieving a few inches at a time and very slowly. Trout will find it.

Being able to differentiate types of rise forms will make it possible to identify which stage of the insect development the feeders are working.

Rise rings also reveal the direction the fish is moving as it feeds, the speed, whether it is feeding on top or just below, and in many instances, the size of the trout. A tiny ring usually indicates that trout are sipping small midges or mayflies. If the rise is dramatic and explosive, it usually indicates larger insects, adult damsels, caddis or some form of terrestrial. A tail and dorsal porpoise-type rise is a trout feeding on nymphs just below the surface.

When trout cruise the shallows feeding on scuds or other insects on the bottom, they often force upheavals of water as though it were boiling. This type of surface disturbance is a key that trout are bottom feeding.

When food is readily available, trout often fall into a predictable feeding rhythm. If they are moving and feeding, it's fairly easy to time the rises and deliver your cast on track in anticipation of the next rise. Feeding trout are seldom in a hurry when there is plenty to pick from. If fish aren't cruising, place your cast next to the rise ring as quickly as possible after the rise. Sometimes a big fish will be content to let food come to it.

Weedy or structured bottoms are obvious areas to look for insect and trout activity. But where the bottom is bare, or when insect activity is minimal, trout will often cruise long distances in search of food--usually opportunistically feeding. Keep your pattern selection consistent with the dominant insects, and you'll do fine.

Reading the rise becomes even more critical when multiple hatches are occurring. Again, close observation will usually solve the riddle not only to insect preference, but to what stage of development the trout have chosen. Wind can curtail hatches on lakes but if the trout continue to feed on the surface, they nearly always face into the wind. Your angle of line presentation now becomes more critical to avoid lining fish.

When wind is not a factor, look for the trout to move in a circular path. This tendency is especially true on small ponds or enclosed areas of large lakes. Mayflies, midges and caddis, although not a high priority in terms of what large stillwater trout eat, are nevertheless the major draws that bring trout to the surface.

When dry fly fishing, it's important to be able to recognize the differences in rise forms, to determine the type of rise, and the stage of insect development trout are feeding upon.

A surface rise, usually small Midge or Mayflies.

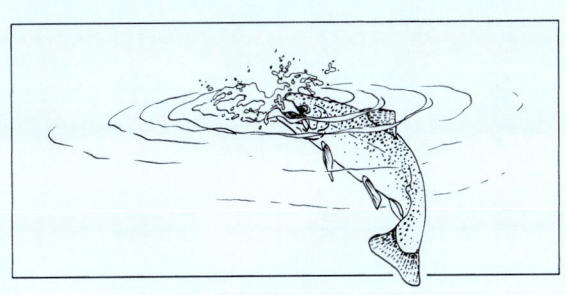

An explosive rise to adult Caddis or Terrestrials

A tail & dorsal rise, usually means trout feeding on emerging duns or the pupa stage of aquatic insects.

It's sometimes easy to misidentify a surface take for a boil actually created by the dorsal fin or tail of a nymphing trout. A boiling-type rise means bottom-feeding trout.

Developing Stillwater Patterns

Most Western lakes support families of callibaetis, tricos or caenis mayflies. The callibaetis is the most important for anglers to imitate because of their wide distribution. For me, the best callibaetis imitation is the Adam's in sizes 12 to 18. High visibility parachute versions have an edge over standard Adam's ties. In my estimation, both will do the trick. Caddis flies are not as widespread as mayflies, but deliver explosive action when trout feed on them. The most active of the extensive caddis family are the traveling sedges. Sedge patterns should be skittered across the surface like the natural and not presented motionless on the surface.

A dry caddis pattern fooled this big rainbow.

In most western lakes, hatches of mayflies and caddis flies take place from June through early September with slight time variations governed by water temperature.

Adult damsel flies appear about the same time as caddis and mayflies, but trout seldom rise to them, preferring the nymph instead. I know of only a few lakes where trout will feed aggressively on adult damsels and seldom is the bite consistent. But when it happens, you'll wish you had a pattern in you fly box.

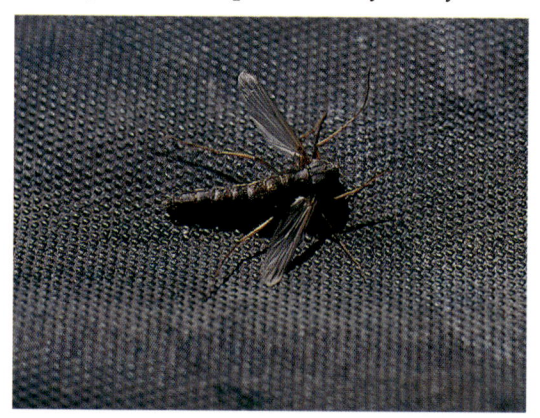

Most midges are small, but adults like this can bring big trout to the surface on occasion.

Adult damsel flies at Crane Prairie Reservoir.

Personally, I don't own an adult damsel pattern because of my preference for the nymph. As for dragonflies, I've never seen a trout eat an adult dead or alive. Perhaps I've missed something, but, as far as I'm concerned, it will be a first when I see it happen.

FLY-FISHING STILLWATERS

Developing Stillwater Patterns

Midges are considered the most important food sources for trout on a year-around basis, but adult midges are not the preferred stage, especially during the summer months when higher protein food sources are more available. More attention is paid to the adults during the fall, winter and spring when other adult insects are absent. Midges are shadow bugs that prefer to avoid bright sunlight. In fact, midges so intently dislike sunlight that they often refuse to hatch when it shines. Luckily, big trout have a fondness for the larva and pupa, especially the pupa.

Terrestrials, especially ants and grasshoppers, are seasonal favorites everywhere. Unfortunately, availability is limited to short, glorious periods. Most Western ant hatches come off sometime in June, and hoppers are seldom available until late August through mid September.

As popular as these two food sources are to trout, I've only seen flying ants on about a dozen lakes and hoppers on just two in 25 years of fishing stillwaters. Keep in mind the availability of any food source is a major factor as to what trout eat and seasonal fluctuations in weather often control which stage and which insect the trout will choose.

A big rainbow looking for emergers near the surface.

There are times when a particular insect will generate enough interest to bring large trout to the surface. During these brief periods, big fish tend to feed on the move, cruising just below the surface. This type of feeding behavior is referred to as "gulping". The term originated on Montana's Hebgen Lake where browns and rainbows from 2 to 4 pounds cruise the shallow flats and bays in search of emerging callibaetis mayflies. Gulpers are less cautious when feeding in this manner as they move about completely focused on inhaling the little duns in prolific numbers.

Inexperienced anglers often cast directly to the rise which is well behind a gulping fish. Because gulpers are on the move, it's critical to lead them a few feet, drop the fly and let the trout come to it. An occasional twitch imitates the struggle of a natural emerging into a winged insect.

There are a number of trophy lakes in the Western states that offer excellent "gulper" action during the summer. Depending on elevation and location, these feeding orgies begin sometime in June and continue well into August. Callibaetis mayflies, caddis and midges are usually the victims, but if ants and hoppers are around, they can offer some exceptional action.

Developing Stillwater Patterns

One major advantage anglers have when trout feed at the surface is seeing where the fish are feeding. "Sight fishing" is fun and not limited to dries, but includes nymphs as well. Whether you're a novice or an experienced stillwater angler, this is exciting fly fishing.

When trout are surface feeding, selecting a fly that matches the natural is one thing, persuading them to eat it is another. Fishing clear flat water with dry flies demands competent skills and presentation technique. You will find there is little room for error with this form of presentation.

Stalking trout under such conditions requires fine-tuned casting, presentation and terminal tackle. Leaders must be long and tippets fine enough to allow the fly to appear lifelike. Cast delicately, place the fly softly on the water and pick up without surface disturbance.

Here's a tip: don't compound a casting error by ripping the fly from a feeding area quickly. Retrieve the fly slowly from the area with as little disturbance as possible. Any unnatural movement only further spooks the trout.

Mastering distance casting is a requirement for consistent trophy trout success, yet it is one skill many anglers seem to lack when fishing stillwaters. On many lakes casts of 40-50 feet will get you by, but you will face many situations where you'll need to cast as far as 70 feet to keep from spooking fish. I've witnessed many opportunities that were lost because the fisherman was unable to make the long cast.

Some anglers like to position themselves in the middle of feeding fish. Not a good idea. This tends to scatter fish, and reduces the odds of getting multiple hookups. Sometimes we scare unseen fish when picking line up for the next cast. It's better to work the edges of a feeding school. Less risk of putting fish down.

There's nothing more difficult when fishing lakes than a mirror-like surface, high sun and feeding fish rippling the water. Under these conditions, the leader becomes a critical part of the presentation. Mirror-like conditions require leaders that are at least 15-feet long, but longer may be necessary if fish are skittish and exceptionally spooky. Tippet size is determined by fly size and external conditions, but on flat clear water a smooth turnover is a must.

Fishing dry flies on lakes can be frustrating at times, but I've never seen a fly fisherman witness a rise and not want to be in the middle of it despite the fact that large fish and tiny dry flies are seldom a successful combination

Dry flies will always be a part of fly fishing lakes and there are countless patterns that will work on stillwater. In my experience the following dries will cover the majority of mayfly, caddis and midge hatches on western lakes.

You will probably need to localize these patterns by substituting hackle and body sizes.

MAYFLIES

Adam's
Hook size: 14-18
Thread: Black
Tail: Grizzly and brown (optional) hackle fibers
Body: Gray muskrat fur
Wing: Grizzly hackle tips
Hackle: Grizzly and brown (optional) tied parachute or standard wrap

Adam's

Developing Stillwater Patterns

Compara Dun

Compara Dun

Hook size:	12-16
Thread:	Tan or olive
Tail:	Moose mane or micro fibers (2 or 3 each side)
Body:	Tan or light olive fur
Wing:	Light deer or elk hair

MIDGES

Adult Midge

Parachute Midge

Hook size:	14-18
Thread:	Black
Tail:	Moose mane or grizzly hackle fibers
Body:	Gray animal fur
Hackle:	Grizzly (four wraps then trim bottom)

Griffith's Gnat

Griffith's Gnat

Hook size:	16-20
Thread:	Black
Body:	Peacock herl
Hackle:	Grizzly tied body length

FOR TROPHY TROUT

Developing Stillwater Patterns

Elk Hair Caddis

CADDIS

Elk Hair Caddis

Hook size:	12-16
Thread:	Tan
Rib:	Gold wire
Body:	Tan or light olive fur
Hackle:	Golden ginger tied body length
Wing:	Cream to tan elk hair tied down over body

Sedge Caddis

Sedge Caddis

Hook size:	12-14 2x long
Thread:	Tan
Body:	Tan or light olive fur
Hackle:	2 light brown or ginger hackle tied body length with excess trimmed below bend of hook and flat on top
Wing:	Lacquered mottled turkey tied over body with V at the end

Developing Stillwater Patterns

STREAMER PATTERNS FOR PREDATORY ANGLERS

In most lakes capable of producing trophy-size trout, forage fish (minnows, chubs, and bite-size fingerlings) make up a large percentage of what big trout eat. Minnows and other small fish excite big trout; they make their gastric juices flow. Because of their size, large trout need a substantial meal to maintain their weight. Burning calories searching for tiny insects is no longer prudent.

In other words, it takes an impossible number of sipped tricos to equal the energy supplied by one gulp of a careless fat head chub.

And that's the major flaw in any dry-fly purist's plans to catch a giant fish on a small floating fly. In my never-ending quest for the perfect big-fish fly, I've learned that there are tremendous differences between the food preferences of small and large trout, differences that should carry over to the fly box of a big trout specialist.

Trout for example, spend most of their early years eating constantly, consuming small insects and other minute life forms. As trout age, their food preferences slowly, but constantly change. Many of the food sources that sustained them early are progressively eliminated, especially those organisms that require considerable energy outlays for the value returned.

Once trout reach a length of about 14 inches, they begin to emerge as predators. From this stage, through the rest of their lives, trout are no longer content to share living space with minnows and other small competitors and become aggressively opportunistic in the search for food. They feed less, but take bigger bites.

From a fly fishing standpoint, this means closing the lid on the box of perfectly-tied light Cahills, and opening the lid on the box of big, shameless, minnow-type patterns.

Any fly that impersonates a forage minnow can be deadly in a big-trout lake. While dry flies and floating lines may define the popular notion of fly fishing, it's streamers and sinking lines that are the tools of the predatory angler.

So what constitutes a streamer fly?

In angling circles, the streamer is defined as any pattern resembling a bait fish that trout eat. The definition has, however, become generic in nature over the years. The streamer and its close cousin, the bucktail, are differentiated only by the materials used to tie them.

Streamer patterns are tied with feathery wings and tails, whereas bucktails, as the name discloses, are tied with animal hair. Marabou feather and rabbit fur are very different natural fibers, yet when retrieved both produce a very life-like motion with each delicate fiber pulsating and creating the illusion of a living creature.

Dan Byford's Zonker patterns and marabou streamers are good examples of suggestive and highly effective streamers with big trout appeal. Streamers and bucktails are typically tied to resemble small minnows, yet they are also taken where the dominant food sources are sculpins, crayfish, frogs, leeches and even grasshoppers and mice. Two prime examples of suggestive flies that impersonate nothing, but generally simulate many food sources are the highly productive Muddler Minnow and Woolly Bugger.

A third streamer style incorporates the colorful creations known as attractors, tied with either synthetic materials or natural feathers and hairs, or a blend of both. Attractors suggest a number of living creatures, but more often than not catch the attention of a cruising trout because of their flashy dress. Excellent examples of attractor patterns that have survived the test of time are the Grey Ghost, Spruce Fly, Mickey Finn, and Royal Coachman Bucktail.

Hundreds of the streamers in use today are local patterns created specifically to match a local food source.

A great many of these local patterns have been nationalized by repetitious magazine articles and seminars expounding their virtues. Many of these patterns have an eastern birthright and their value in the West is largely accidental because they happen to resemble a local food source. Patterns I include in this category are the Back Nosed Dace, Light Edison Tiger, Black Ghost, and Mickey Finn.

FOR TROPHY TROUT

Developing Stillwater Patterns

The West has also got its share of provincial patterns, including the endless variations of sculpin flies, the flashy Matukas, Grey Ghost, Woolly Buggers, and various Marabou Muddler patterns.

Nearly any decently-tied streamer, I've found, will get a trout's attention. It's how you present and retrieve the fly that determines whether or not that trout responds positively to your presentation.

Streamer Strategies

Some 20 years ago I read the late Joe Brooks book, *"Fly Fishing."* In the section on streamer tactics, one particular sentence stood out as the key to presentation with streamer patterns. *"The best way to present a streamer or bucktail,"* Brooks wrote, *"is broadside so the fish see the fly from head to tail."*

I've found his words to be excellent advice. Brooks' point was based on experience and so is mine. The number of days I've spent fishing streamer flies in front of trout seem endless. Frankly, I believe the profile presentation is the key to angler success on a consistent basis. Few fish of any species take their prey head on or from behind. They chase it down, grab it in the middle, crushing or stunning it, then turn it and swallow it headfirst. This maneuver, I suppose, prevents the prey from flaring its fins and lodging in the trout's throat.

Mike Dehart's 12-pound rainbow was caught on a streamer pattern while chasing minnows in shallow water.

The problem with a profile presentation is that it's tough to pull off unless you're sight fishing. Many times trout will chase minnows to the surface, and believe me, it doesn't get any better than this. These feeding frenzies produce extremely aggressive strikes and if there is a down side, it's that the bite doesn't last long enough.

When you can't sight fish, which is usually the case, you can still make a presentation that delivers the fly perpendicular to a holding area. One of the ironies of this type of fishing is that trout feed most actively when wind, darkness, or other cover protects them from being seen by above-surface predators--and that includes you.

Developing Stillwater Patterns

Consequently, we blind cast during these periods, secure in the faith that fish are feeding, gambling that our faith is on line.

It's crucial to cover as much water as possible when searching with streamers for unseen cruising fish. A trait, actually more of a flaw, of inexperienced anglers is that they beat one area to death because in the past they caught a good fish there. Experienced anglers will cherry pick a series of hot spots, continually moving until they find feeding fish.

Retrieving a minnow imitation that mimics the swimming motions of forage fish typically requires a strip and pause motion. I recommend varying the speed and length of the retrieve, especially when searching, but not on the same cast. I start with a medium fast two-foot pull and pause and vary the speed and length of subsequent pulls until I find a combination that works.

When fishing minnow-type patterns, I prefer an intermediate line and rarely use fast-sinking lines since most attacking trout maneuver their prey towards the surface usually in relatively shallow water.

Denny's Seal Bugger, visible in the corner of the mouth, fooled this 8-pound rainbow which had been chasing minnows in shallow water.

Leader lengths are determined by water conditions and weather patterns in place at the time as well as the size of fly used. With streamers, I like to use a leader section 10 to 12 feet long.

Longer leaders may be necessary if the water is low and clear. Tippet sizes should also be balanced to the size of the fly, but again, conditions will determine what limits you have to play with. Trout generally throw all caution to the wind when chasing minnows and since strikes can be quite savage, 2X and 3X tippets are not out of line.

The size of the streamer pattern should be comparable to the bait fish in the lake. Matching a minnow's size can be just as critical in streamer fishing as when matching the hatch with a dry fly. The key is to match the size and color as well as the motion (retrieval speed) of the bait fish you're trying to imitate.

Fly sizes from No. 4 to No. 8 will match most forage fish found in stillwater fisheries. Shallow, clear water often requires smaller patterns to avoid spooking fish. Trout are naturally more wary in shallow or clear water and often spook when large flies enter their space.

Whether you tie your own flies or buy them at a retail outlet, remember a sparse dressing is better than over dress. Too much bulk compromises fly action and will dramatically reduce the number of strikes. I learned this lesson years ago when fishing the East Walker River in California's Eastern High Sierra. For three straight weeks following opening day I had enjoyed

Developing Stillwater Patterns

outstanding action using No. 4 and 6 marabou muddlers. One night, at the vise, I gave in to the bigger-is-better theory, and tied up some No. 2 patterns heavily dressed.

During the preceding three weeks my normal evening fishing with smaller flies produced 6 to 10 hookups on browns to 6 pounds with an occasional larger fish. I was expecting even better and bigger results as I stepped into the river that evening with my bigger, bushier variations. I cast, and cast, and cast. Nothing. It took an hour of thrashing the water with my overly-dressed patterns before I realized that something was out of sync. A quick change back to the lightly dressed patterns, renewed the interest of the heavy fish.

It's easy to make the mistake I made. Just don't assume bigger is always better, and when the question is how much dressing, the answer is nearly always less.

A streamer can be tied and fished to resemble a number of different minnow types. In the hands of an experienced angler, streamer flies are a serious threat to the longevity of any big trout. Anticipate big fish and arm jolting strikes. If you haven't fished them before, you'll find fishing streamers is not only addictive, but rewarding.

Here are some proven patterns with color options, that I recommend for trophy-trout in stillwaters.

STREAMER PATTERNS

Zonker

As minnow imitations go, Dan Byford's Zonker is as close to the real thing as you're going to get. It's the best I've ever used for big fish. The rabbit fur breathes, creating that life-like motion that draws strikes even from non-feeding fish. I do best with non-weighted Zonkers because I fish them mostly in the shallows where big trout hunt for little fish.

Try the Zonker in various colors to match the forage fish in the lake you're fishing. A long two-foot strip seems to work best for me, but you may have to experiment. I rarely fish this pattern on anything but an intermediate line concentrating on the top 6 feet or along shallow shorelines early or very late in the day.

Zonker

Hook size:	No. 4 to 8, 4X long
Thread:	Same as the wing color
Body:	Mylar tubing (Coat the hook shank with head cement before tying the body on)
Wing:	Rabbit fur extending from the head to an inch beyond the bend of the hook
Collar:	Red, yellow or orange hackle
Head:	Same as the wing color (painted eyes are optional)

Developing Stillwater Patterns

Denny's Shiner Minnow

The Shiner Minnow is a pattern I developed while trying to handle those huge rainbows of Upper Klamath Lake in southern Oregon, which has a little bit of everything in the way of minnow life. This pattern has also been very consistent for me when matching little shiners so prevalent in many lakes in the West. I prefer marabou for body motion, Flash-a-Bou for an attractor over the wing, and either Mylar or Crystal Chenille for the body. It's a simple but deadly pattern that deceptively matches many small fish. I prefer it in white with a little gray marabou over the top for the back. I find it fishes most effectively with an intermediate line and long slow pulls with extended pauses between pulls.

I use this pattern in the top 6 feet or in the shallows next to shore where big fish search for small fish.

Hook size:	No. 4 to 8, 3X or 4X long
Tail:	White marabou
Middle wing:	White marabou
Top wing:	White marabou with a little dark gray added on top then a few pieces of pearlescent Flash-a-Bou over the gray marabou
Body:	White crystal chenille or pearl mylar tubing
Head:	Black or match wing color.

Shiner Minnow

Matuka

An import from New Zealand, the Matuka is a versatile fly that resembles bait fish in many, if not all, lakes. The dominant colors are brown or olive. Body and wing colors can be varied to match local bait fish.

Hook:	No. 4 to 8, 3X or 4X long
Thread:	Same as wing color
Body:	Olive fur
Wing:	Two large grizzly soft hackles died brown or olive, extending from the head to an inch beyond the hook bend.
Rib:	Copper wire, or olive tying thread wrapped through wing feather.
Collar:	Red or orange hackle.
Head:	Black or olive.

Matuka

Developing Stillwater Patterns

Denny's Chub Minnow

Denny's Chub Minnow

This is a pattern that my close friend, Jay Fair, helped create for the big rainbows on Upper Klamath Lake. I've tried it on other lakes with equal success because it resembles so many species of forage fish. The use of marabou wings gives the fly a life-like appearance regardless of what retrieve style is used. I prefer the use of Flash-a-Bou over the wing instead of Crystal Hair which tends to mat the marabou, reducing the breathing motion so critical with suggestive patterns.

Hook size:	No. 4 to 10, 4X long
Thread:	Olive
Tail:	White marabou
Middle Wing:	White marabou
Top wing:	Olive marabou
Body:	Short pearlescent crystal chenille with 8-10 strands of rust Flash-a-Bou tied on top
Head:	Olive or black

Developing Stillwater Patterns

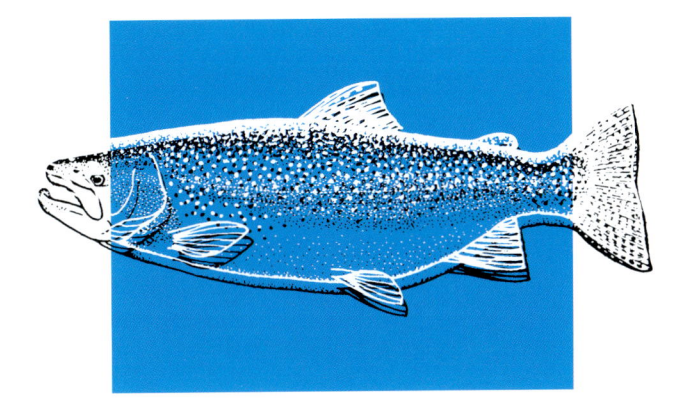

Long casts are a must when fishing over large spooky trout.

Chapter 7

CASTING FOR DISTANCE
The Required Skill For A Big Trout Specialist

Learning to cast is one thing, learning to cast for distance is a different skill altogether.

Distance casting is a challenging sport all by itself. It is a critical skill that must be developed if you are to become proficient enough to consistently outsmart trophy-size trout. Many anglers are excited about the challenge of stillwater fly-fishing, yet come up short of their expectations because they lack the skills to make the long cast.

The deadliest fly pattern is useless to the caster who can't put it in front of a feeding trout. Casting for distance is a skill few anglers learn well especially those who are used to the limited casting demands of streams and small rivers. Most fly fishermen have difficulty on lakes where clear, calm water conditions and vulnerable, spooky trout often require that you cast 60 feet or more. Sixty feet is a long way, probably about 20 feet farther than most anglers can cast well.

The ability to cast 60 feet or more is critical for trophy-trout specialists.

The inarguable truths that show up at officially measured distance casting-competitions have polished off more self-described 100-foot fly-casters than heart attacks.

Bruce Richards of Scientific Anglers is one of the finest casting instructors in North America. He stresses several points that are critical not only to good casting, but to distance casting as well.

The first and most important step to achieving greater casting distance, according to this professional caster, is to understand the dynamics of a fly line. Even the rawest beginner has learned that it's the weight of the line, not the fly, that is cast. The most critical factor, and least understood by novice and veteran anglers, is that it's the shape and angle of the moving line on the back and forward casts that largely determines accuracy and distance.

Casting For Distance

Gravity and air resistance are the limiting factors of distance casting, and casting techniques have been developed that, if properly executed, will overcome both problems. During the casting of the line, arm and wrist motion forms the shape of the loop and applies power to the line. The size and weight of the fly helps determine whether a tight or somewhat open loop is best.

In most instances, certainly in all on-the-water situations, the best way to minimize the effects of gravity and air resistance is to throw a tight casting loop. The tighter the loop, the less wind resistance and the greater the casting distance.

The size of the loop is determined by the motions of the casting arm and wrist. To form a tight casting loop, it is essential that the tip of the fly rod travel in a straight line during the applied power phase of the cast.

If too much wrist motion is used during the power stroke, the rod tip travels too far and opens the loop. Keep the wrist stiff and tight against the rod butt. The size of the developing loop is directly proportional to the vertical distance the rod tip travels during the power stroke.

The less wrist motion, the less vertical travel and the tighter the loop. It's important to remember that vertical travel only applies to loop control during the power part of the stroke, not the total arc of the rod tip.

Wrist movement is also a major part of building line speed which is critical to achieving distance.

As power is applied, the line travels in the direction in which the power is applied by the rod tip. *Figures 1 and 2* show how the amount of rod tip travel during the power stroke determines the size of the casting loop. By making the power stroke as short as possible and by limiting the wrist movement, the size of the loop can be restricted.

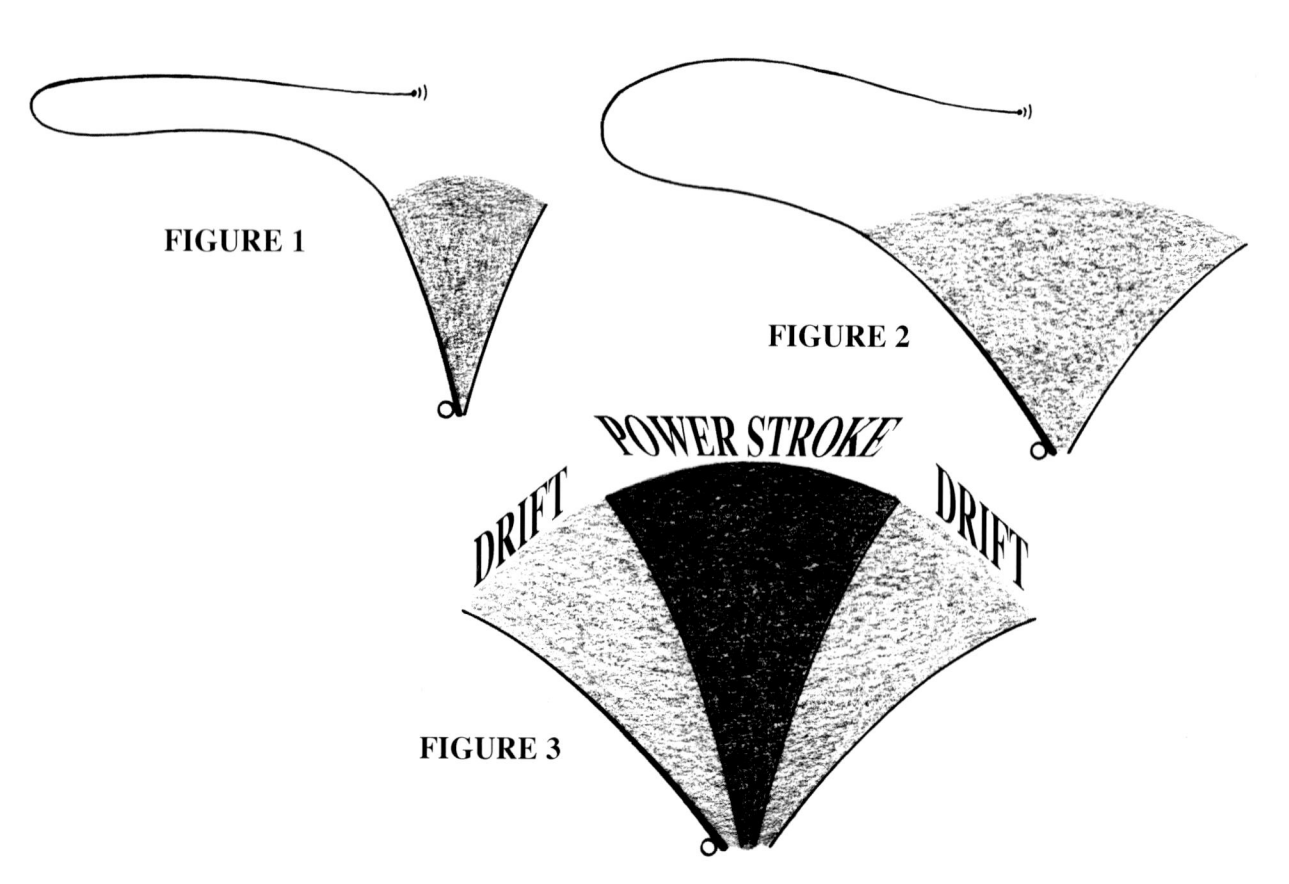

FIGURE 1

FIGURE 2

FIGURE 3

FLY-FISHING STILLWATERS

Casting for Distance

Remember, as you practice, that any curve in the line represents slack in the line. If curves are allowed to form during the forward power stroke, the slack will steal power and shorten distance. To make long casts, it is essential that the line be allowed to straighten on the back cast before the forward power stroke is applied. Otherwise it will be difficult to make an efficient forward cast.

To make a smooth tight-looped cast in either direction, it's critical that the power stroke be smooth and fully straightened (this loads the rod) before changing directions.

Practice by turning to watch the back and forward casts as they unfold. When the loop has nearly straightened, begin a slight drifting motion with the rod in the opposite direction. This pulls on the line, removing any slack that may have formed, and slightly pre-loads the rod, reducing the amount of power that must be applied with the wrist during the power stroke. It is important to remember that the drift motion is a slow non-powered move. If the rod drift is too fast or has too much power, the loop will open. The risk of slack line during a cast is highest when there is a lot of line working in the air. Sometimes a longer drift is needed to pull out the slack of a long line. Power most efficiently transfers from the rod to a slack-free line. Every inch of slack reduces power.

Almost as critical as loop control is the ability to develop high line speed, which is best accomplished by incorporating a single or double haul into the cast. The shape of the line loop must be tight or wind resistance will rob you of distance. In addition, applying power on the forward cast too abruptly will result in tailing loops which make distance impossible.

If you can't cast a 6-weight line, 60 feet consistently, my best advice is to enroll in a casting course, available in most regions through community colleges, parks departments, or fly-fishing clubs. There are hundreds of how-to books and videos on the subject that would be worth the investment.

Don't get me wrong, not all stillwater fishing requires long distance casting. Shorter casts may be adequate when lake water is clouded from nutrients or algae, when the wind creates surface chop, or when utilizing the cover of darkness.

This 5-pound rainbow was the result of a 70-foot cast over flat water.

Casting For Distance

Long casts, however, are in order when fishing during one or more of the following conditions or situations:
- When the water is flat and the sun is overhead, your mistakes will be magnified, especially when moving shadows are visible to fish.
- When trout are surface feeding, avoid getting too close, and spooking a scattering fish, ruining the bite.
- When trout are feeding in shallow water. Big trout are exceptionally cautious in the shallows and will panic at the slightest alien sound or vibration.

Learning to cast well is a prerequisite for enjoying the sport. Learning to cast for distance is a required skill for trophy trout specialists.

When the wind is a factor and is blowing from the angler's right to his left, merely extend the right hand above the head and turn the wrist so the rod extends over the left shoulder. When done correctly, the wind will never be a negative factor again.

Cast viewed from the front

This is the correct rod casting position to compensate for a wind blowing from the angler's right to his left

FLY-FISHING STILLWATERS

Casting for Distance

COMMON CASTING PROBLEMS
And How To Correct Them
(Reprinted From Scientific Angler's Fly-Fishing Made Easy Handbook)

All of our casting difficulties are the results of mistakes. If you use the proper form you will avoid most of them. All of us, however, occasionally get into bad habits. Some of the most common, that are particularly troublesome to beginners, are listed here along with suggested solutions for correcting them.

Low Back Cast

Cause: Hitting the water or ground on the back cast is caused by continuing to apply power too long through a wide arc, thereby driving the line down; also by insufficient line speed to turn over the back cast.

Correction: Make the back cast with a brisk backward movement, holding the wrist stiff. Stop power application abruptly when the rod reaches the one o'clock position.

Wind Knots,
Hooking Line,
Hitting Rod With Fly

Cause: Most commonly, knots in the leader are caused by punching the rod during power applications.

Correction: Concentrate on accelerating the rod smoothly through its arc; don't apply all of the power at once.

Piling Up Line and Leader
At End Of Cast

Cause: Piling up line and leader is caused by an inefficient wide loop. By powering the rod through a wide loop (often from three o'clock to nine) a wide loop is formed which cannot transmit enough energy to fully straighten the line.

Correction: Accelerate the rod briskly from 1 to 11 o'clock, stopping the rod abruptly. Remember, don't let any line slip from your left hand during the power application, only after.

Snapping Off Fly

Cause: Snapping off flies and cracking the leader on the back cast are caused either by starting the forward cast too soon, before the back cast has time to straighten, or else by failing to use sufficient force in the back cast. In this case, it would never straighten, no matter how long you waited.

Correction: Watch the back cast and start the forward cast when line and leader are straight behind. Use sufficient force in making the back cast so it will straighten.

Slapping Water

Cause: Splashing the line, leader and fly down on the water, sometimes hard enough to sink a dry fly, is caused by aiming the forward cast too low.

Correction: Tilt the arc of power application backward a little so the forward casts straightens two or three feet above the water, then settles gently. In other words, aim your cast higher.

FOR TROPHY TROUT

Casting For Distance

Line Won't Go Out

Cause: When the line won't go out and straighten even 30 feet of it, one or both of two casting faults committed by all beginners are nearly always to blame. The first is waving the rod through a great wide arc, instead of pushing it briskly through a narrow one. The second fault is permitting line to slip through the guides during the application of power.

Correction: Again, make sure that you are powering the rod through a narrow arc, not a wide one. If your loops are large, you are using a wide arced stroke. Having someone watch your cast and tell you what you are actually doing with the rod can be very helpful. Also, if you are working out line, you must not release the line from your left hand until the power application is completed.

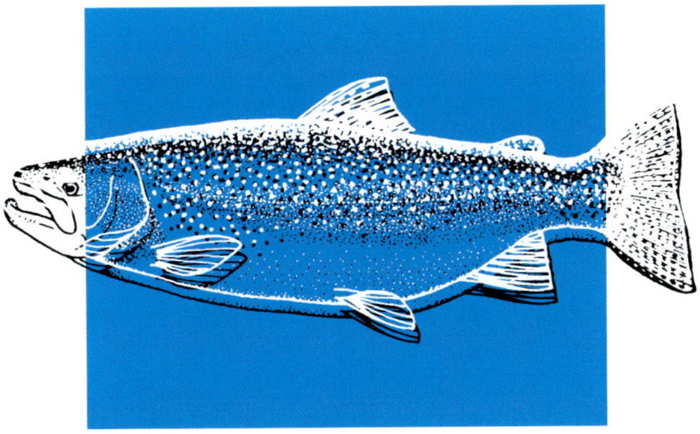

Weedy shorelines offer trout ideal cover from predators and a variety of food sources.

Chapter 8

WHERE BIG FISH HIDE
*The Ultimate Challenge;
Finding Giant Trout In Stillwater*

Face it, lakes are intimidating. The bigger they are, the more intimidating they become. Yet large shallow lakes are more likely to harbor true trophy trout: pot bellied memory fish so thick one hand won't span a side, and so rare you won't bother telling anybody because they never believe you anyway.

Many fly fishermen take one look at the flat, unbroken surface of big lakes and are overwhelmed at the idea of unraveling the trout paths in such waters. Unfortunately, many anglers are so wracked with indecision that they shy away from exploring what could be the most rewarding trophy fishing they will ever encounter.

Unlocking the secrets to a lake's big trout is not as difficult as our imaginary fears would lead us to believe. The first job of a novice lake fisherman is to overcome the fear of tackling a large unknown for the first time. The uncertainty that comes from the first outing on a big lake is a lot like a small child's fear of a dark room. As soon as you begin to think of a giant lake as nothing more than a series of small ponds, the lights begin to come on.

Although it's the size of most lakes that intimidates stillwater anglers, locating trout in lakes remains the single most important challenge awaiting fly fishermen. All lakes can be a frustrating mystery and like the first year of school or marriage, there are more questions than answers. The answers are hidden beneath acres of flat, often unbroken water, a perfect disguise when compared to the easily read character of moving water.

Which way to the fish? Are they in close or off shore? Near the surface, stratified, or belly-down on the bottom? Nymphing or inhaling sucker fry? Cruising, feeding, or at rest? Where do you start?

Nearly three decades ago, the first few times that I fished lakes, I was soundly trounced and sent home in humbled defeat by these mysteries. I was as baffled and bewildered as any other traditional fly fisher in love with moving water.

Streams and rivers are what most fly fishermen equate with trout fishing, yet wherever I've fished the truly trophy-size fish were in stillwaters. They grow long, fat and old in an environment rich in nutrients, multiple food sources and protective cover. They always have lots of room to dodge predators along with the opportunity to relocate with seasonal changes in habitat and food conditions.

When I first became interested in Western stillwater fly fishing, the only reference books that I could find dealt almost exclusively with waters on the eastern cuff of North America, and the amount of information that applied to my waters was at best, limited.

It was clear that if I wanted to learn how to locate trout consistently in the West's vast number of natural lakes, reservoirs, impoundments, beaver ponds and mountain lakes, it was going to be a solo learning adventure. It would have to start in ignorance, hopefully rising to solutions that would unravel the mysteries of these big beautiful trophy trout waters.

Where Big Fish Hide

It was and still is an engrossing, consuming challenge, yet the pieces have slowly fallen into somewhat predictable patterns. The first couple of years my prospecting and research could only be described, and then generously, as suffering in comfort. I'll spare you the roller coaster thrills of my occasional highs and crashing failures and head straight for the bottom-line where I began to detect patterns of consistency. Consistency led to standardized answers that I have successfully applied to almost every stillwater fishing mystery.

There is nothing, absolutely nothing more important in fishing stillwaters than knowing how to locate the fish. When you read those six words--knowing how to locate the fish--the logic appears elemental, even simple to the point of possibly being insulting.

Believe me, there is nothing simple about it, or else why would so many otherwise meticulous fly fishermen squander their time lashing water for fish that aren't there.

If you retain nothing else in this book, be sure you understand that the single most important challenge confronting stillwater trophy trout anglers is learning to consistently locate trout. This includes any lake, during any season, or under any external influence.

Typically, anglers new to a lake wander from point to point, trying this, trying that. They catch a few trout, but most of their fishing time is wasted making great casts and text book retrieves in troutless water. The deadliest fly pattern ever pulled from a vise is worthless if trout don't see it.

PREY ON THE PREY
You Are The Predator: Adjust

The first adjustment is mental--a realization that the biggest difference between trout in stillwater and trout in moving water is feeding behavior. It sounds simple. It's not. For most fishermen, myself included, accepting the difference between flowing and frog water means uprooting and modifying years of imprinted fishing behavior.

Lakes, unlike streams, are harder to read because the keys to locating fish are not so obvious. In moving water, holding areas are more easily defined. Trout can hide and let the current bring the groceries to them. But, in lakes trout must move, always hunting, always changing locations.

Trout spend most of their time feeding when conditions are acceptable to them, sometimes selectively sipping, and sometimes inhaling everything that resembles food. A trophy trout fisherman must be able to catch under both feeding patterns and also recognize apparent changes in feeding behaviors, not for what they appear to be, but for what they are.

Talk to any group of fishermen and you will hear episode after episode of how they were enjoying great action when the bite began to fade and eventually died.

For years, I too thought that was what was happening. Because I was always exploring, I continued to move and fish through some exceptional action as well as the hot bites and dead periods. Soon I began to discover that with a few rare exceptions, the bite doesn't die, it moves.

The sudden variation in the feeding patterns that most anglers mistake for the end of the bite, often marks the start of a new feeding period, a new hunt. Quite often this happens at the same time in, not only one area of the lake but in many others as well.

Remember, when a trout feeds in stillwater, it usually moves to the prey. What we mistake for the end of a trout bite is nearly always a case of trout feeding away from our casting zone, or giving up the dregs of a fading surface hatch for more plentiful nymph action developing down below.

We should be following these changes and taking advantage of new feeding patterns. Instead, we put down our rod and reach for a sandwich, blissful in our ignorant confidence that the bite is as dead as a stonefly stuck on a windshield.

Where Big Fish Hide

The clues for unraveling secrets of trout movement in stillwater are found in water temperature, structure and habitat. These three factors could also be called oxygen, shelter and food -- the three basic needs of every healthy, catchable trout.

Most fly anglers are familiar with these three requirements for survival. The skill that separates the fishless majority from the successful minority lies in the ability to recognize and to understand the impact of external factors.

These external factors can, and often do, have as much influence on trout movement as the basic three. To get a comprehensive "read" of the water look for:

a) *sources of food*
b) *protective cover*
c) *oxygenation / temperature*

After determining the status of these basics, you can then narrow the search [and leave most of your fellow fishermen far behind] by factoring in atmospheric conditions, barometric pressures, water depth, temperatures, water clarity, wind [velocity and direction], light intensity, time of day, and seasonal peculiarities which could include spawning, water temperature extremes, and seasonally dominant food sources.

A trout's movements are directed entirely by the strengths and weaknesses of these factors. They in turn become our keys to not only where and when to fish, but to tackle selection, choice of fly patterns and presentation techniques.

When you begin to take seriously this pursuit of big fish, you will learn to enjoy and then look past the ambiance of the sunrise, water smells, croaking herons, and ain't-it-great-to-be-alive aura. You will begin to focus on and to recognize the forces that are dictating every movement of a trophy trout.

When you know why, where and when a trout moves, you will be able to invest most of your fishing time casting to water with big fish in it. And that is the first key to consistently hooking trophy trout in stillwater. The operable word here is consistent. Anyone can luck into a bragging-size lunker, and that is exactly how most fishermen get their fish of a lifetime. To consistently catch trophy trout, we cannot afford to depend on luck. Anglers who fish aimlessly across a lake may catch a fish or two, but they spend too much time fishing unproductively.

Locating trout in lakes should never be left to chance. We need to depend on factors within your control--information and skill.

We need to understand how food, cover and oxygen/temperature needs affect trout behavior.

FOOD SOURCES
Find 'Em Or Forget It

More than any other influence, the desire for food directs a trout's movement and preferred locations. Besides food, only the sheer terror of a predator can drive a big, wary trout away from the safety of protective cover or to briefly tolerate uncomfortable water temperatures. Terror, however, is temporary. The need for food is perpetual, a dependency that we have absolutely no qualms about taking advantage of.

The need for food drives trout into the areas where we expect to find them. But it's not as easy as staking out a likely looking area and hooking the first trout that moves in. The order and density of insect life varies widely within a lake and are influenced by a number of conditions that will determine how important they are to your fishing success.

Where Big Fish Hide

There are 28 orders of insects, five of which are entirely aquatic, and all of which can wind up as trout food--some more often than others.

Metamorphosis of these insects [even within the same order] takes place at varying rates, times and areas within the same lake.

In the area where you are fishing, the stage of each insect [larval, emerger, dry, spent] and the rate of metamorphosis are governed by water temperature, wind, oxygen saturation, barometric pressures, and the time of day or night.

If you are to match the existing food source, there are slivers of fact that must be taken into account. If this all sounds a little too cerebral for our pastime, then add the sunlight factor and see how these few paragraphs can put 15 pounds of brown trout on the end of your tippet.

Light, more accurately sunlight or the absence of it, is the single most important influence in triggering stillwater insect activity and is especially critical to hatch development. The hatches of many of our most popular hatch-match patterns are totally dependent on the degree of sunlight penetration and subtle increases in water temperature from that penetration.

Because lakes are a varied lot, with a mix of depths, shade and structure, light penetration is never the same all over the lake. This should work to your advantage. At several of my favorite big fish lakes, it's possible to fish the same feeding pattern in several areas of the lake by progressively following the sun, and fishing the same order of insects patterns as the sun sporadically develops hatches across the lake.

Quite often, we can reverse the pattern for evening hatches. Fish the first shade, beginning in the areas of the lake where the sun first leaves the water. Often this occurs along the west bank in the long shadows of tall trees. Follow the shadow lines and the ensuing evening hatch as darkness creeps across the water.

Trout, especially big predatory fish that require large gulps of protein to survive, often move into an area of insect activity and begin feeding on nymphs or emergers before the surface hatch develops. Conversely, these big fish are often slow to abandon a food source and will hang around for a bit after the hatch, cruising for opportunity. In both instances, I've found the fish to be unusually aggressive, especially toward large attractor patterns.

My favorite patterns in this situation are color and size variations of leech, seal buggers and minnow imitations. These are workhorse patterns, and when fished on an intermediate line, these flies are deadly, especially for big trout on the hunt. There is no question that big trout are caught sipping No. 20s, but in my experience each catch is the rare exception.

When I pursue big trout, I often use a seal bugger, and frequently when I tighten up, it's on a fish that will show me my backing. Flying in the face of popularly held theories on exclusive selectivity during major dry-fly hatches, is the number of times I've had bruisers literally inhale this pattern in the center of an otherwise selective feeding binge.

It's been my experience that average trout often become maddeningly selective. Exceptional size trout, however, are opportunists and are more vulnerable to well-presented wets in larger sizes. More protein per gulp I imagine.

Between feeding binges, trout hold up in the safety of cover which can be depth, weed beds, rocks, wood, or shoreline brush.

In lakes, trout do not seem to be nearly as territorial as their relatives in moving water. It is not unusual, however, for trout to remain in a specific area of a lake for extended periods. Trout, and especially big trout, are never far from food where the hunting is easy. They rest in areas where there is cover and the water temperature and dissolved oxygen levels are more preferable. This temporary territorialism will normally change with the seasons.

In my hunt for big fish, I've found it essential to determine the locations of these holding areas and to do that requires looking away from the trout and concentrating on its prey. Understanding and recognizing the habitat requirements of the dominant food sources narrows my focus to potentially productive areas and eliminates water with less than ideal prey habitat-which is the majority of any lake.

I eliminate the acres of unproductive water by recognizing the preferred habitat of a specific food source, and understanding the time of day or season when that particular piece of protein is most abundant.

As an example, on Upper Klamath Lake in southern Oregon, leeches are a prime food source for the huge rainbows that thrive in the rich shallow waters. During the spring, leeches abound along the shoreline and the giant rainbows are in tight to shore feeding on them.

For years though, I didn't see this seasonal predator-prey relationship and dropped my flies in the traditional holding areas offshore a hundred yards from where I find fish in the spring. Eventually, I learned that this area was a hot summer fishery because the big 'bows were concentrated where cooler water temperatures prevailed.

In the cool weather near the first of the season, however, neither trout or leech had reason to be out in the deeper, cooler water.

My "fishing luck" changed drastically for the better the spring I discovered giant leeches were thriving in the sun-warmed water around the tule beds and willows. Hungry spring trout were thriving on them. Learning can be so slow and painful. I take solace in the fact that I'm not the last slow learner. Every spring, while I'm teasing and being teased by 7 to 12 pound rainbows in the shallows, I'm within sight of dozens of fishermen working the unproductive cooler water a hundred yards away from trout that look like footballs.

Once I understood the key to locating big trout is locating their food source, success got a lot easier and targeted fishing areas a lot smaller and more focused. The lake, once a giant intimidating mystery, is now divided into vast sweeps of unproductive water between slivers of productive targets.

Let's consider those areas where trout feed, the same areas where big fish specialists must concentrate their time.

Shallows/Shoal Areas
A Conspiracy of Wind, Waves and Weeds

The shallow areas of any lake, sometimes referred to as shoal areas, are the most prolific food-bearing regions in the entire stillwater environment. Nutrient-rich and saturated with a multitude of insects, these areas, especially those along shorelines, are one of the few places big trout routinely cruise, hunting for an opportune gulp.

The shallows are warmer than the rest of the lake, an ideal condition for most aquatic insect life. This wealth of water insects, augmented by a seasonal load of fat terrestrials like ants, bees and hoppers, attracts small bait fish which in turn attract large opportunistic trout.

The more weed growth (protective cover) that exists in shallow water the better for finding trout. Because big trout spook easily in here, it's wise to concentrate your fishing efforts during first light or late afternoons when the sun rays are diffused. One of the great natural events that you can hope to fish occurs when wind and waves churn clouds of silt along shoreline areas, dislodging minute food sources while generating a protective covering of off-color water.

Many times I've seen this combination of wind, waves and weeds trigger feeding binges that can only be described as savage. This is the food-chain at its most dynamic moment. In the shallows, under these conditions, you are as likely to hook a record-size trout as a 10 incher. Watch carefully and you should be able to spot the backs and fins of the largest fish jutting just above the surface.

Where Big Fish Hide

The greatest food producing region of any lake is in shallow water.

Littoral Zones
A Gathering Place For Trout

In every lake there are specific, well-defined areas that literally teem with trout food. Except for deep-water marl beds and freshwater shrimp zones, these areas will be located between the high and low water marks a region scientifically described as 'littoral zones." These zones are nothing more than an extension of the shallow regions of a lake.

Littoral zones typically support a rich mix of aquatic and terrestrial life forms (plant, animal and insect.) These zones can extend from the bank to the depths, sometimes up to 30 feet depending on water clarity in natural lakes and the extent of annual water draw downs for non-fishery uses, primarily agricultural irrigation in reservoirs.

The deeper extremes of littoral zones support less life [food] than the shallower areas and normally will attract fewer large fish. The exception is during the heat of a summer's day, when big trout may retreat to the cooler more comfortable water in the depths at the far edge of the littoral zone.

If the water temperature and oxygenation is comfortable, these deep-water hides are an ideal holding area for midday trout. Sunlight penetration is minimal, there is some food for opportunistic feeders and it's a short swim back to the food-rich shallows once the sun slants. I rarely fish deep-water littoral zones, not because I don't catch fish there, I just find the shallow areas more productive. When the sun is bright, temperatures high and big trout tough to come by, I wouldn't hesitate to recommend probing the outer edges of pronounced littoral zones.

Fishing for big trout in shallow water is a demanding exercise. You learn to stalk trout using all your skills including those you are about to develop.

Big trout are uncomfortable feeding on the surface and, will often hit quickly and streak back into cover.

A good example occurred several years ago at Eagle Lake in northern California, one of the most intimidating big trout lakes there is for fly-fishing. There are hundreds of acres of water and miles of shoreline.

Each November, I fish the lake with Jay Fairs, a resident guide. On this particular morning we motored across the lake to a quiet little bay, beached the boat and began working the shoreline on foot.

Jay had fished the bay the day before and his exploratory casts had produced eight thick rainbows, the smallest around three pounds, the largest six pounds.

I'm no beginner on this lake, but I'm no Jay Fairs either. I waded offshore until I was about crotch deep in the cold water and began casting to where I expected to find cruising trout.

After a few casts, I heard Jay chuckling. He was still standing on the beach. "Denny," he said, "the fish are behind you."

When I waded back to shore he turned over a few rocks in a foot of water revealing hundreds of tiny freshwater shrimp *(scuds)*. The trout, he explained, were gorging on the shrimp in knee-deep water along the shoreline

Instead of blind casting, we quietly walked the shore watching for nervous water, tails or any other sign of active feeders. We cast my stillwater nymph, an excellent imitation of a scud, to specific cruising fish. The takes were soft and the fish incredibly large.

That cold November lesson stuck with me, and it's been good to me over the years. Now, in similar weather and water conditions my first thoughts are fishing shallow waters where big trout prey.

Where Big Fish Hide

Weed Beds
Not Just For Bass

Weedy areas in lakes solve two of the trout's basic needs, food and shelter. They also help solve a problem for the angler by concentrating fish in a definable area. In weedy areas, insects also abound and big trout, very big trout, can make a decent living with minimal effort.

But for some convoluted reason, most trout fishermen steer clear of weedy areas, missing the same fishing potential that bass and panfish anglers zero in on, realizing what super water it is.

I often get the opportunity to fish as I travel the West researching stillwater fishing and delivering how-to seminars. Invariably, I see local anglers beeline for the uncluttered deep water away from those nasty hook snagging, leader tangling weed beds along the bank.

Their haste to fish deep water is directly away from the food factory, and from where the biggest trout in the lake may be feeding.

I'm fortunate. My education about weeds was forced on me by my home lake. The lake is spring fed, covers more than 100 square miles, with less than two percent of that water deeper than 25 feet. Most of the lake supports both a rich aquatic environment with acres of tules and assorted vegetation both above and below the surface.

If I was going to fish anywhere but that dinky two-percent I would need to learn how to fish the weedy areas. It didn't take too long to discover that trout, especially large trout, are as comfortable in weeds as any largemouth bass or bluegill.

About the only thing that will drive big trout from the protection and food sources that are found in and around weed beds, is water temperature. If the temperature is trout-comfortable, trout will favor the cover of weed beds over the exposure of open water, every time.

A weedy shoreline area produces lots of insects and attracts a lot of hungry trout.

FLY-FISHING STILLWATERS

Like all productive water, weeds have their own special challenges for fly-fishermen forcing anglers to choose between multiple options concerning lines, patterns and most importantly, presentation.

Line selection is determined by the dominant food source, and at times may require a floating, sink tip, intermediate, or full sinking line.

There are two types of trout-holding weeds: free-floating and subsurface beds. Big trout are inherently wary and prefer to feed beneath a floating mass of weeds where they are protected from surface predators.

Subsurface weeds provide big trout with two requirements-- food and cover.

This is generally short-line fishing, and with a decent presentation it's possible to fish a fly beneath the weeds. Unfortunately, one of the paradoxes of this type of jungle fishing is that these suspicious fish often demand a light leader. I've had to go to 6X at times to draw any serious action and then take my chances playing the fish. Break offs are common.

Whenever it's possible, I prefer to drop my fly into small clear holes between weed masses. Trout frequently hide along the edges of these holes to ambush prey. It can be a real challenge to work a big fish out of the jungle, but that's where the fish are at these times.

Reconcile yourself to the fact that when you fish for big fish, you're going to lose big fish-- sometimes in an explosion of water, weeds and snapped tippets that will leave you shaking. I've hooked fish in tiny holes that literally destroyed my tackle. I've hooked others that simply sucked in the fly and bolted for the bottom. You never know.

At times, I've found that a countdown system is one of the most dependable techniques for fishing weeds. Count the seconds between the time the fly lands on the surface and when it hits the top of the underwater weeds. I have my best luck when I time the retrieve so the fly just skims the top of the weeds.

Intently watch the line where it enters the water throughout the retrieve. Keep your rod tip in or at the water's edge and set on the slightest deviation. In this type of fishing, takes can be aggressive or soft depending on the pattern and retrieve used. Unless you're working a tight line, missed strikes and break offs will occur often.

Where Big Fish Hide

Weed bed strikes are often explosive, with break offs common.

Springs
It's The Oxygen, More Than The Temperature

During mid to late summer when the water in most lakes is at its warmest, trout move into the coolest areas because the cooler water has a higher oxygen content.

Oxygen, more than water temperature, is what determines where fish are located. If the water in a lake is a uniform 60 degrees it would follow that trout would be uniformly dispersed throughout the lake. Yet, any trout fisherman smart enough to not sit on a wet boat seat can assure you that is not the case.

When you're trying to learn what it is that motivates a trout to be in one place or another, remove the food factor, and what you have left is the oxygen content, not necessarily the water temperature. But it's difficult to think of one without the other. Temperature importance is a critical influence on trout behavior, yet in my estimation it is greatly misunderstood. I believe a great many trout fishermen spend too much time fishing depths where the water is cold enough to attract trout, but is so devoid of oxygen that trout can't survive there.

One area that is a consistently great mid-summer producer in just about any lake is around springs. It would be easy to come to the conclusion that it is the temperature, the pocket of cool water in an otherwise uncomfortably warm lake that attracts the fish.

I don't necessarily agree At least, temperature is not the sole driving force.

After extensive research and comparative test fishing, I'm convinced that trout hold in spring areas not just because of temperature, but because of an increase in oxygen created by the influx of highly-oxygenated spring water.

Once you understand that principle, it follows that springs will be productive throughout the year, not just in the dead of summer. And that is another one of the least understood principles in fly-fishing. Springs are just as promising when the snow flies, leaves fall, flowers bloom, or when the sun bakes the bank mud until it cracks. Not only do underground springs offer trout, well-oxygenated water, but they are also an attraction for other food sources.

Underwater springs like these are favored holding areas during the summer for trout, especially big trout.

Where Big Fish Hide

This 26-inch rainbow was one of the smaller 'bows I found holding near a spring in the Pelican Bay area of Upper Klamath Lake.

    The problem with springs is locating them. In some of the best trophy lakes, there are maps with spring areas marked, which will narrow the search to general areas.

    Underground springs have several obvious signs that mark their locations. Small bubbles on an otherwise smooth surface film is perhaps the most obvious clue.

    In areas with good water clarity, pick a day with no surface disturbance and, using polarized eyeglasses, slowly move through your fishing area watching for bubbles and rounded mounds of light colored material showing against the dark bottom. Water clarity is best in the winter (no algae) and this can be a good time to locate springs for in-season action.

    Summer draw-down can help fishermen locate springs as water levels drop. I have learned a ton about lakes during low water that paid big dividends the following year when water levels returned to normal. This is one of the best times to pinpoint spring locations.

    Most spring areas are also marked by temperature changes in the water. I've used everything from electronic temperature sensors to hand-held thermometers, including that old standby just sticking my hand in the water. As a last resort, if the water gets warm enough for summer swimming, plunge in and when you feel a sudden chill in the water, you're over a spring.

    When fishing a spring area deeper than 10 feet, I prefer to work flies very slowly and use a Uniform Type II full-sinking line. This line sinks at a predictable rate and is easily controlled, which is exactly what's needed when the target area is both deep and small.

    When fishing between the surface and 6-feet deep, I prefer an intermediate line and will use two types of retrieves. The first retrieve is an agonizingly slow hand twist that works well with small flies. The second is a short-quick one-inch pull. If one retrieve fails, use the other. Sometimes I'll start the retrieve with slow twist and after covering a couple of yards, switch to the short rapid pull. This imparts a darting action and is especially effective with my Stillwater or A.P. Emerger nymph patterns.

Understanding Inlets
Stream Fishing In Stillwater

Incoming rivers, streams, and spring creeks offer trout much the same benefit as underground springs. Flows are cooler than the lake water, more saturated with oxygen, and will carry food organisms sufficient to hold the attention of a large trout.

When lake water temperatures exceed 70 degrees, oxygen content begins to diminish and lake fish move into the inlet areas, sometimes in great concentrations.

Most of these fish are small and include a variety of suckers, minnows and other forage fish, which in turn attract trophy-size trout.

There are several important rules to successful inlet fishing, rules, that when properly applied, provide anglers with the ability to catch trout consistently.

River Inlets are often concentration zones for big trout.

Approach inlets quietly. Watch for any surface activity that will reveal the main concentration of fish. If the flow is substantial expect the trout to be facing into the current, as they do in rivers. When I fish major inlets in lakes, I cast up and across the current and work my fly down exactly as if I am river fishing because even in lakes the trout will face into the current

On shore or in a boat I stay as far away from the holding water as possible. These fish are always spooky, and I make long, soft casts that will allow the fly to dead drift just off bottom toward the feeding stations. [Minnow imitators, of course, require action-retrieves].

Where Big Fish Hide

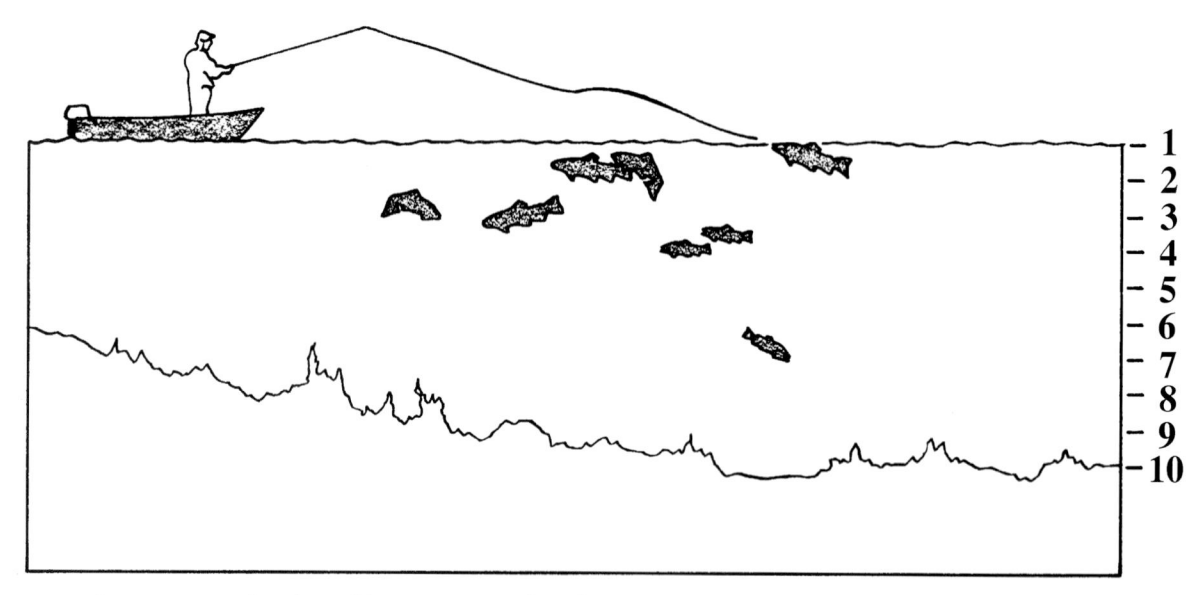

A common mistake of inexperienced stillwater anglers is casting over unseen fish to reach a visible working fish. Called "lining", the line strikes the surface and will put down subsurface feeding fish.

I try to place the fly line off center of the holding area to avoid "lining" fish. Running the line or the line shadow directly over trout is a sure bet that you'll be looking for another area to fish shortly. Once you spook them, forget it.

I've found the new transparent fly lines specifically designed for stillwater fishing to be a tremendous asset in this situation.

In my home water lake, the inlet streams support large populations of small shiners, a good forage fish. Most of the shiners are concentrated around the tules and willows in the transition seam where the river becomes the lake. In spring and fall, many of the lake's largest rainbows move in and gorge on the shiners.

Matching the bait with a Zonker pattern in the spring or my shiner minnow in the fall, I've had many days landing a half-dozen rainbows over 5 pounds and few that pushed the 10 pound range. These fish were all taken in less than 6 feet of water, and were invariably stuffed with inch-long shiners.

Adult rainbows will also begin to concentrate near the inlets when spawning season nears. Pre-spawn rainbow rarely feed, but are short-tempered, aggressive and seem to love to unload on big streamers.

Inlets are worth prospecting at any time of the year and are one of the first places I try when fishing unfamiliar water.

Old Stream Bed Channels
Casting With More Than Blind Faith

Every man-made lake, reservoir or impoundment in the West has at least one and sometimes several channels etched into the bottom, and these channels usually are fish-holding honey holes. Most have multiple channels, but all have at least one--the original stream bed. Finding these channels can be as easy as marking them with a depth finder or following a tributary stream offshore.

In shallow lakes, any indentation in the bottom--from a few inches to several feet--has the impact of a channel and can be fished the same way. When I use an electronic depth finder to locate channels, I look for structure, not fish. Fish move, structure doesn't.

Again, my favorite time to locate these premium fish-holding areas is in the late fall or winter when most impoundments are drawn down to their lowest point of the season. At times I can literally walk along the bottom and see what I'll be fishing next spring when the lake's full.

On hot summer days or during low water periods, trout take refuge in the deeper water of a channel bed and this can be awesome fishing with dragonfly nymphs, streamers, or attractor patterns. Late fall, when water levels are at the lowest, trout are forced into channels. This is also a prime time to find aggressive brown trout.

This 6-pound brown was chasing minnows in a sunken stream bed channel when it took the big streamer visible in its mouth.

These fall spawners are notoriously energetic in October and November and seem to be especially defensive about sharing a select piece of channel bottom with an intruding streamer pattern.

Every year in late October, I've landed browns up to 12 pounds taken from the original Deschutes River channel in the shallow bottom of Oregon's Wickiup Reservoir. Even bigger fish have been hooked and landed. In the heavily dammed West, where irrigation reservoirs are a way of life, this is not a rare occurrence. In fact, you can expect the biggest fish in any impoundment to be holding in the most favorable water of the river channel every time there is a draw down.

Where Big Fish Hide

Low water is not the only time to concentrate on these channels, however. Even when lakes are at their seasonal normal levels, large trout still prefer to put enough water over their backs to feel safe, and in many lakes, this is channel water. I've found that predator trout will leave the channel to herd minnows into a nearby shallow area where they devour the trapped fish before returning to the safety of the channel.

Channel fishing is a time for big flies, heavy leaders, and full-sink lines. This is no-holds barred trophy trout fishing and you can expect to be abused a few times by fish too big to brag about. But you can try.

Ledges 'n Drop-Offs
The Art Of Ambush

Drop-offs in one form or another are common on most lakes, and I've found that the techniques that have evolved on Pyramid Lake in Nevada are the most effective tactics for fishing this type of structure wherever it's found.

Pyramid Lake, located on the eastern flank of the Sierra north of Reno, is one lake where your chances for landing a trophy trout are determined by your ability to cast far enough to reach a series of ledges and drop-offs.

This lake is so large that it's clearly visible to the crews onboard orbiting space shuttles. Its entire shoreline seems to be a series of stair steps leading into mysterious depths.

The lake is home to a giant strain of cutthroat trout known as Lahontans. These heavily marked cutthroat are native only to this area of Nevada and California. These trout thrive in high alkaline desert lakes where other trout struggle, Lahontan's have been successfully stocked in alkaline lakes in other states.

This is significant only because Lahontan's are the largest subspecies of cutthroat in North America. The Pyramid Lake official record is a 41-pound fish landed in 1925 by a Piaute Indian, John Skimmerhorn.

It's rare today to catch a Lahontan that exceeds 20 pounds. But still, if you want to catch a very large cutthroat, Pyramid Lake is a good place to fish.

These giant trout cruise the lake following the rows of ledges, feeding and hiding along the drop-offs. Pyramid cutthroat are adept at using the rocks and ledges as cover to ambush bait fish.

Wading is the traditional method of fly-fishing these ledges. Casting is accomplished with both feet either on the bottom, or on the rung of a small stepladder set up in the water well offshore. The added height gained by standing on the ladder allows fishermen to increase casting distance. It is possible to fish these ledges from a boat, but the ladder system seems to be the most effective technique.

Many of the ledges require casts from 60 to 70 feet while others can be reached by wading to within easy casting reach. If you do not reach the ledges, you do not catch fish. This is a fact that Pyramid has in common with nearly every lake with similar ledges and drop-offs paralleling the shoreline.

Rigged with large woolly worms or woolly buggers, fly fishermen put their backs to the shore and hurl fast sinking lines or shooting heads lakeward, strip out the slack and let the fly settle to the bottom. A good cast will hang momentarily on the edge of a ledge before it pulls free.

Flies are retrieved with a mix of strips that cause them to dart and dip representative of feeding bait fish. Typically, the big cutts follow the fly a long way and take near the end of the retrieve when the fly rises off the bottom.

In deep lakes, trout, sometimes very large trout, can often be found cruising ledges and drop-offs using the rocks for both ambush points and protective shields against predators.

Remember the last time you hooked a big fish near a ledge? I'd be shocked to learn the fish did anything but streak directly away toward the protection of deep water. Deep water seemingly makes a trout feel secure, which is why you want to fish the deep-water side of a ledge if possible while fishing from shore.

Big trout, like this 9-pound rainbow, often cruise the edges of drop-off ledges.

Cast beyond the ledge and let the fly settle a few feet before stripping back the retrieve. The strike zone, that area where trout are most likely to hit, is near the top of the ledge. In this situation, I hook most of my fish just as the fly darts over the top of the rocks. The rest I hook as the fly moves from the top of the ledge toward the surface. I can't overemphasize the importance of maintaining a tight line when the fly is in the strike zone. You can often detect ledges or sharp drops by the surrounding topography. A hill or point of land that runs into a lake very likely continues at nearly the same angle below the waterline.

Rocky, sharp dropping points tapering from the bank into the depths are some of my favorite ambush sites for trophy-size trout. Normally, some of the largest fish in the lake, any lake, will cruise and feed on the smaller fish attracted to this protective structure.

In 1977, when Utah's magnificent Flaming Gorge Reservoir was earning worldwide fame with giant brown trout, many in the 25 to 30 pound range, I witnessed some of the most impressive big brown trout feeding binges that I have ever seen, or probably ever will see!

The bottom structure in the area where I was fishing dropped quickly in a series of steep, deep ledges. For three days a friend and I watched brown trout well over 20 pounds hide in the rocks waiting in ambush for chub minnows to feed within striking range. These browns were huge, sag-belly trophies and to see so many of them feeding so aggressively on big chubs was an incredible sight.

Where Big Fish Hide

I fished for these huge predators with large bucktail streamer patterns, casting as far as I could, letting the fly settle and then bringing it back in foot-long pulls that imparted a chub-like dart and dodge swimming motion. The browns would unload on the fly as soon as it came over the rocks and if they missed, I would continue stripping and these nasty-tempered giants would chase the escaping fly into the rocks if necessary.

It was great! Just great!

I wish I could report that I landed one of those coveted 30-pounders. Instead, I can tell you I now know what it feels like to set the hook into several of these monsters and then have them beat you silly before finally snapping the tippet. I was close a couple of times, very close.

That was the only time in my life that I ever landed a 10-pound trout on a fly and felt like I had settled for something less.

Those lessons learned in the monster fish ledges of Pyramid and Flaming Gorge have done well for me over the years. The cast beyond and retrieve over the rocks technique has provided me with a number of big fish under some difficult fishing conditions. To feel the solid tug of a fly stopped in the mouth of a cruising hog-like monster will keep you wired long after your nerves have returned to normal.

Dave Freel worked a rocky ledge with a Denny's Seal Bugger for this 12-pound rainbow in a small lake in northern California.

Where Big Fish Hide

PROTECTIVE COVER
Recognizing Big Trout Hide-a-ways

The second basic need of big trout deals with shelter. All fish inherit survival instincts and one of the most acute is the ability to hide from predators.

Shelter, cover, structure--call it what you will, is as important to growing exceptionally large trout as good genes. Trophy-size trout don't get to that size if they become protein for another predator.

For trophy-trout seekers, a trout's instinct to conceal itself should be taken into consideration and given just as much importance as a trout's better known sensory systems which include sight, smell and sound.

In open water, I believe a trout depends mostly on its sight, on its ability to see predators and prey. If you doubt my belief, then try this. Using any colored fly line, cast a fly onto calm, clear water and then look for fish. I'll guarantee there won't be a trout within 30 feet of where your fly lands.

In clouded water or where the cover--like dense weed beds--is thick enough to compromise visual senses, trout rely on receiving and interpreting sonic vibrations. Anything that moves in the water sets off a chain of vibrations that trout, and other fish, catch in a series of pores positioned in a line extending from behind the gill plate to the tail along their side. This series of sensory pores is commonly called a lateral line and it is a marvel. The receptors within the lateral line are responsive to low-frequency vibrations--such as those made by changes in water flow, another fish, predator, or fly.

Most of the big fish in my home lake respond instantly to such noises as vibrations of an anchor rope rubbing a gunwale, or a fly box falling on the floorboards. Boat noise and careless wading probably save more monster fish than barbless hooks ever will.

Sometimes I am convinced that trout are nothing more than a bundle of nerve endings collected in a wrapper of scales just waiting to explode. Trigger any of their protective senses -- sight, sound, smell-- and they head for shelter.

The instinct to find shelter is strong and there is not a trout in the world that won't run to shelter when its sensory system picks up possible danger signals. The older the fish, the quicker it heads for shelter, which is exactly why a trophy-trout specialist needs to learn to identify and fish shelter areas that appeal to a trout's survival instincts.

Some of these shelter areas are obvious--weeds, rocks, logs, channels. Many of the most productive, shelters though, are not so easy to detect. These areas are created more by external factors than hard structure.

Examples of these somewhat intangible big trout shelters will include: periods of low light (dawn, dusk, overcast); surface disturbances (ripples, wind streaks, waves, rain); and water discoloration (algae bloom, mud, snow melt).

[For More Detail Refer To Chapter 9]

Under these sheltering circumstances, trout--especially large predatory trout--become more active, apparently feeling more secure under the protective cover. I've also found that in these peak activity periods, fishermen can better disguise their presentation when cover remains intact. In other words, when trout are active, there's a bigger margin for presentation error and the trout gods are more forgiving as long as there is a security blanket in place.

In July of 1990, I was at Crane Prairie Reservoir which is five square miles of excellent big trout water in the Cascade Range of southern Oregon doing research for this book. It was good duty, and not without surprises.

The morning sun had burned through a light mist triggering a hatch of Callibaetis mayflies. Within an hour damsel flies began appearing and I reached for my fly box and a damsel imitation.

Where Big Fish Hide

Crane Prairie Reservoir is known for many natural features: Hundreds of acres of flooded standing timber, a world-class concentration of ospreys, very big rainbow and brook trout, and outstanding damsel fly hatches matches to name a few.

My eagerness gave way to confusion, then despair, as I watched rainbows in excess of 10 pounds cruise just beneath the surface, refusing both the naturals and my imitation. By noon, a thundershower that had been threatening all morning began to move in. Big rainbows began to feed all around me, but I only hooked a couple of 12 inchers, frustratingly small fish when I could see 10 pounders boiling just beneath the surface.

My increasingly frantic casting moved the fish almost outside my casting range. Each long, powerful cast only spooked the fish further away. The surface was flat and the wind was absolutely still. I was fishing on an unforgiving mirror and the slightest disturbance from line, leader, fly, or shadow sent the big paranoid 'bows lunging for cover.

By early afternoon I had managed to hook only a few more eager pan-size trout. To complete my defeat, the storm arrived. The sky darkened, thunder rumbled, and vanguard breezes rumpled the mirrored surface. Tiny waves began to dance on the mirror.

With an apprehensive eye on the fast advancing thunderhead, I fired a long cast toward a patch of wind riffle. One foot into the retrieve and my fly stopped so suddenly and unexpectedly that I almost broke-off on the strike.

A rainbow of nearly six pounds shot through the surface in a spectacular series of head over tail acrobatics and went deep into the backing before the eventual release.

A 6½-pound rainbow from Oregon's Crane Prairie Reservoir, one of the best lakes in the West for both classic trout shelter and big trout.

For two hours I fished the incoming storm front, landing seven of what I consider to be trophy-size rainbows, the largest just a shade over eight pounds. The trigger to this bite, I have no doubt, was the advancing cloud cover and the rising breeze that ruffled the surface.

The feeding intensity picked up in direct correlation to the improvement in shelter as the storm clouds and advancing breeze negated the bright sun and glassy surface. It was spectacular fishing but, without the environmental boost, the bite probably wouldn't have developed until late evening when the sun finally slipped off the water.

WATER TEMPERATURE/OXYGEN

This Is Perhaps The Most Important Section In The Book--
Read It-Again and Again
and Again!

The third and most important of all trout needs is water temperature/oxygen. Understanding the effects of water temperature on trout behavior is as critical to angler success as the line, pattern, or retrieve. Talking or reading about temperature is, to most, drudgery, boring, a science project. But because of its impact on trout location and migration patterns, let's push on.

Make no mistake, water temperature is the key to where and how we fish a lake.

For some mystifying reason, most trout anglers either don't understand or choose to ignore the importance that water temperatures play in determining their successes and failures.

Water temperature is one of those key factors that most of us are aware of, but actually know little about. Yet, the more I learned about factors critical to catching large, bragging size trout, the more importance I began to attach to the impact of water temperature.

Water temperature and oxygen levels are leading indicators to where fish will be, what food sources will be available, when they will be active, and whether or not trout will feed on them. This in turn tells us which flies to use, what depth to fish them at, and the speed they should be moved.

Joe Humphrey, a well-known big trout specialist from Pennsylvania, once described a common thermometer as "a modern angler's Geiger counter." He believed it could reveal year-round trout holding waters as accurately as the Geiger registers uranium deposits.

Water temperature has such an impact on trout, and their environment, that it is a major indication of not only what is happening in the water, but what will happen.

Since water temperature affects the amount of oxygen in water, it becomes almost impossible to refer to one without considering the other as they are so closely related. Together they not only affect trout survival, but influence migration and spawning patterns throughout a lake system. Trout are attracted to areas where there are adequate levels of both oxygen and temperature. Too much or too little of either and fish will abandon that area.

It takes enormous self discipline to actually incorporate water temperature monitoring into your standard fishing ritual. I've fished with many anglers who enjoyed great success without consciously taking the temperature of the water. Some thought it was simply too much bother, while others said it was too much like a science project, an analytical intrusion into their peaceful ambiance. But, I believe that without paying attention to water temperature, too much time is wasted fishing unproductive water.

If the goal is to catch trophy-size trout, the biggest trout in every puddle, then being aware of oxygen content and water temperature is a mandate, a key piece of the big fish puzzle. It is one of those critical lessons that when learned will separate top trout fishermen from the herd.

Where Big Fish Hide

Keep in mind, this doesn't have to become a daily ritual unless you are a nut for statistics. I usually check temperatures when I'm fishing new lakes, after major fluctuations in weather patterns, or when the bite is off and I think it should be on.

When water in one area of a lake is colder or warmer than a trout's optimum comfort zone, fish become sluggish, quit feeding, and begin to cruise searching for more comfortable oxygen and temperature levels.

As cold-blooded animals, the body temperature of fish is the same as the surrounding water. Body temperature, as anyone who has ever had a leak in their waders will testify, directly affects the body's function and ability to move.

Drawing one of these cruisers away from their mission and to your fly is the real challenge. Understand, that adequate oxygen and water temperature are critical factors in a trout's survival and in order to interest a cruiser in your fly, means that trout has to repress survival instincts. Accept that trout rarely sidetrack from their mission until they find what they're looking for. By keeping track of oxygen/temperature levels and migration patterns prime holding locations become more easily defined and that is where you should be investing your fishing time.

Occasionally, you will see a truly giant trout lethargically cruising. Your blood pressure will rise, your jaw will drop, and because you are a trout fisherman, your willpower will collapse. But, you will rise to the challenge like a brook trout to a Royal Wulff. When it happens, tie on a gaudy attractor pattern and tease the bruiser. Occasionally, you will provoke a response, perhaps a vicious strike.

Most fishermen pay attention to water temperatures yet only rarely monitor oxygen levels. Which is why we often trick ourselves into investing fishing hours prospecting in water with the ideal temperature, but insufficient oxygen levels. The most common setup for this situation is when fishing deep or in deep water.

In deep lakes, I've often found that although the water temperature is ideal near bottom, oxygen levels are too low to support trout.

After several years of eliminating options, I'm convinced that trout holding near the bottom actually move up through the water column when oxygen depletion occurs.

In small, easily patterned waters, you can often get away with blind casting, but in big waters or at depths beyond 20 feet, electronic depth finders are about the only reliable and efficient way to identify the stratification level where trout are holding.

In this situation, when stratification zones may be located anywhere in a lake, I believe electronics perform the same function as your eyes do when fish are homing in on visible structure.

Electronic depth, temperature, and oxygen sensors have long been standard equipment for boat fishermen.

If you gasp at the idea of compromising with electronics, don't use them. Electronics, after all, are not required. They are an option that will even the odds when trout have homed in on elements invisible to you. In lakes less than 20 feet deep, I can sometimes locate these stratified trout with a sinking line, retrieved vertically, in a pattern that covers all water levels. This is the toughest way, in my estimation, to find trout that hold at a certain depth and is actually no different than following a hunch.

Personally, I try to avoid deep lakes, especially when trout are holding deep. As a rule, they don't fly fish well. I find shallow, nutrient-rich lakes far more rewarding.

When you consistently locate trout that are holding at roughly the same depth over a wide span of water, you will be able to select the correct line type, and work your flies with the confidence of knowing that you are fishing the zone with the right mix of oxygen and temperature to hold active fish.

Water temperature also has a major impact on the food sources trout eat, specifically insects.

Many insects hatch in extremely narrow temperature or time slots. When these magic periods of activity fall within the optimum feeding temperature of a trout species, the table is set for outrageous fly action. As a predator of big trout, your task will be simplified by monitoring water temperature in the lakes you fish, understanding the temperature limits of fish and prey, recognizing when these requirements will intersect, which in turn keys feeding behavior in trout.

Simple, huh!

When you can incorporate these awareness factors into your fishing ritual, you will have a better understanding of where the best fishing will take place, which species of trout will dominate, which fly patterns will be productive, the type and speed of retrieve, and the appropriate depth to fish these patterns.

Trout, as a family, have specific temperature requirements and those requirements narrow even more when applied to the individual species within that family.

There is always some disagreement among any collection of experts, but as a good fishing rule, you can determine that the optimum feeding temperatures for North America's dominant trout and char are:

Rainbows:	61°- 68°
Browns:	61°- 68°
Brookies:	57°- 61°
Cutthroats:	60°- 65°

There are many factors that come into play and influence the levels of feeding activity, but these temperature are a good place to start.

As the chart shows, most species of trout are comfortable when the water temperature is in the mid 60s. When the temperature rises above 66° oxygen depletion becomes a factor. When temperatures reach 70° or higher, trout begin to migrate. I've found that trout, especially rainbows, will tolerate 70° water if food is present, but only for a short period of time.

To understand the importance of oxygen, realize that a trout can exist for long periods in water temperatures below or above their optimum range and can remain healthy for months without feeding. Without sufficient oxygen, however, they will die within minutes.

DON'T KILL BY ACCIDENT

I'm an unrepentant disciple of catch and release fishing, especially where old, trophy-size trout are concerned.

I wasn't always such a strict c&r advocate. I have my share of beautiful mounts taken years ago and I can understand killing a representative wall fish. That once-in-a-lifetime memory fish is not my concern or the reason I'm standing on this soap box in the temperature/oxygen section of the text.

My pet peeve is how many anglers inadvertently kill trout because of tackle and fighting styles. In summer months throughout the West, the oxygen levels in many stillwater areas are severely depleted. There are areas of high oxygen content, but when measured against a lake's entirety, this content is at its seasonal low.

A fish hooked, fought, and landed in mid-summer, in most lakes, rapidly depletes the oxygen level in its blood supply and is slow to replace it because of the reduced oxygen content in the water.

If a large fish is fought long on light equipment during the summer, the odds are very good that fish will sink to the bottom and die of oxygen depreciation shortly after release.

During low-oxygen periods, use fly rods and tippets that are heavy enough to land a fish while it is still fresh enough to recover. This is not the time of year to display your fish-playing skills with light gear. Hook the fish, land the fish, release the fish.

Please, don't play it to death.

--DR

When water temperatures slowly rise, there is a corresponding increase in how fast a trout's digestive system processes food. A big trout becomes more active, utilizes more calories, and increases the need to feed.

Once the water temperatures exceed the optimum levels, fish activity diminishes at a correlating rate. The higher or lower the temperature rises above or falls below the optimum, the less active trout become, the less they feed, the less opportunity you have to catch them.

This depends on the sky more than the season. On overcast days, surface water temperatures often fluctuate very little throughout the day. On clear days, I've found that surface temperatures can rise and fall as much as 15° within 24 hours. This is why the most difficult period to hook a slab-size trout is at high-noon on a bright blue-sky day. Even most of the insects quit hatching during the heat of mid-day in the summer, deferring to the more temperate periods of mid-morning and late afternoon.

I've seen gray skies trigger massive mid-day hatches and feeding binges in the dead of summer, especially when the overcast follows an extended period of hot weather with an unrelenting sun.

Relief from a scorching sun sometimes seems as welcome by the fish as by fishermen. On a more practical note, the reason trout activity picks up can be traced directly back to the three keys--**Food** (moderate day-time temperatures trigger hatches), **Water Temperature** (surface temperatures will be several degrees cooler on overcast days), and **Shelter** (less light penetration).

Successful summer fishing is often a matter of good timing and if you're headed for a lake to fish a specific hatch, it's important to pay close attention to air and water temperatures. Success depends on it.

If water temperatures warm early or remain cooler than normal because of seasonal weather variations, such as an incoming front or barometric surges, the timing of hatches will almost always be altered.

Changes in water temperature occur more gradually than air temperatures, and the effect on insects and feeding trout is also much slower. It may take a day or two of consistent overcast to alter water temperatures enough to modify the timing of hatches and feeding periods.

In the fall and spring, when water temperatures dip below 50°, trout respond to these below optimum temperature levels much the same as they do when temperatures exceed the preferred limits during the summer months. The colder it gets, the lower their metabolism rate, the more sluggish they become and the slower they move. Even their digestive system slows to a crawl, depressing their need to feed. It's a balance carefully struck to maximize trout survival, and unfortunately minimize fly-fishing success. However, even then, big trout can be caught.

Resident trout will continue to feed even when temperatures hover just above freezing, but at a much slower pace.

Trout will move slowly now and seem to become more selective, demanding precise fly presentations before they can be coaxed into expending the energy it takes to eat.

On extreme weather days, when temperatures are near freezing or unbearably hot, the limiting factor is more often our commitment to catch fish, not whether trout can be caught. Compared to every other animal in nature, including fish, fishermen are fragile, with a much more narrow window of comfort. Most fishermen have the good sense to head for the fireplace or the A/C when this comfort window shatters, which is probably why most of the trophy trout specialists appear a tad short of good sense. They fish in weather extremes that separate the ultra-dedicated from the rest. This is when big-trout fanatics pay their dues and earn the fish that others only dream of catching.

I can't emphasize enough how critically important water temperature is to not only trout, but even more importantly, a trout's source of food. Understanding and reacting to the symbiotic relationship between a big trout and its prey is to understand the difference between successful fishing and whatever is left.

Anything that affects a trout's prey, affects the trout and that affects you, the trout fisherman.

Remember, the most educated credential-carrying angler in North America doesn't understand as much about trout and trout food as the dumbest trout in the lake. Listen to what the trout say and structure your fishing techniques and tactics accordingly. Whenever a bite or lack of it occurs outside the norm, I consider the conditions and how those conditions will affect trout behavior.

This means recognizing the impact various atmospheric conditions have on water temperature and trout behavior. Most importantly, catch trout the way they want to be caught, not the way you want to catch them.

It's senseless, in my estimation, to pound the water with perfect dry-fly patterns because that's the way you prefer to fish, when the big trout are hunting three-inch sculpins on the bottom.

Like any predator, trout are aware of when certain food sources become active, inactive, available, or unavailable. They adjust by moving to where the food, temperature, and shelter is optimum. We adjust by reading the water, weather, and seasonal signs, then changing fly lines, patterns, and retrieves accordingly.

Once you understand the variables and recognize how they fit into a trout's survival requirements and feeding routines, locating trout ceases to be the challenge. You'll know you're fishing where the fish are.

Now, what you need to know is if you're fishing during the right time.

Trophy-size trout, like this 12-pound rainbow, actively feed during early morning hours.

Chapter 9

SOLVING THE TIMING PUZZLE
How To Pick The Best Hour For Big Trout

Knowing where to fish a lake is as critical as any part of solving the stillwater puzzle, but it's not enough unless you also know when big trout are most vulnerable.

Lakes, much like streams, go through cycles of activity when the aquatic life, including trout, roller coaster through periods of high and low activity.

Learning to catch big trout depends on successfully learning not only when trout can be caught, but when to apply our best efforts.

I've found that all lakes have periods when trout are aggressively feeding and periods when they sulk. Except in rare situations, you can identify these periods by recognizing and identifying tell-tale indicators. These indicators or conditions are what I refer to as "cover." Examples include low light conditions, semi darkness, riffled water or surface chop, and water colored by nutrients, algae, or runoff.

Trout, especially big trout, prefer to feed when a light wind riffles the surface or during low-light periods (dawn, dusk, or overcast). As a big trout predator, these are the times to be on the water. Trophy-size trout may not feed during every period of low-light or surface disturbance. However, and this is important, these conditions are nearly always in place when they do feed.

Big trout became big trout by being selective about the food they eat, and when they eat it. These are the feeding time frames they control, and that's what pushes their feed buttons.

Trout aren't suckers for the first riffle or cloudy day and you shouldn't expect to set the water on fire from the friction of a 12-pound rainbow ripping line through the water just because some form of cover is present. It can happen. Prepare for it. Just don't be disappointed when Big Kahuna doesn't show.

From an angling perspective, you can fish with confidence knowing that trout are less cautious when there is a good chop, feel more secure in shallow water when light conditions are minimal, and will often be far less selective when the water is foggy from nutrients or algae.

The more I fish, the more convinced I am that the existence of good cover is a much, much greater factor than we traditionally gave it credit for.

As obvious as light penetration factors appear, you would be amazed at how many people I meet in classes, seminars, or at the casting end of my guide boat, who never give it a thought, and, in fact, want to pick up and head for home just as these factors are beginning to develop.

I really can't blame them, I guess. Not too many people get a kick out of casting in a wind, or from a rocking boat, just the ones who want big fish. Everybody else heads for shore until the wind dies, the algae bloom drifts off and the water calms.

When the average fisherman does consider the impact of light penetration, it is usually in a very limited way. That usually means getting out the sun screen or putting on the shades, but even the beginning student of sport-fishing understands that at noon you catch fewer fish than at dawn and dusk.

Solving The Timing Puzzle

Advanced fishermen extend that thinking to include murky water algae bloom, plankton, shade shadow, heavy overcast, and discolored run-in from a tributary.

These conditions come and go each day, yet we often fail to recognize or take advantage of them.

There are many factors, in addition to semi-darkness and surface riffles that influence trout feeding behavior. But none are more important than the availability of food itself.

As important as food is, its mere presence has never been instrumental as to whether or not fish feed. In fact, they will often leave cover to search for food, but are hesitant to feed unless there is adequate shelter to protect them from predators.

In clear water lakes with sand or rock walled shorelines, sometimes the only adequate cover is depth and darkness.

This helps to explain why big fish are rarely caught during daylight hours.

Small trout, those dinks and feeders typically categorized in the outdoor columns as *"pan-size trout"*, are comparable to human teenage kids, and are dominated by involuntary appetites in order to satisfy the craving of a metabolism seemingly gone mad. These growing trout are literally eating machines and will feed whenever conditions are anywhere near acceptable. They may entertain you for hours, sucking down your elk hair caddis or Adam's floaters from the surface film even while the sun is high.

But, give these aggressive juveniles a few close brushes with diving loons, feeding otters, or a caddis draped around a No. 12 barbless hook, then add a few inches of girth, a few pounds, and slow the metabolism down to a maintenance level, and this is the fish you're after.

Remember, this fish, this old mossback, is not going to be hooked while frisking with the little fish in the heat of the day.

The magical hour.

Solving The Timing Puzzle

Trout At Dark

Ask a fisherman when they expect to be home and they'll tell you about dark, a phantom hour found almost exclusively on fishing and hunting clocks.

The actual hour of dark may be only imaginary but the hour it denotes is certainly real. And unlike most hours, this one comes around twice a day: just before full dark, and again just before sunup.

The first and last hour of the day is so magical and packed with potential that fishermen and hunters patiently wait out the other 22 hours.

For me, this period is a good opportunity to stalk big fish. The first light of a new day, or the dying light of a spent evening, is so packed with big fish potential that I do not believe any true trophy-trout enthusiasts would miss either of these periods.

Since I was a youngster dangling a juicy worm over bluegills, early morning has been a special time of high expectations. Over the years, I have landed enough fish, especially big fish, during this period to justify such expectations.

This big rainbow was hooked under the cover of low light just after sunset.

This period has always been a primary feeding time for trout. The biggest trout in every lake will be on the move, feeding in the shadows or along the edges of shallow water while daylight and darkness struggle for dominance.

In shallow water, the primary food sources are scuds and small minnows. Scuds avoid bright sun and the peak of their activity is often early or late in the day. Minnows, themselves predators on a much smaller, but equally voracious scale, are also hunting under the cover of near-darkness.

Trout seem to sense this and, being very much in tune with their environment, know well in advance which food sources will be available and will continue to feed until their protective cover disappears with the rising sun. At this point, they begin retreating to the protection of the depths which for trout is just another form of cover.

It's not unusual, I've found, for big trout to continue feeding as they slide into the depths in direct opposition to the rising sun. The darkness of the depths, replaces the darkness of night as satisfactory cover and fish will continue to feed as long as the food is available. The problem is, however, that food is seldom available in deep water.

Expect, however, that a fading bite will only last a few minutes before deteriorating com-

FOR TROPHY TROUT

Solving The Timing Puzzle

pletely--not so much because the fish quit feeding, but more because the cover has been removed. This is a typical reaction to any combination of flat water and bright light.

As big fish specialists, we need to be able to recognize this situation and to focus on areas with more permanent cover: weed beds, tules, logs, boulders, ledges.

During extended periods of flat water, trout are normally inactive despite an abundance of food. You will see a few small trout sipping insects from the surface, but the big trout will be deep and holding, a survival trait that allows them to grow old.

Unless an errant wind stirs a surface riffle, these flat water periods can last for most of the day. It's been my experience that trout will hold, sometimes actually stratifying in deep water until there is some kind of environmental change.

As the sun begins to sink, trout begin to move and the movement is in direct correlation to the setting sun. When the sun is completely off the water, big trout will reappear in the shallows hunting minnows or looking for bugs near the bottom.

One of the most overlooked factors that good fishermen must be aware of is the difference between the dawn and dusk feeding periods.

The heat of the day, preceding an evening bite, produces heavy insect activity, actually creating a surplus of bugs in some areas. Where this happens, the evening feeders have the luxury of becoming highly selective. This is when I go to a suggestive pattern, usually a seal bugger, stillwater nymph, or leech, and continue to fish into the darkness.

The timing of an evening bite can be affected by the extreme of outside temperatures. During an unusually hot, still day, surface water temperatures often creep up a degree or two, enough to keep big trout from entering shallow water on schedule.

A simple rule to follow is the hotter and brighter the day, the longer it will take for an evening bite to develop.

The dawn bite is rarely as selective as the evening, and while it may be cut short by a bright rising sun, it is more likely to be extended by nutrient-clouded water or the filtering mist of morning haze.

These early and late feeding periods are fairly predictable especially during the summer months. Add some type of surface disturbance and you have ideal conditions for hooking some really big trout.

Under The Cover Of Wind

Wind is rarely considered an ally of fly-fishermen. It dumps our casts, blows our flies off target, turns good presentations into skittering wakes, rocks our boats, blasts grit into our eyes, and generally makes fly-fishing a living tangled hell.

When surface chop develops, big fish usually begin to feed.

Solving The Timing Puzzle

On the other hand, wind can also be the edge a fly fisherman needs to set the hook into a tail-walking memory.

To experience how wind can become an ally, don't fight it, take advantage of it, make it work for you. Look at it this way, a good breeze is just another form of cover: a form that trout need, that we can exploit, that can create an unexpected feeding binge.

When you stop dwelling on the annoying irritations that develop when air moves, all that remains is a scuff on the water, a surface disturbance that can diffuse light penetration, provide protection from predators, dumps airborne insects into the water, and conveniently concentrates aquatic and terrestrial insects into a trout's version of an all-you-can-eat buffet.

Wind, in moderation, is every bit as effective as advancing cloud cover, discolored water, or an algae bloom in triggering trout feeding sprees.

Here's why.

When sunlight penetrates deeply into the water, trout show little interest in feeding, despite an abundance of food. When a breeze pushes a ripple across the water, light beams are diffused and trout will begin to concentrate on food instead of safety.

This condition, if it intensifies, will stop the emergence of hatching insects with the first puff of moving air, but does not reduce a feeding trout's interest in subsurface nymphs or other food sources.

I've found that wind-triggered bites are exceptionally aggressive.

Using the ruffled surface water as a protective shield, big trout abandon much of their usual caution, move rapidly, and feed heavily while they still have the advantage over predators such as ospreys, eagles, herons, and kingfishers.

There is little margin for error when fishing flat water under clear skies. These conditions demand your best presentation.

FOR TROPHY TROUT

Solving The Timing Puzzle

These fish are motivated and have a single purpose--to eat: and what they eat is anything and everything that moves and looks like food. At times this feeding spree goes beyond the binge stage and crashes into what can only be described as panic feeding. It's as though trout have developed an instinctive recognition that wind is temporary and speed is necessary.

We fly-fishermen, as predators ourselves, need to exploit this time frame as trout will be less cautious or selective regarding what they eat or how it is presented.

Wind is an ally wherever you find it, but is at its best when it's bashing the shoreline shallows. Wave action slamming into shoal areas, stirs the bottom, spinning minute food particles every which way while simultaneously stirring up enough sediment to hide even the biggest trout. That is why I put up with the irritations and tackle-tangles inherent in casting flies into the invisible, unpredictable turbulence of moving air and will fish water where the waves are piling, the bottom is stirring, and the big trout are feeding with the zest and abandon of a young, uneducated fish.

I learned how to fish windy conditions after more humbling mistakes than I care to remember, most of them on my home water on Upper Klamath Lake in southern Oregon.

During July and August, tremendous numbers of huge rainbows, and I define huge as 8 to 12 pounds, move from the main lake into Pelican Bay where cold-water tributaries and springs maintain water temperatures at a comfortable 50° to 55°. At times, this water is 10° to 12° cooler than the main lake.

Most of the depth of Pelican Bay varies only slightly between 5 and 7 feet and it's fairly weedless. When the water is flat and clear, it's common to see giant trout darting away from the shadow of the boat or fly line.

Getting one of these monsters to eat under calm, clear water conditions is just a notch above impossible. Believe me, I've tried. I've offered these fish to some of North America's most famous and accomplished fly fishermen and we've all been handed our hats and sent home to re-evaluate our skills. These are tough, spooky fish.

These are also the fish that taught me most of my stillwater skills: the value of wind riffle, long-casts and clear-fly lines. The riffle provides the necessary cover, while casts of 60 to 70 feet allow you to reach fish without spooking them.

Fish lose much of their caution while feeding under the cover of wind waves and cloudy water, but they are not suicidal.

After decades of trial and error, I'm convinced that fly-line color makes a difference. The extent of this difference is determined by water disturbance and clarity.

When the water is clear and still, the effect of line color on fish will be dramatic.

When fishing in crystal clear water without a boost from a friendly breeze, I've watched big trout panic and flee when they see a brightly-colored fly line moving overhead even before it hits the water. After much experimentation, I believe that bright lines have about the same effect on trout as "lining", laying the shadow of your fly line in front of or across a fish. A shadow is often the last thing a trout sees before it's converted into osprey protein. As you would expect, survivors of these attempted "conversions" have a healthy fear of moving shadows.

I don't have a problem using colored lines and long leaders in disturbed water, but rarely use them when it's calm and clear. Pastel colored lines, such as pink, yellow or soft blue, and bright lines such as green, fluorescent reds, oranges, and even white, reflect light in the air and will put down fish before the fly ever hits the water.

I have witnessed this so many times in the clear waters of Pelican Bay that I no longer question it, or waste time arguing with those who claim that line color doesn't affect fish.

In my estimation, one of the most progressive innovations in all of recent fly-fishing has been the development of translucent (clear) fly lines. Clear lines now in general use came from the laboratories, test tubes, and oscillators of 3M scientists at Scientific Anglers, in St. Paul, MN. They developed a specialized line for stillwaters that is colorless and allows me to work on huge, spooky trout, in clear, calm, shallow water until some form of cover develops. Ideally, the line creates little if any shadow.

I've found the Stillwater line casts well--at least as well as you have a right to expect--under windy conditions. It cuts a sharp, fast path through headwinds, has enough weight to argue with a backwind, hits the water with minimal commotion, and doesn't splatter a cable-size line shadow across a trout's hunting grounds. I like all of those features, and in fact, when I started using SA's Stillwater lines my success ratio for banging trophy trout in clear stillwater took on a new dimension.

Consistent big fish success takes time, patience, education, and a willingness to fish when other anglers have given up the hunt.

To feel the jolt of one of these huge fish, to just see them hanging in the air pinned to your line by a tiny hook, to have the satisfaction of knowing that if there is a fish in the water that is remotely interested in food, you can catch that fish--that makes it all worthwhile.

When The Algae Blooms

Probably the most overlooked, under fished hide-out of big fish in the West is under the algae bloom that fills many western lakes in the summer. There is a direct correlation between the density of algae and the pH/dissolved oxygen levels in nutrient enriched water that affects the feeding behavior of trout. If the algae is so thick that it looks like you can walk on it, the pH will be too high and you can expect a slow bite. But, if visibility extends a foot or so into the water, fish hard--you can expect active fish.

The murky water visible in this photo is created by nutrients, providing the cover this big rainbow needed to feed.

If you have never fished the bloom, you are in the unfortunate majority.

Algae are pond scum, by definition of Webster's Ninth New Collegiate Dictionary, a non vascular, chlorophyll impregnated plant, that drifts around stillwaters in giant clouds that resemble squalls of brown or red snowflakes.

Solving The Timing Puzzle

The flakes of plant life are as dependent on the rays of the sun for their food, as big trout are dependent on insects and minnows. They grow fat on the process of photosynthesis, where the energy of sunlight forms carbohydrates in the chlorophyll-containing tissues.

For a fisherman, all it means is that when the sun shines, algae is thick, and when the sun wanes, so does algae. Algae is an important form of cover for feeding trout, and that makes it a worthwhile target for big trout specialists. Although algae growth is a slow forming process, it makes fishing shallow water a lot less difficult.

Under a blanket of green algae, trout are safe to feed and cruise in open water, protected from overhead predators.

They are also protected from most fishermen, fishermen who avoid the "scum" at all costs, who have little patience with cleaning hooks and knots of green goo, and who will probably look at you as though you've just lost the best part of your fish sense when you suggest fishing in algae clouded water.

So go without them.

It took me years of exploratory fishing and textbook analysis before I realized just how productive a moderately dense algae bloom can be and why it is. Believe me, it's worth the minor agitation, inconvenience, and less than satisfying ambiance to plunge a fly into the algae swill of summer green.

An algae bloom appears to have the same effect on trout as an exceptionally heavy overcast day. Most trout can't see more than 6 feet in a heavy bloom and they are secure in that invisibility, both as predator and prey, which narrows the productive fishing zone to manageable proportions.

Algae conditions change daily, sometimes even hourly, because they are sunlight dependent. There is a fine balance between algae densities that attract trout and densities that actually repel trout. That's because algae can get so thick the oxygen level is reduced to a point where it is insufficient to support trout.

Many times in late summer or early fall when lake water temperatures are cooling, I have found trout concentrated under

Trout prefer to feed under cloudy skies, which is another form of overhead cover.[Sheely Photo]

FLY-FISHING STILLWATERS

Solving The Timing Puzzle

algae clouds where the water temperature is actually a little higher than neighboring clear water.

Not fishing algae-clouded water is a mistake that nearly all trout fishermen make, and one which many refuse to correct. In many lakes, a summer algae bloom is a blessing. The shallow, greenish water is what a big trout needs to continue daylight feeding even in the heat of summer when daytime fishing success is meager in nearby clear water lakes. I've been amazed at the number of otherwise solid fishermen who are unaware how productive this type of fishing condition can be.

To fish algae water effectively we must learn to ignore our love of clear, clean waters, and the attendant bias that the trout we love must also favor clear, clean waters. Even more than good water quality, trout demand a good source of food and quality cover in which to hunt without fear of becoming the hunted. For fly-fishermen who don't mind a little green goo on their fingers and hands, this can be a prime fishing place, at a prime fishing time.

An algae bloom offers these big fish a well-defined food base of minnows, leeches, and a slew of aquatic insects.

Except in rare instances, when you fish the algae you will be blind casting to fish at least a few feet below the surface. Remember that algae is often concentrated in a layer that only extends a few feet into the water. It's entirely possible that the trout are feeding in less clouded water below the algae.

Algae is a transient and moves in and out of areas. If you caught trout in an area when the water was clear, fish it again during the bloom. The favorable structure, water temperature, or food sources that attracted trout in clear water, will similarly attract them to the area during algae blooms. There is another plus for algae anglers: you can fish very effectively without worrying about distance casting. Those beautiful, delicate 60 and 70-foot casts that were so necessary to fool those spooky mid-summer predators hunting in the shallows at dawn and dusk, are not necessary in the algae bloom.

Trout will continue to feed aggressively because they can't see you or your casting mistakes. Short bad casts are just as potentially lethal as long perfect casts.

When fishing a bloom bite, you can expect some surprise strikes to occur at the end of the retrieve. Because the fish can't see you, sloppy presentations will sometimes work. You can expect to catch some unusually large trout, and be prepared to fish alone.

From a presentation perspective, I find it is best to use one-piece tapered leaders to reduce the number of goop-collecting knots. I also recommend full sinking lines and expect the strike when the fly begins to ascend. I have a couple of theories on why algae-fish strike on the upswing, but they are still too thin to bother you with. What I do know, is that many strikes occur on the ascent, often, I suspect, as a last second pounce just before the fly escapes or emerges into a winged insect.

This reminds me of a third fact, actually, an unfortunate price that must be paid in lost fish and flies. Break offs are common when fishing the algae bloom because the strikes are on short, tight lines. But what a thrill when a big trout aggressively pounds your fly just a few feet off the rod tip.

That kind of strike will make you sit down for a bit. It can make you forget to breathe. I know, because that's how I fish much of the time.

An algae bloom is just one of several types of transient and spontaneous cover elements that big trout specialists need to remember and take advantage of.

That Explosive Thunder-boomer Bite

Right up front, understand there is no way that I will ever recommend fishing on open water, waving 9-feet of graphite rod over your head when there is even the most remote chance that a thunderstorm is in the area.

In fact, I'll tell you not to do it.

FOR TROPHY TROUT

Solving The Timing Puzzle

Lightning strikes, while not anti-fisherman per se, have put the brakes on more lake fishing jaunts than dried up lakes, and rightfully so. I don't have to explain the nasty ramifications of getting a little lightning touch on the back of your neck, or the possibility that your favorite long fly rod will become a short lightning rod if you wave it in the nose of an approaching storm.

My advice is to leave the water whenever a storm front looms, and bear in mind that lightning strikes have occurred 30 miles away from the storm front. Go to shore!

That said, let's consider the effect that a storm has on trout.

Just before and sometimes shortly after summer thunderstorms, trout go on a feeding rip that I can only characterize as explosive.

No one seems to know or understand why trout behave this way. There are a number of theories. Barometric flutters and ion-charged atmosphere are the usual suspects, but that's for scientists.

We're fishermen and all we really need to know is that storm fronts turn trout on! And if you can fish a thunderboomer, without risking a little lightning strike, you can have the greatest fishing of the season compressed into just a few explosive moments.

I experienced just such an occasion while fishing a lake in western Montana, and I still break out in grins when I think about it.

I had enjoyed some very good early morning action fishing the shallows with my stillwater nymph pattern. Big rainbows and browns were cruising the shoreline inhaling tiny freshwater shrimp. After a couple of hours and enough trout to make the day, a high sun and flat water moved the cruisers away from shore into the cover of deeper water.

I motored a short distance down-lake to a shoal area that supported a large weed bed some 30 yards offshore. I slowed the boat and drifted quietly into the weeds. Small callibaetis mayflies were bouncing on the surface. Occasionally, there was a gulp that sounded more like a bucket of concrete slipping under the water, than a tiny mayfly being inhaled. I quickly changed flies, replacing the stillwater nymph with my callibaetis nymph.

Over the distant mountains I could see a white boil of clouds, the unmistakable top of a turbulent summer thunderhead. A few minutes later the thunderhead had wrapped itself around the mountains and was sliding slowly down the valley toward my lake.

Small rainbows to 14 inches were sipping duns in the surface film, but I could plainly see much large trout cruising just above the weeds a few feet beneath the surface.

A half-hour of steady casting slipped by. I had only one take and I managed to miss that. The thunderhead was getting uncomfortably close and I was just about to head for safety on shore when a heavy fish jolted every taut nerve in my body. I have no idea why I didn't lose it. Luck I guess. The fish was 20 inches long, thick through its dark green shoulders and the tail was square and heavily spotted. I slipped it back in the water, checked my fly and leader, fixed one worried eye on the approaching storm and with the other spotted a feeder.

While I was working out the line, thunder bounced through the mountains on both sides of the valley. Time was short and fishing incredible! I kept track, and during 20 minutes I never put a fly on the water that was not struck. The fish were all 18 inches plus (I have no idea where the pan-size fish disappeared to) and to say they were aggressive would be to seriously understate their ferocity.

The sky blackened, lightning lit up the mountains, cattle turned their backs to the wind, and fish were everywhere, eating everything that didn't run or fly. This was a frenzy in all of its primal glory. No insect, alive or dead, was safe. These trout were sucking flies off the surface then crashing back to take an emerger several feet deep.

It was glorious, simply, fantastically glorious.

This was the rarest fishing of all and it would be insane to leave the bite, but it would be even crazier to stay. I finally dashed for cover just ahead of a furious downpour and electrical display.

That was a special day. I pushed my luck to the limit, was rewarded with the explosive success befitting the gamble, and did it all without getting fried to my boat seat.

The result of a thunder-boom bite.

Over the years, I've had the thunder-boomer bite develop exactly like that enough times to know that it's predictable, and while the feeding may or may not be frenzied, it will always be among the best days of the season.

I still like to fish the frenzied bite on the edges of thunder-boomers, sometimes pushing the odds a little more than I should. But now, I make it a point to get off the water well ahead of the fury of summer storms.

That is, most of the time.

In the microscopic underwater world of stillwater trout, fishing success is tied directly to an angler's presentation skills. [Sheely Photo

Chapter 10

PRESENTATION
The Most Critical Skill Of Them All

When you make the conscious decision to pursue big trout in stillwater with a fly rod, no other skill is more critical to success than your ability to make the fly look and act like a natural food source.

We call this presentation, and it's the one obvious skill factor that will set apart the expert fly fisherman from all others.

Novice fly-fishermen should spend less time on fly-tying techniques, equipment worship, and catalog shopping, and re-allocate that time to those elements that make up a decent presentation.

The sorry truth is, I've found that most fly-fishermen present their flies poorly, often for lack of practice because they have no measuring stick for what is necessary to be successful. Consequently, they settle for something less.

Complacency is a luxury big fish specialists cannot afford. Trout fishing success anywhere, but especially under the microscope of stillwater, is tied directly to your ability to make a good presentation. If you're not catching fish, the odds are it's because you're not presenting the fly the way you should.

Presentation is nothing more than a three-part system;

1) tackle selection
2) casting ability
3) retrieve styles

These three parts must be addressed independently and then together as a balanced one-piece unit: an incorporation that will deliver your fly to the fish at the depth they want it, and have it retrieved as a totally natural simulation of the real thing.

Real Things Don't:
- splatter onto the surface.
- alight daintily amidst coils of line.
- shred 10 yards of surface film lifting into the air.
- spin when they swim.
- move like they're snubbed to a cable.
- swim through the water at the wrong time of year.
- drape themselves with moss.
- arrive with 20 feet of line shadow.

The key to effective presentation is choosing the right tackle and techniques for the situations and conditions present. This means having balanced tackle that will deliver your fly to the fish, retrieving it in a way that simulates the natural insect, and with a line that will suspend your fly for an extended period at the depth fish are feeding. Because a lake's chemistry and external conditions are constantly changing, your ability to adjust presentation becomes not only necessary but critical.

Presentation

Just as there is no single line, fly, or rod for all situations, there is no one form of presentation. Mother Nature keeps shuffling the deck, forcing stillwater anglers to constantly make adjustments.

Often we fail to recognize nature's effect on trout behavior and don't make the necessary modifications in our presentation. When trout refuse the fly, it's not a question of should we change, but what should we change. Sorting out the options can be complex, but is not as difficult as it may appear.

It's almost impossible to make adjustments in presentation without considering the relationship between fly, retrieve, and line. If any one of these three factors is out of sync, the entire presentation breaks down.

Fly selection is not generally considered a part of presentation, but it requires careful consideration whenever changes in presentation become necessary since the fly is relative to the retrieve and line being used.

When trout refuse a fly, the first instinct is to change flies, but often the problem is not with the pattern, but how it is being retrieved or the depth at which it is being fished. Quite often if the bite is slow, I'll change the retrieve or line before I change the fly.

In order to understand the importance of presentation, we have to understand the components of this critical part of the stillwater puzzle.

Tackle

Knowing the limitations of your tackle and matching it to the conditions is a major part of presentation. It's important that every angler understand that the conditions and situations we encounter on the water mandate our choices of tackle. You would never consider pitching a 4-weight system in a heavy wind any more than you would use a fast-sinking line in four feet of water.

Line selection is the one element of our tackle that seems to be least understood by stillwater anglers. The purpose of any line other than getting our fly to the fish, is to hold your fly at the depth where fish are feeding for as long as possible. The depth at which fish are holding may extend from 2 to 4 feet below the surface, but once your line and fly pass through that zone, the odds of getting a strike diminish quickly since trout never look down for food.

Imagine that you make a 50-foot cast with a fast-sinking line. If the trout are suspended 24 inches below the surface and the fly line is sinking three inches per second, how much time would you have before the fly slips below the holding depth? The answer may surprise you. You can effectively hold your fly in the feeding zone for only 8 seconds. If you attempt to retard the rate of sink by increasing the speed of retrieve, the movement of your fly may look unrealistic to an approaching trout. What could be worse, only 6 to 10 feet of the retrieve will be fished through the zone in which the trout are holding. The remaining 40 feet will be retrieved unproductively as the fly sinks below the trout and will never be seen.

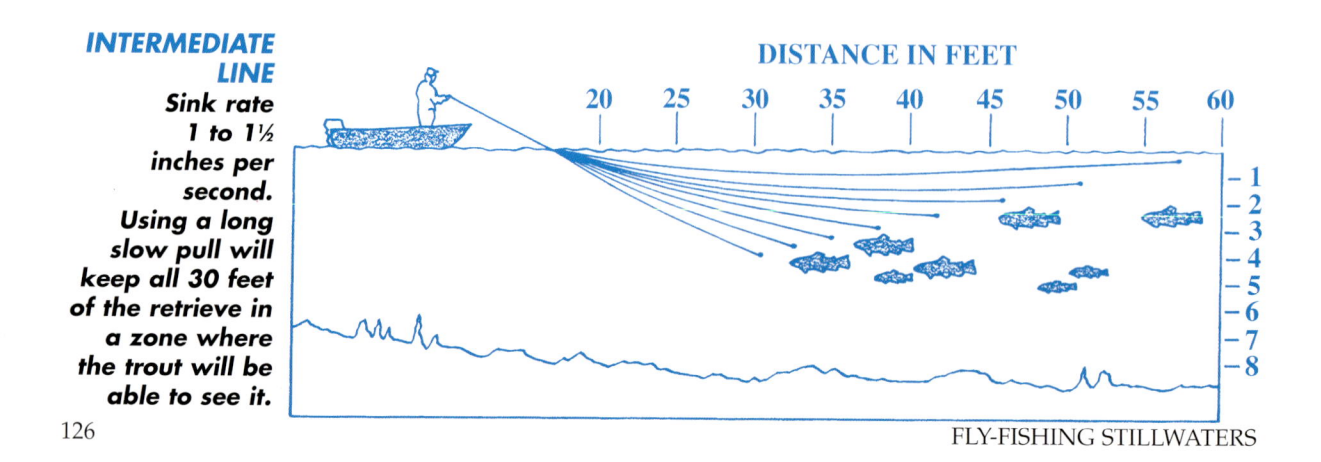

INTERMEDIATE LINE
Sink rate 1 to 1½ inches per second. Using a long slow pull will keep all 30 feet of the retrieve in a zone where the trout will be able to see it.

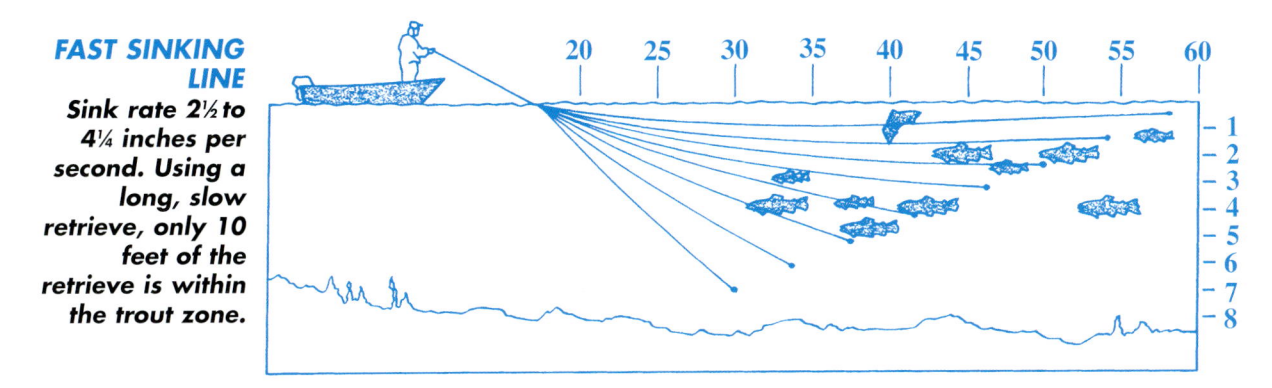

FAST SINKING LINE

Sink rate 2½ to 4¼ inches per second. Using a long, slow retrieve, only 10 feet of the retrieve is within the trout zone.

As I said earlier, the challenge of any fly line is to hold the fly at the depth at which fish are feeding for as long as possible. Remember, once your fly sinks out of that zone, you're no longer fishing productively because stratified fish look up not down for food.

This problem smacked me in the face a few years ago at Dry Falls Lake, a premium brown and rainbow trout lake in semi-arid northcentral Washington. It was early morning with a light mist rising off the water.

A few midges were bouncing on the surface attracting an occasional rise. I decided most of the feeding was going on underwater and rigged up a seal bugger on the full-sinking Stillwater line. In an hour I landed seven rainbows between 14 and 18 inches, before the bite began to slow. Within minutes the reason became obvious when callibaetis mayflies began appearing and trout were right on schedule, intercepting the emergers as well as the duns on the surface.

It was obvious that a change in both pattern and retrieve was necessary. I switched to my callibaetis nymph and a hand twist retrieve, but stayed with the Stillwater sinking line. Twenty minutes of casting and I was still fishless. I was going to change patterns again, but I knew the fish were hitting emergers and the nymph was a good imitation.

And then it dawned on me, the problem wasn't the fly---it was the line. The faster-sinking line was pulling the fly below the level of the feeding activity during most of the retrieve. These fish were looking up for food and I was fishing down. The only half-hearted takes I'd had were when the fly passed through the feeding zone en route to the surface.

I changed spools to an intermediate line, attached my callibaetis nymph, and landed five fat rainbows up to 4 pounds which reinforced a critical lesson in presentation. The relationship between line and depth is just as important as the choice of pattern or retrieve.

Because lakes and trout are moody, we need variety to match those moods--whatever they may be. I am convinced that the number one fault of 90 percent of all unsuccessful stillwater flyfishermen is giving the fish what the fisherman wants to give, not necessarily at the speed or depth the fish wants.

If you like to fish a sink-tip line with a chironomid pattern, but the trout want a full-sinking line with an undulating seal bugger--well, you see the problem. And, hopefully, the solution as well.

Casting

As we discussed in Chapter 7, learning to throw a long line isn't a luxury for lake fishermen, it's a necessary skill. Because trout are constantly on the move in lakes, casts of 60 to 70 feet are often necessary to reach fish without spooking them. The biggest fish in any lake are also usually the first to be spooked by anything out of the ordinary.

Anything less than long, quiet, straight casts that unfold and land with the lightness of dragon-fly feet will put these big fish down. In my 15 years of guiding on lakes, I've seen far more people who couldn't cast, than those who could. Many never had to make a long cast because their fishing, until that time, was restricted to small streams.

Presentation

I've found that there is a direct relationship between how many big fish an angler catches, and how well they can cast a long line.

How long is long enough? That depends on the conditions. Wind, sunlight, water clarity, surface disturbances all of these factors dictate distance requirements. As a rule, remember, as these factors change, the need for long casts may increase or possibly decrease. Because each of these elements produces cover for trout to feed under, the more cover in place, the less need there is for distance casting.

If you can consistently throw a 6-weight line 50 feet, your potential rate of success will be about 70 percent. In other words, hypothetically, you'll be able to reach 7 out of every 10 fish within your area regardless of conditions. At other times, a 60 foot cast may be necessary to reach a higher percentage of fish.

Unfortunately, the upper 10-percent of that scale is where most of the trophy trout will be found.

When fishing flat, clear, shallow water I've often found it necessary to use long leaders and cast of at least 70 feet. If I approach any closer, the fish spook. Sure, there are times when weather conditions are all on my side. On a few occasions, I have been able to sneak right into their cafeteria and pull the trigger on a monster trout with only 20 feet of line out.

Yet, if I waited for those conditions to create that ideal opportunity, I would be a long time waiting between fish. I've found it a lot more rewarding to learn to make a long cast, as well as a good cast.

Chapter 7 relates to the importance of casting distance. There are hundreds of books and magazine articles, casting clinics, and seminars that do a fine job of that already. I suggest that if you are serious about stalking big fish, you take advantage of as many of these instructional opportunities as possible. I teach casting, and still I find ways to improve by watching other instructors.

Perhaps the biggest advantage for learning to cast far is that you increase the number of trout that you show your fly to on every cast.

For example, let's assume that you can consistently cast 50 feet. George, your fishing partner, can cast only 40 feet.

While we're enjoying assumptions, let's assume that in the space of that extra 10 feet, you will show your fly to two fish more than George does with his shorter cast. If you make 15 casts an hour and fish an eight-hour day, you will show your fly to 240 more trout than George.

The chances are that quite a few of those 240 fish will bite your bug.

Now, imagine if you can consistently stretch your 50-foot cast into 70 feet or more on a consistent basis. The potential is intriguing isn't it.

Another advantage for making long casts is when using a sinking line, the line will sink steadily throughout the retrieve. For some reason, big trout love to nail a fly just as it turns toward the surface at the end of the retrieve. I suspect these fish have been following this curious intruder and strike only when it looks as though it's about to escape, or because that is when the fly looks the most natural, like an emerger angling to the surface.

Some fishermen stoutly defend a belief that they can offset the need for long casts by using a weighted fly and allowing it to sink on their shorter casts. The problem with this theory is that big trout are the spookiest trout and only rarely come that close to you without skittering away to some hideout unless some form of cover is in place.

The third advantage for the long-caster is keeping the fly in the water where the fish are, while reducing the number of casts made in a day. Saving the arm and shoulder muscles can be very important on a multiple-day trout trip.

If I can pound two lessons about presentation into your fishing style, let it be these next two.

Regardless of the distance you cast it is critical that as soon as the fly hits the water you pull out all line slack. All of it!

Presentation

As soon as the cast hits the water, all slack (left) must be removed immediately. Slack line presentations result in drag, missed strikes and break-offs. A tight line (right) helps to detect strikes and maximize the time the fly is in the strike zone during the retrieve.

I've watched thousands of fishermen, and they, almost to a person begin their retrieve before pulling out slack, which means their fly is sinking on a slack line for several seconds. If the cast is reasonably decent and lands softly, there is a distinct possibility that a trout will eat the fly before the line tightens. You'll never know, because you will never feel the take before it's rejected.

As soon as the fly touches the surface, strip out every inch of slack. The effectiveness of all flies improves when the leader draws taut, especially wet flies descending on sinking lines.

The second rule of presentation is to position the top few inches of your fly rod in or at the water's edge as you start the retrieve.

CORRECT

Stillwater angling requires that the tip of the rod be placed in the water during the retrieve to maintain a taut, sensitive, slack free line

FOR TROPHY TROUT

Presentation

INCORRECT

If the rod tip is suspended in the air, slack develops in the retrieve decreasing sensitivity which results in missed strikes and poor presentations.

There are four solid reasons why a wet rod tip is a must when fly fishing in stillwaters:

1) Tension is maintained between rod and line. Slack does not develop as the tip bobs during the retrieve and you'll detect the lightest bite. That is because most bites will be even lighter than you probably expect. Big trout don't "strike" most bug patterns. They don't have to. Most insects aren't going anywhere fast. Trout simply inhale most organisms, a soft sucking action that you'll never feel 50 feet away if there's any amount of slack in the line to dampen sensitivity.

2) Eliminates line bounce on the water during the retrieve. Again, we're working against line slack. Any style of strip retrieve will cause the rod tip to bounce and each bounce creates a few inches of slack increasing the risk of break offs.

3) If the rod tip is positioned hip-high, three feet above the water the power of your retrieve is reduced by two thirds. In other words, if you pull a 6-inch strip, the fly will move about 2 inches. The other 4-inches of your retrieve absorbs the slack and the fly sinks instead of moving forward.

4) Fewer strikes are missed and fewer leaders snapped when the line is held taut by water tension.

The Retrieve

In moving water, a well-built trout fly breathes, constricting and expanding with the impact of various currents as it passes through moving water. A stillwater fly, however, will lay in the water like it was strangled, unless the angler imparts the action, which brings life to the fly. The type of imparted fly action depends on the type of retrieve.

The purpose of any retrieve is to make the fly simulate the natural movements of those food sources living beneath the surface.

Because fly patterns represent not only different insects, but varying developmental stages of each insect, we need to learn as much as possible about each bug and how it moves at each stage of development.

And how we imitate that movement is a product of presentation, the relationship between the retrieve, the line and the fly.

With trout being opportunistic feeders much of the time, a fly that acts like a natural insect has much greater appeal than one whose movements appear unnatural.

Caddis and mayfly naturals emerge from bottom silt, resting only occasionally on their jour-

Presentation

ney to the surface. To match this movement, requires a sink-tip or floating line, weighted fly, and a leader that is twice as long as the depth of the water.

The presentation puts the fly on the bottom, on a tight line, and then moves it toward the surface in a staccato series of short, rapid, little pulls, punctuated with brief pauses between each pull. This simulates the jerky start-stop-start motion of a natural.

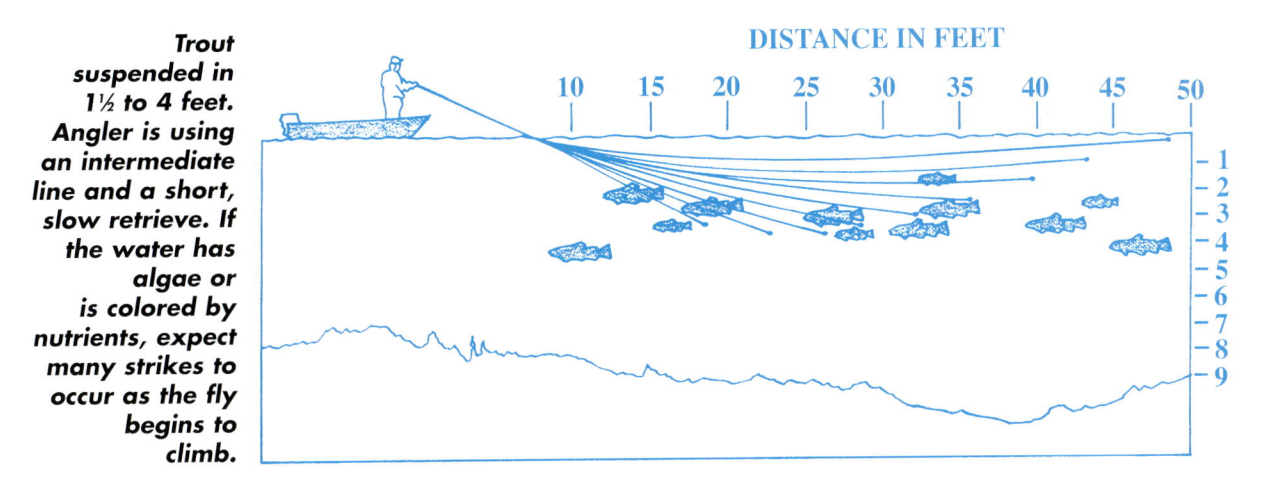

Trout suspended in 1½ to 4 feet. Angler is using an intermediate line and a short, slow retrieve. If the water has algae or is colored by nutrients, expect many strikes to occur as the fly begins to climb.

On the other hand, intermediate and full-sink lines do a better job simulating the horizontal swimming motion of other insects such as dragon and damsel flies, scuds, leeches, plus small bait fish.

I won't say that you will never catch a trout by using a mayfly imitation with a full-sink line, but I am convinced that you will enjoy a more consistent level of success by using tackle that allows you to match the angle of ascent as well as the movements of the naturals.

Trout will sometimes, in fact quite often, take a fly even though it doesn't resemble their primary food source, if the pattern is retrieved in a manner that emulates a natural food. If the fly is moving too fast, or too slowly it's usually refused, regardless of how exactingly it's tied or what it imitates.

This massive buck rainbow was a direct result of a tight line retrieve. If the rod tip had been out of the water it is likely the light take would have been missed.

FOR TROPHY TROUT

Presentation

Not all patterns need movement to attract fish. In fact, many of our most popular stillwater angling techniques are with floating lines and emerger patterns fished either on the surface, in the film, or suspended just below the surface. This is a favorite technique of fishing chironomids in southern British Columbia for Kamloop-strain rainbows.

Despite the fact that most aquatic nymphs move very slowly, most of us retrieve our flies too quickly. It's a matter of impatience and usually a lack of knowledge or concentration on our part. I know most of us love to feel the rod working out another cast, but forget the romance and concentrate on creating the most lifelike presentation possible. Slow your retrieves and keep the fly in the water longer, and I'll bet you catch more fish.

Sometimes, however, the opposite is true, and a fast-moving fly will trigger a latent strike response from these predators. In fact, it's not a bad technique to rip a couple of retrieves through the water when a bite falters, especially if you're about to leave the water. What's to lose?

Experienced stillwater fishermen master and depend upon a series of basic retrieves. Each retrieve can be divided into three parts: speed, distance, and timing. The speed of the line being retrieved, the length of the pull, and the amount of time or pause between each pull are the significant parts of any retrieve.

Each part is independent, but must be worked in perfect harmony with the other two. There are also variations within each part necessary to match the movements of naturals.

The two basic swimming directions are parallel to the bottom and ascending. When trout feed on the surface or in the film, little if any action should be imparted beyond the slight strips needed to draw out slack. Retrieves that bring the fly to the surface or crawl it along the bottom should be equally slow. Among the other zillion factors to remember, bear in mind that external weather factors always dictate which retrieve speeds are best: the colder the water, the slower the speed, and vice versa up to the point where oxygen depletion slows trout reactions.

If it's not working, before you change patterns, make a few casts and vary the retrieve speed, distance, and pause. Sometimes all that's needed is a minor adjustment.

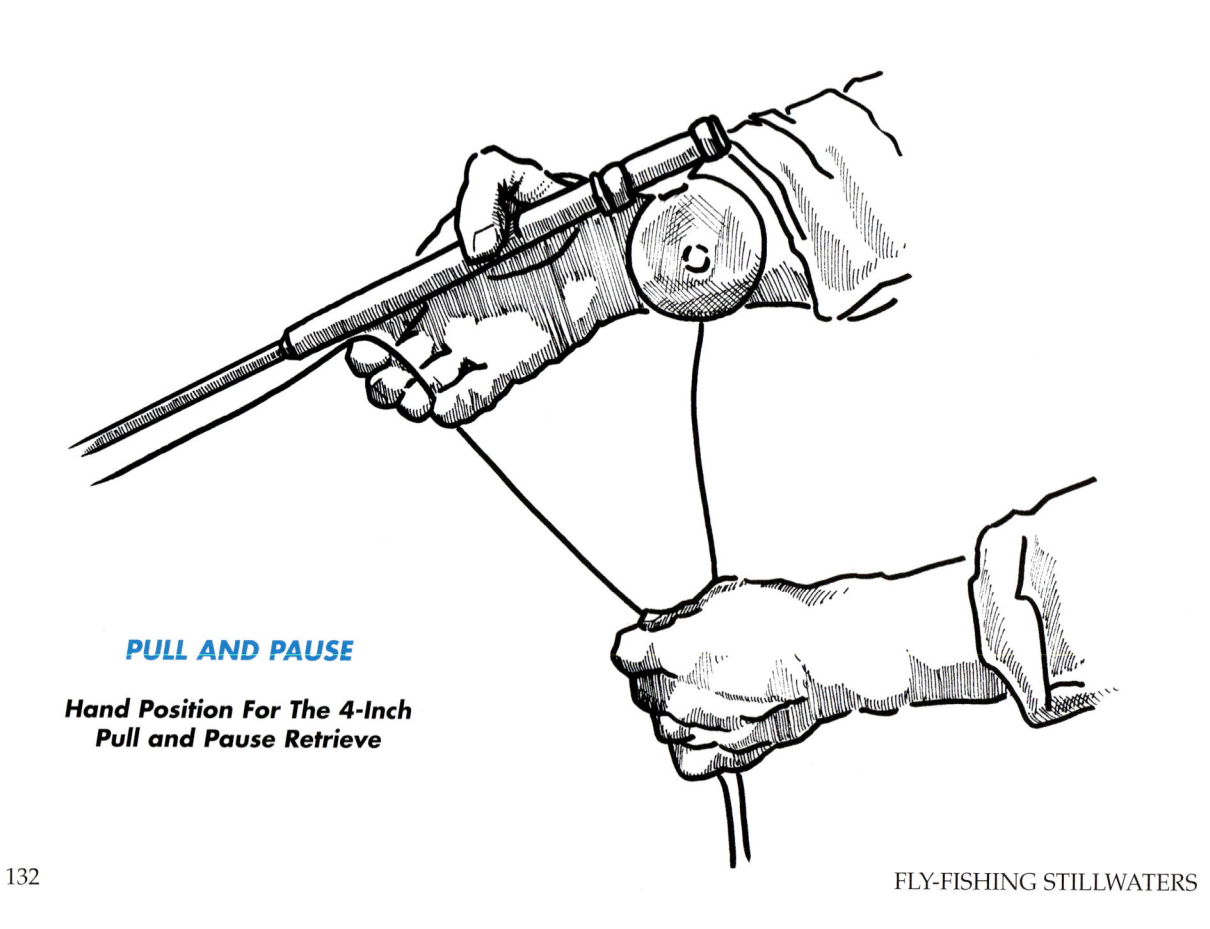

PULL AND PAUSE

Hand Position For The 4-Inch Pull and Pause Retrieve

Presentation

4-Inch Pull 'n Pause:

This retrieve is at its best in the top 6 feet of water with the Stillwater or intermediate slow sinking lines. Presentation emphasis is on speed, or the lack of it. The pull should be s-l-o-w and the pause definitive.

I believe that the 4-inch pull-pause retrieve, in its multiple variations, is the best retrieve when using No. 10 to 16 nymphs, regardless of water temperature. The explanation is simple; it works.

A four-inch pull and pause retrieve convinced this trophy trout to strike a Denny's Stillwater Nymph.

The strength of this retrieve is in its versatility. The imparted movement imitates an entire host of aquatic nymphs throughout the season. The take can be soft, hardly detectable one time and vicious the next. If strikes are inconsistent you may need to experiment with the pattern selection.

This retrieve may not be the absolute ultimate in every situation, but it is consistently productive enough to become a major part of your standing presentation.

Long, Slow Pull:

I believe that this is the least understood retrieve style, yet it's absolutely deadly with some of my favorite patterns--specifically, leech, seal bugger, and minnow imitations.

The long, slow pull retrieve simulates the idling indifference of a great many insects. Because trout aren't used to chasing their prey, strikes will be sipped instead of aggressively eaten. Trout, especially those very large trout that husband their energies, simply idle up to the loafing lunch and suck it in. It's important to keep a tight line, especially with this retrieve.

The retrieve consists of long pulls--24 to 30 inches from start to stop. The trick with such a long pull is going slowly enough and pausing between pulls a little longer than normal until it feels right. The trout will let you know if you are doing it right. They will also tell you if you are doing it wrong.

FOR TROPHY TROUT

Presentation

The long, slow pull works best with flies that are weighted at the head. During the pause, the off-balance fly will dip and drop slightly. Many strikes will occur as the fly drops. I always try to anticipate the strike, so that when it comes I won't overreact.

This undulating motion creates a very life-like imitation that trout find difficult to resist.

I prefer to use an intermediate line with this retrieve, especially when fishing shallow water. Most sinking lines will work, though.

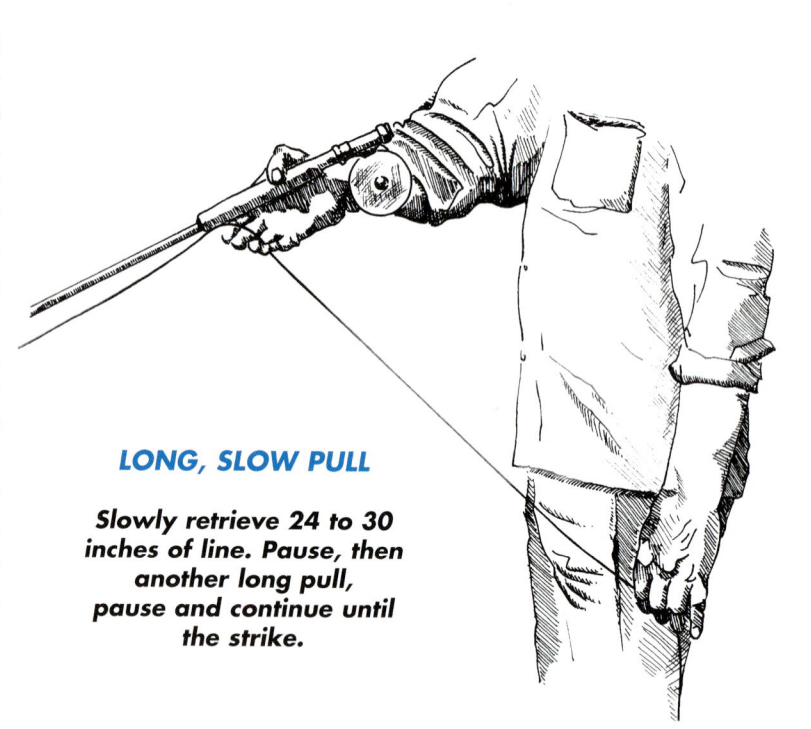

LONG, SLOW PULL

Slowly retrieve 24 to 30 inches of line. Pause, then another long pull, pause and continue until the strike.

Streamer Retrieve:

This is the basic retrieve used for fishing minnow patterns in rivers, but there are some deadly variations we can use in lakes.

When I'm fishing a streamer, such as the popular Zonker patterns, I prefer to use a long, 24-inch semi-rapid pull interrupted by obvious pauses.

This retrieve will match the swimming motion of most bait fish, such as small shad, minnows, shiners, and chubs. To imitate the little shiners and daces, the streamer retrieve needs to be shorter (8 to 12 inches), slower and the pause should last only about a second.

After years of experimenting, I found that the fly lines most effectively incorporated into this presentation are intermediate or transparent stillwater sinking lines. These lines really shine when you're fishing big streamers over weed beds or shoals. The lines hold the flies on a course parallel with the bottom and can be fished at specific depths. It's a big mistake to use a floating line when stripping minnow patterns because of the surface disturbance created. I usually don't use fast-sinking lines because minnows are not found in deep water, only in shallow water or near the surface.

I love this style of presentation; it's effective, exciting, and the fish go crazy. It surprises me how few of today's anglers fish streamers in stillwater. It's getting

The author nailed this broad-shouldered rainbow using the long, slow retrieve. Conditions and patterns dictate the retrieve speed in most lakes. [Photo: Dave Freel]

to be a forgotten art. That's just as well, because those of us who remember, also remember that this technique usually brings a response from the largest trout in lakes and reservoirs.

Rapid, Short Pull:

If there is one retrieve that stimulates aggressive strikes, this is it. The quick, jerky movements of the fly simulate an insect about to emerge or trying to escape, and strikes are fast, hard, and extremely violent. I like that.

A medium, slow, erratic retrieve enticed this big brown to hit a streamer. [California Department of Fish and Game Photo]

The problem, if you want to call it that, is that trout quite often break off on the strike.

While a slow moving insect may be carefully selected and sipped by a cautious trout, speeding prey sometimes gets annihilated. To most trout, I'm sure it must appear as though the fly is trying to emerge or escape, motivating an aggressive strike.

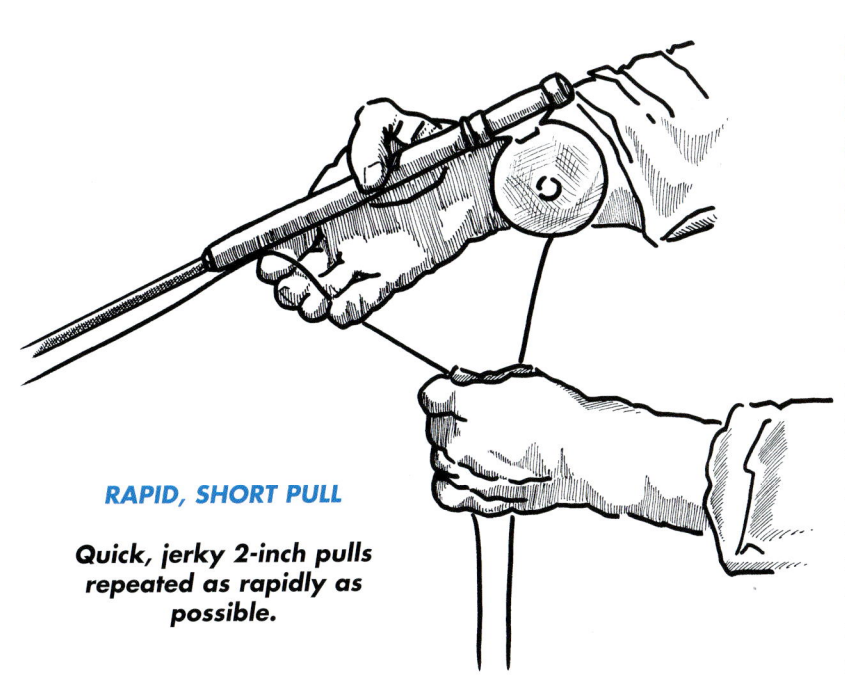

RAPID, SHORT PULL

Quick, jerky 2-inch pulls repeated as rapidly as possible.

To work the retrieve, position your line hand directly below the hand holding the rod. With the thumb and index finger, grasp the line and pull straight down in rapid 2-inch pulls. Because your rod tip is in the water, the line won't bounce and wrap the tip top because there is no slack in the retrieve. Bring the fly stuttering back to within 6 feet of the rod before recasting. This retrieve is at its best when fished in the top 4 feet and it's not very effective deeper than 6 feet. Bear in mind that insects are much more active in shallow water than deep.

Because I'm rarely fishing deeper than a couple of feet with this retrieve, I prefer an intermediate or the translucent Stillwater specialty line from Scientific Anglers.

When water temperatures are between 54° and 63°, my deadliest patterns with this retrieve have been my Seal Bugger, A.P. Emerger, Stillwater Nymph, Black Diamond Nymph, and leeches. But any jointed fly or pattern with a long tail will work explosively with the rapid, short pull retrieve.

Most strikes take place within the first dozen pulls, especially if you're fishing the edge of cover structure, like weed beds. This retrieve is not a guarantee for success, or the answer to all fishing problems. It is, however, consistent for me in most water, under most conditions.

Presentation

Hand Twist:

This retrieve is almost as old as the fishing reel. It was popularized by the late Ray Bergman and is still a favorite on stillwater. It's about the only retrieve I know that's consistently effective when fishing chironomids and it's deadly for me when working small nymphs in shallow water, especially when I'm wading a lake.

Floating lines and long (15'-20') leaders get the best out of hand twist retrieves with tiny nymphs or emerger patterns fished near the surface. Spend a moment watching the water and you'll see why this slow, erratic style is so effective. Just about every insect worth eating moves this way.

There are several versions of this slow-motion retrieve.

Short, rapid pulls will often trigger aggressive strikes, sometimes carrying the fish exploding through the surface.

This 7-pound rainbow unloaded on the fly when the author began a short, rapid, 2-inch retrieve.

136   FLY-FISHING STILLWATERS

Presentation

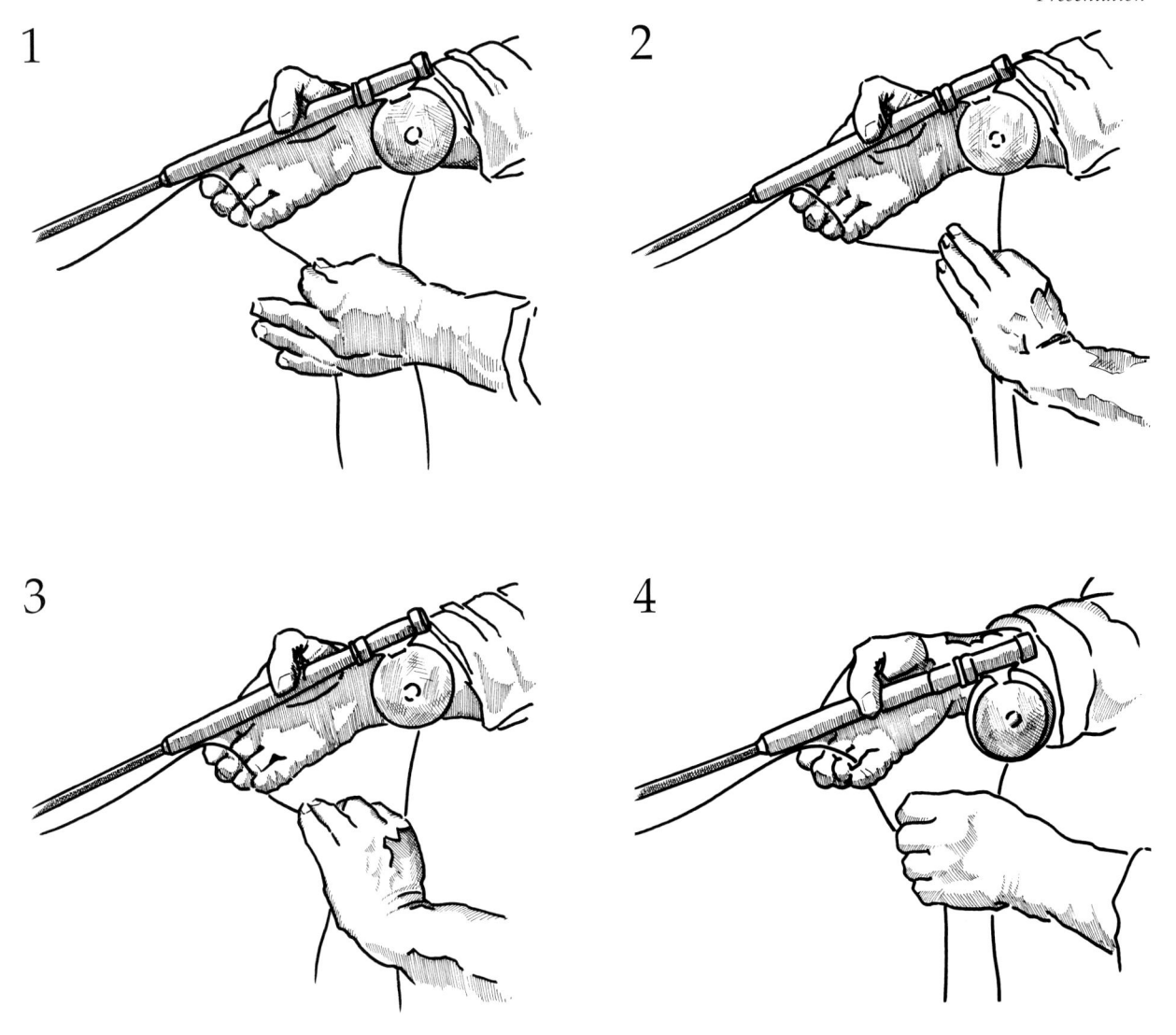

The four critical movements of a hand twist retrieve

I've had good luck by holding the line between the thumb and index finger. With the remaining three fingers, pull an inch or two of line at a time into the palm of your hand. As with any retrieve, the key is to move the fly on a tight line.

Vary the speed, but always go slowly. Slow sinking lines also work with this retrieve, but the fly pattern makes the final determination. Any time I use this retrieve and fail to get a response within a reasonable period of time, I start to work in small variations in speed and twist length until I find that day's magic spot.

Strike Indicators:

Using a strike indicator to suspend a wet fly or indicate a strike falls more under the classification of presentation than retrieve. This form of fishing requires only slight movement of the fly, then a tightening of the line to remove slack. The idea of fly fishermen sitting on boxes under umbrellas and fishing their flies in the same manner they would drown a worm, is not--in my estimation--fly fishing. We could just as well be using a piece of corn, or a chunk of dog food, while waiting for the indicator to signal a strike. But, like it or not, indicator fishing is effective. Nothing wrong with it. It's just not fly-fishing.

Presentation

This trout hit an emerger in the surface film, a productive technique that requires little or no fly movement.

In clear, flat water and a high sun, an indicator and patience was the right combination for fooling this big rainbow.

Presentation

But whether or not I like it, doesn't alter the fact that strike indicators are a very effective, very simplistic form of fishing. Indicators are built with foam flotation, come in many colors, shapes and sizes. Simply attach the indicator to your leader so the fly is held forever at the depth you pre-select. Trout bites are generally passive and there may only be a slight bump to the indicator. Concentration is a must, while attention should be focused on the indicator, not where your line or leader enters the water.

While I probably never will be a fan of strike indicators in stillwater, more and more anglers are using them and that's a testimonial to their effectiveness.

Irv Wheat of Chester, California, is the very best I've seen at using the indicator presentation. He is absolutely deadly with this technique. I've seen him take trout after trout while no one else could draw a strike.

Irv feels the indicator is at its best when the lake surface is calm or just slightly riffled. A professional tier, Irv favors his "Woodduck Nymph" pattern with the indicator, but I think he could catch trout with a safety pin and feather using this method.

Author with a nice brown trout from southwestern Montana's Clark Canyon Reservoir. [Sheely Photo]

Chapter 11

STILLWATERS BY BOAT, TUBE AND WADERS
How You Get To The Trout Does Matter

On good stillwater-fishing lakes you can't afford to wait for the trophy fish to come to you; you must go to them. Mobility is something you're going to have to think about before you ever see the water, not after you get there.

The aquatic definition of mobility is flotation, and flotation is an expandable noun that can stand for anything from a drifting log to the ruddered pontoons of a float plane. But in the end, for a stillwater fly-fisherman, fishing lakes comes in only three forms, boating, float tubing, and wading.

Which of these forms of approach you select on a given piece of water can have as much impact on your success as the fly you select. In fact, I believe that how you get to the fish should be given serious consideration along with all of the other pieces of the presentation puzzle: lines, rods, reels, tippets, flies, water clarity, light penetration--the lot.

Each option has advantages and disadvantages and specific applications. Sometimes we get lucky and lakes will have restrictions, imposed either by the managing entity or by natural obstacles, and happily the decision is made for us. That's usually not the case though. Most big trout lakes, especially the public ones, are also big, equal-opportunity lakes and can be fished any way you care to challenge it.

So which is best?

There are a few standard clues as to the most effective way to fish stillwater. A lake's surface size, amount and type of shoreline cover, vegetation, depth, remoteness are all factors that need to be considered. Often mother nature, always the maternal dictator, will funnel our option to the right choice--sometimes the only choice.

For example, wind, or lack of it, often plays a major role in not only angler success but can determine if fishing from a boat or float tube are even feasible. A high sun and flat water that moves fish into deeper water during daylight often eliminates effective presentations from shore. The same could be said when uncomfortably warm summer water moves trout offshore to spring areas or deep-water ledges and shoals, taking wading fishermen out of the game. Standing timber, shallow water, weed growth can just as easily block boat access. That's why I rank the flotation decision high in priority. What you choose to fish from will influence your presentation, tackle selection, choice of fly pattern, and retrieve, all of which will affect your ability to reach and hook cruising fish.

These are some of the considerations I mix into my decision.

Trailered Boats

Fishing from a small boat, 8 to 16 feet long, is the most common form of fly fishing stillwaters. It isn't always the best way or the most popular method, but it's one way of reaching all the fish in the lake.

Drifting flies from a boat is extremely popular in England and to some extent is common in

Stillwaters By Boat, Tube And Waders

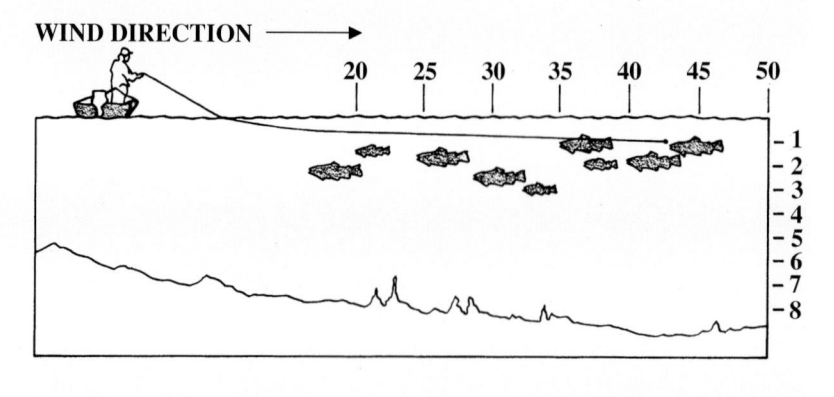

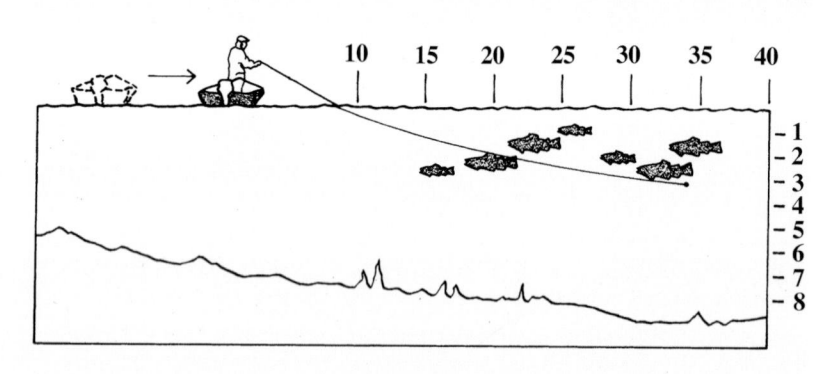

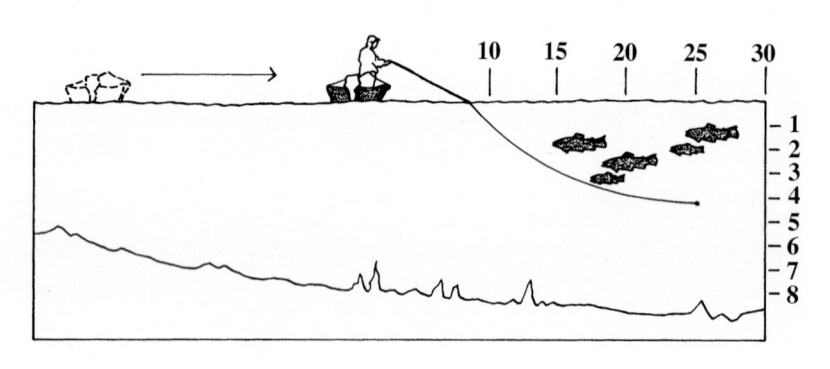

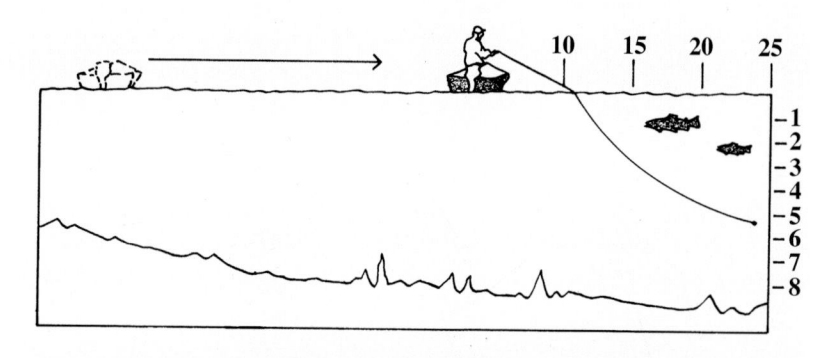

The boat is drifting into the cast, creating slack. The retrieve merely removes this slack without moving the fly. As a result, the fly continues to sink below the level of the feeding fish.

the United States as well. But drifting flies, although sometimes successful when fishing on top, is not as effective below the surface. The problem is wind, which is often prevalent on lakes. The solution is to anchor the boat, fore and aft, in order to make a consistent presentation.

Here are your options if you still choose to cast from a drifting boat.

1) If you cast downwind in the direction you are drifting, getting a controlled, effective retrieve is impossible. Because you are drifting into the cast, most of the retrieve simply goes into removing developing slack caused by the speed of the drift.

2) If you cast upwind, there will always be an area directly behind the boat that will be void of fish, because trout naturally move away from the boat when it drifts over them. Another problem with casting directly upwind is that feeding trout tend to face into the wind awaiting drifting insects. An upwind cast puts the line over the fish, "lining" them. It's a hardy trout that won't spook when lined. Even if the trout doesn't see the line hit the water, every fish between your boat and fly will be on alert because the boat is drifting down on them.

3) One of the two remaining casting directions, depending on whether you are right or left handed, is not really an option because it creates the risk of being hit by your own cast as the wind snatches the fly and dumps the backcast, possibly into

FLY-FISHING STILLWATERS

your ear. It's the right angle to cast, just not necessarily the safest.

4) This leaves but one direction, crosswind. And even this isn't good because as the boat drifts, the movement creates line bow which develops drag. Drag is just as devastating to the presentation of a fly on a lake as it is on a stream.

To me, these are four good reasons why drifting boats should only be used for reading, napping, lunching and day-dreaming. Unanchored boats cannot be fly-fished from effectively while drifting during windy periods.

The best option is to find a likely spot and anchor. When the anchor line pulls taut (two anchors stabilize better than one) you immediately reduce the number of variables, simplify the complications and your presentations are controlled, consistent, and correctable.

There are several points that must always be evaluated when fishing from a boat on stillwater.

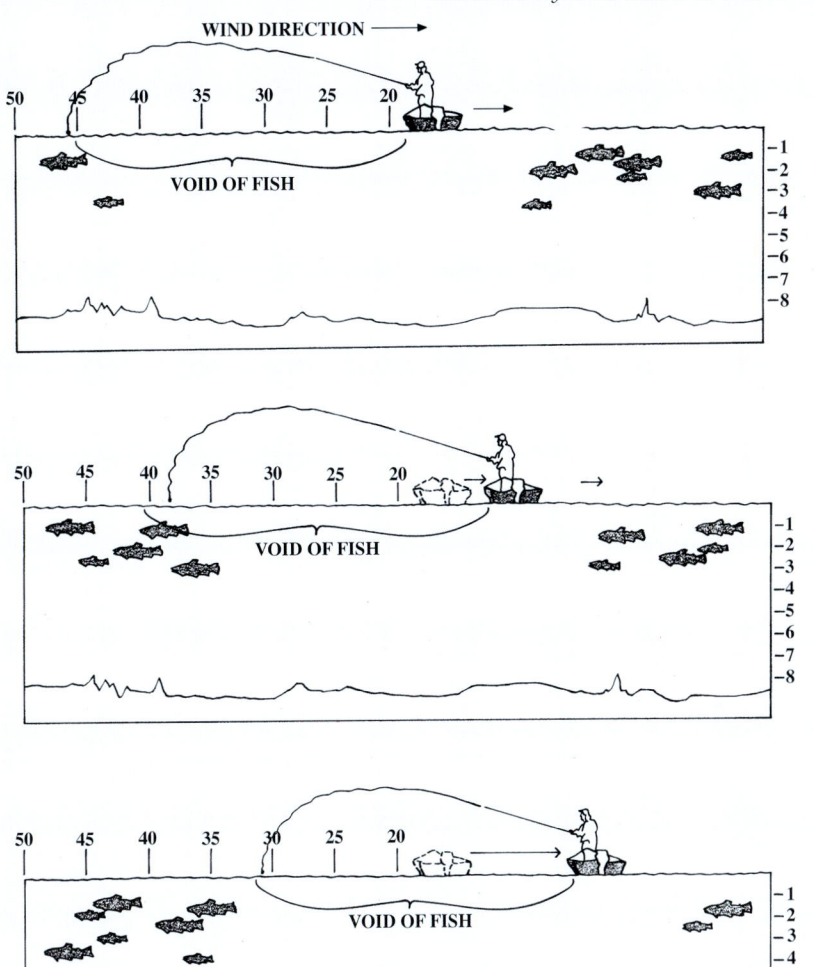

• Mobility is critical. The best areas are often miles apart and when trout stop feeding in one area, they may be just starting in another. Being able to move quickly is often the difference between a few fish and large numbers of fish.

Casting into the wind is dangerous and distance is difficult to achieve. Trout will move as the boat drifts over them creating, a fishless void behind the boat.

• Never stay in one spot if you're not getting strikes. Adopt a policy of moving 20-30 yards every 30 minutes or if the bite even begins to slow. Trout tend to shy away from the area around a boat after a period of disturbances created by casting, playing fish, setting anchors, etc.

• Take advantage of cover such as surface chop, algae, low light, or semi darkness. Fishing from a boat in flat water with a high sun is as tough as it gets. If you can't make 60 to 70-foot casts, chances of getting bit under these conditions will decrease dramatically.

• Sit down. Unless you are fishing off-colored water, avoid standing as much as possible. Your arm and rod waving against the sky will move fish beyond the casting range of most anglers.

• Approach an area as quietly as possible. Trout associate unnatural noises and vibrations with danger.

Stillwaters By Boat, Tube And Waders

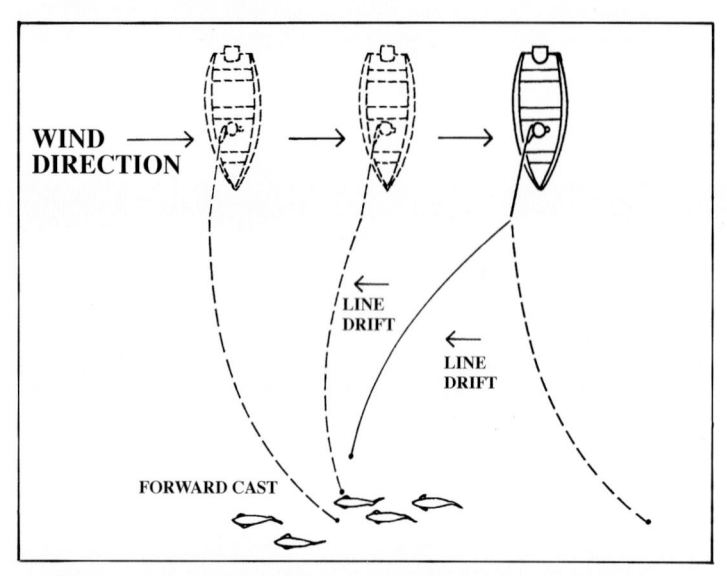

This is the right angle to cast from a drifting boat. It is, however, still dangerous and the angler and passenger can be hit by a windblown fly.

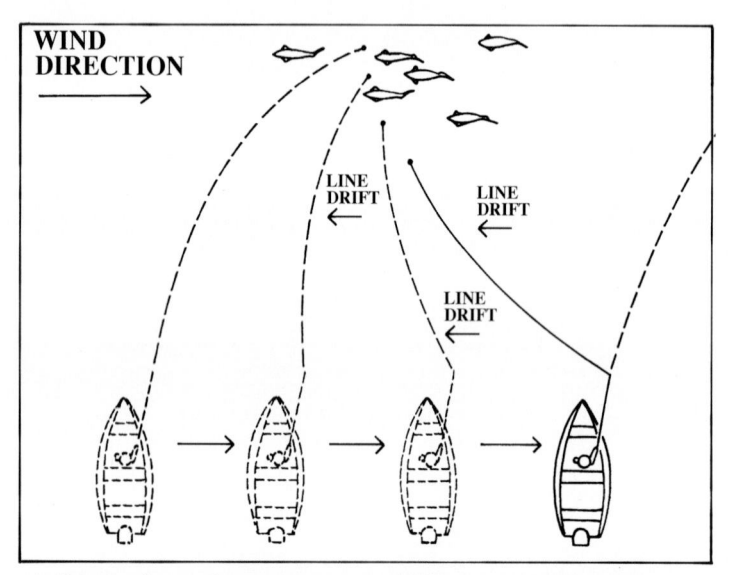

This is the safe and best angle for presentation from a drifting boat, but it's still not good. As the boat drifts from left to right the line bows, because of drift, reducing effectiveness of the fly presentation.

• Choosing the right spot to anchor should never be haphazard. The choice should be deliberate, and determined by the variables of weather, time of year, water levels, cover, and, of course, the presence of trout.

Float Tubes

Many stillwater fisheries are inaccessible to trailered boats and because of weedy shorelines or marshes cannot be waded or fished effectively from shore. Float tubes, kick boats, and one-person pontoon boats are the ideal crafts for this type of water. Light, portable, quiet, maneuverable: the belly boat or float tube has exploded on the stillwater scene, allowing anglers float access to lakes previously considered inaccessible. The innovations that have led to the float tube revolution are largely responsible for the numbers of anglers turning to stillwater fishing in past years. As versatile as they are, there are advantages and drawbacks. Here are a few points to consider.

• Under windy conditions, float tubes can be difficult to control. The high-riding one man pontoon boats, even those equipped with oars, are almost entirely at the mercy of wind. Float tube expert Steve Probasco, has tried nearly every tube and one-man flotation device in North America and his advice is to carry shoes so that when the winds comes up and pins you to the shore furthest from the car you can walk back without wearing off the feet of your waders. There are small float tube anchors being marketed as an option but in a strong wind they could create a safety problem.

• Some fishing presentations are difficult to make from a tube. Tube drift can make it extremely hard to maintain a tight line Even the slightest movement will make it difficult to detect light takes.

• On large lakes the limited mobility inherent in non-motorized tubes is a major disadvantage. To cover a large lake from a tube is impractical. It's easier to get out and walk between honey holes, drive to another launch point, or have a motorized boat available as a shuttle between tubing spots.

Stillwaters By Boat, Tube And Waders

Exact presentation is a must when fishing in gin clear water for trophy trout like this 7-pound rainbow.

When fishing from a boat, a long cast is often necessary to reach spooky fish.

• Because your profile is low to the water, trout are spooked less by tubes than boats and it's not as necessary to make long long casts. The bad part is that tubes don't provide the leverage most fishermen need to make long casts when they are needed.

• The major advantage of float tubes is the ability to fish lakes or pieces of lakes that boaters and waders have to pass up.

• Float tubes or similar craft are soft, flexible and generally much quieter than boats, without the disturbances created by motors, oars, anchors, etc.

Wading

Some lake areas must be waded to be fished effectively. Because of the abundance of insect and minnow life found in shallow water, trout cruise these areas daily during feeding periods. Shallows are also the first zones to warm especially during the fall, winter, and spring months. As a result, wading becomes the best option for exploring these regions. On lakes without inlets,

Stillwaters By Boat, Tube And Waders

Using a float tube allowed Bob Johnson and a big trout to fight it out on Montana's Duck Lake.

This 6-pound rainbow could only be caught with the aid of a float tube on a small, difficult pond in Oregon. A float tube is often a necessity for fishing many of the best trout waters in the West.

trout seek shallow gravel areas to spawn. All good reasons to wade.

Wading things to remember:

• When shoreline water is calm, an intermediate fly line or a floating line with a 15-20 feet leader will minimize surface disturbance.

• Trout are extremely cautious when feeding in shallow water. Learn to move slowly and quietly within casting range of trout whether visible or not. Sound vibrations travel five times as efficiently through water as air. Clumsy wading, banging a staff against rock, splashing, stamping feet, or kicking obstacles will clear out trout quicker than a heron on the hunt.

Dave Freel found that his Super Cat was the best approach for this 3-pound brown at Washington's Dry Falls Lake.

Stillwaters By Boat, Tube And Waders

Sight fishing for cruising cutthroat along the shore of Mann Lake in eastern Oregon.

• Wading requires stealth and subtle approaches. Practice moving quietly and slowly with splashless casting and pickup techniques.

• Trout in the shallows are constantly on the search for food. Your targets will be cruising and you have to learn to lead fish without lining them. The toughest target is a trout going directly away from you. This is such a difficult cast to pull off without lining the target that I advise passing it up and waiting for a better shot. Line a fish going away and the odds are awesome that fish will blast right through the rest of the feeders and spook the lot.

• When water is without a riffle, any movement on the surface or just above it will be noticed by cruising trout. Avoid waving the rod and use the absolute minimum number of false casts. I prefer to reach a cruising fish with no more than two false casts to extend the line.

Stalking trout in shallow water demands patience and your best presentation.

FOR TROPHY TROUT

Stillwaters By Boat, Tube And Waders

Ray Beadle releases a 14-pound rainbow he caught from shore using an olive damsel on South Lake at Sugar Creek Ranch in northern California.

Pat Hoglund, Oregon editor of Fishing and Hunting News, landed this 10½ pound male rainbow while wading in two-feet of water on a small lake in southern Oregon.

• Drab clothing will blend you into drab backgrounds, and it helps. But it's really movement that frightens fish. Move slowly especially if you're in a position where fish can distinguish you from the background.

• In shallow water, with the sunlight bouncing off the bottom, I find it a rule of thumb to move my fly very slowly, keeping it just off bottom.

• Color selection can sometimes be critical in clear, shallow water. Trout may have short memory retention, but it is often sufficient to make one color useless after a while, and another deadly. When the bite slows, change colors and sizes.

Regardless of how you choose to fish a lake, success is really a result of making the right decisions then performing the right functions on a consistent basis.

If you are serious enough about catching big trout in shallow water locate a great blue heron. Watch. Learn.

Hap Scollan plays a big April rainbow on Montana's Mission lake

Chapter 12

FLY-FISHING THROUGH THE SEASONS
Twelve Months Of Big Trout Tactics

Fly-fishing lakes for trout, especially oversize trout, means adapting to and fishing through change, constant change.

In the course of a year, not one thing about lakes remains static, and a successful angler is the one who recognizes when it's time to change and then makes the changes necessary.

New fly-patterns, changes in lines, altered leaders, modified presentations--nothing remains the same and change can occur hourly, daily, and certainly between seasons. That's because all lakes are susceptible to seasonal fluctuations in weather, temperature and other external factors, all of which influence the behavior of all living things below the surface.

Even the most inexperienced fly-fisherman has been made aware that the tactics that produced spring trout, are not necessarily the tactics that work in summer, fall, or winter. But sometimes the adjustments required are much smaller than what we make.

For example, a retrieve system that moves a specific pattern slowly in cold water may also be fished successfully in the warmer water of summer simply by increasing the speed of the retrieve to compensate for the change in metabolism. Sometimes the adjustments we make are small and at first appear insignificant. Admittedly, such minor modifications often work better with suggestive or attractor patterns than imitators that match specific seasonal hatches, but you see the point.

Being able to make the correct adjustments to meet a constantly changing environment is the challenge of fly-fishing.

The ability to recognize that a change is in order is one of the reasons some anglers succeed and others are jealous. It's not only what we do, but when we do it that makes the difference.

I have a system for approaching the changes in a season, and a fair share of that system comes with the understanding that changes taking place below the surface occur more gradually than those on the surface. Yet, underwater variations are heavily influenced by what's happening on top.

We need to prepare for both. If you enjoy the challenges of stalking big trout, you will have plenty of opportunity to be a player in this game.

SPRING
April Through Mid-June

Although some may argue that spring fishing begins in the first balmy days of March, the lake's environment, the food sources, and the temperament of the fish still operate under winter rules and a couple of days in the sun won't change that schedule.

Spring offers some interesting opportunities for big trout.

Early spring is a period of temperamental lakes, transitions in water temperatures, insect activity, and plant growth. It's not the predictable seasonal change that affects our fishing, but

Fly-Fishing Through The Seasons

the way those changes influence our fish and our presentation.

Early spring trout are sluggish and often the bite is spotty, inconsistent and notoriously unpredictable. Strangely, it is also one of the peak periods for catching big fish, if not the biggest trout of the season.

Spring Tackle

For most fishermen, the first few casts of the new year are awkward, often clumsy attempts to get a fly to the fish. Luckily, trout are also a bit off-stride and it all works out to the point where your less-than-expert presentations will be enough.

While shaking off the winter doldrums, trout are more interested in eating than what is on the menu. Even giant trout are not, as a rule, shy or selective. If a fly looks edible and moves naturally, it is usually eaten.

It's more a matter of presentation than pattern.

One of the oddities of spring is that the warmest water in a lake is the deepest water. The colder water is on the surface and the trout are down where you need a variety of sinking lines to reach them.

I prefer to start with an intermediate line and explore the top 6 feet first. If I turn up empty after a reasonable number of casts, I'll switch to the all clear or transparent line and probe the next 6 feet of depth. Depending on water conditions, I rarely fish deeper than 12 feet and will move to another area before investing the time required to work a search pattern below 12 feet.

I have found that changing fly patterns at this time of year should not be the first consideration. If your fly is an established, productive pattern, stick with it. Otherwise, consider other presentation options.

At this time of year, these trout aren't picky. It's just a matter of locating them.

Trout are seldom leader shy at the beginning of the season, and I usually can get by with a 4X (6 lb.) during this time. If I'm going to make a change, I'll make it at the tippet, and depending on water conditions may go up as high as 3X (8 lb.) when I'm working large fish with large flies.

Twelve-foot leaders are spring standards for me, but if you prefer 10-footers, I won't stop you. It's best to let the size of the fly and the weather and water conditions determine the length of the leader and strength of the tippet. My early fishing is with a 6-weight, 9-foot graphite rod with progressive action and a medium soft tip. This is a fairly stout rod, but it's a good early-season choice because of the sinking lines, larger diameter tippets, bigger flies, and deep water exploration required.

Spring is also kite-flying weather, and with these stout rods I can make the long cast under windy conditions. Still, while I'm not as disciplined in the spring as I'm forced to be in summer, I try to match my rod to the size tippet and flies being used, not to the size of the fish.

I know this thinking may cost me a few fish, some probably monsters, but I'll hookup more often, and with heavier gear I might not. All things being equal, I usually can handle even a monster trout on 6-pound tippet. After all, in 1984, the early days of monofilament line development, Craig Archer whipped a 39-pound, 12-ounce chinook salmon on 4-pound test, and in 1981 Stan Shanker landed a 27-pound, 9-ounce brown trout with 4-pound test. That same year, Washington's Cowlitz River surrendered an 18-pound, 4-ounce steelhead to Larry Johnson's 2-pound test line. Those lines were prehistoric compared to the quality control lines on the market now. Sometimes, I fear, today's ultra strong, ultra thin fluorocarbon tippets might make the impossible boring, but not really.

Spring Fly Patterns

I like this time of year because practically everything in the fly box, including most of last winter's adventures in creative fly-tying, can be fished with a degree of optimism.

Big flies and big trout are a natural match in the rough and tumble of early spring.

Fly-Fishing Through The Seasons

Every lake will be a little different from the next lake, but spring trout will always, no matter where they live, be found where the food is concentrated. That food, now, is either leeches, scuds (shrimp), midges, or forage fish such as sculpins, chubs, or shiners.

I match these foods with a **seal bugger**, sizes 6 to 8; **stillwater** and **callibaetis nymphs**, sizes 10 to 12; **marabou leech**, sizes 6 to 10; and a variety of **streamer patterns** (Matuka, Zonker) in sizes 4 to 8.

To be visible in the often turbid water of spring, I prefer dark colors on my buggers and leeches and shades of olive on my nymphs. Streamers seem to produce the most hits with a white or pearl body and wings of white, light gray, or olive.

Spring Casting

Regardless of the season, fly-fishermen who can throw the long line--a minimum of 50 feet and preferably 70+ feet, will, on average, out-fish those who can't. Of course, other factors play heavily on the outcome, but distance casters will have the advantage in most instances.

Not to be redundant, but those forms of cover, wind, light, and nutrient-type water, along with other conditions, will dictate your distance casting needs. Remember, you will catch more fish, and some of those fish will be very big fish when you can consistently make the long cast.

If you can't cast 50 to 70 feet then practice until you can. There is no second option for the trophy trout specialist.

Locating Spring Trout

This is the tough part, finding fish when they could be anywhere.

Springtime is, in my estimation, the toughest time of the year to locate feeding trout.

To shorten the search, go back to the basics covered in Chapter 5, water temperature/oxygen, food, cover.

A colorful 5-pound male rainbow trout caught in early April at Montana's Battle Creek Ranch

FOR TROPHY TROUT

Fly-Fishing Through The Seasons

Just don't expect to locate spring trout where you left last year's summer fishery. Too many environmental variables are at work here for that. I've always found that high, cold water tends to break up the schools and scatter trout, while low, warm water concentrates them.

On shallow lakes, it's been my experience that trout hold close to shoreline cover or near inlets early in the spring. That's because trout are often attracted by the slight change in water temperature in the shallows--a warm area that will also be the first to develop insect life. If your favorite lake doesn't have a defined inlet, then look for gravel areas. Trout, especially pre-spawn cutthroat and rainbows, will be close by.

In deep lakes, trout tend to hold in the deeper water. As spring lengthens, however, the shorelines will warm faster than offshore surface water, and trout will move in to hammer the emerging food sources. If you are fishing a new lake, plan on spending some time looking for them. It's called "paying your dues."

Best Time To Fish

Another nice twist about early spring fishing is that like all good sports, it is best pursued at a civilized hour of the day.

On my home lake in southern Oregon, I often see spring anglers, bouncing on the enthusiasm and promise of a new fishing season, heading toward their personal hot spots at the first blush of dawn and sometimes fishing until the last weak ray leaves the sky. If it were summer, this would be perfect timing. In early spring, however, not only do you not get extra points for crawling out of the sheets before daybreak, but you'll probably have points taken away.

In my experience, when fishing early spring, there's not a lot sense in being on the water until the rising sun has had a chance to warm it a bit. Spring water is cold, and cold-water trout are lethargic, insects don't hatch and fishermen get cold fingers.

Opportunities for catching spring trout are considerably better after the sun has been on the water for a few hours. There will be a slight, but definite, increase in water temperature, food sources become more active, trout begin to feed, and fishermen smile.

By late afternoon, the spring sun is canted well into the southwestern sky, a chill settles over the water, and the bite dies for the night. Go home, eat dinner, tie flies, mow the lawn, or whatever makes you happy. If you insist on fishing, don't expect much of a bite. There are, of course exceptions, but as rule don't worry about being on the water until a decent hour the next day.

Spring Presentation

Because early spring water temperatures are under the chilling influence of winter, our early presentations more closely resemble winter tactics than summer.

In April, feeding periods are short and infrequent. The pace increases with every week of increased sunlight, progressing toward summer activity levels that begin sometime in early June.

When the water is colder than the comfort zone of your specific species, trout movements are miserly and require fewer calories to fuel. Because trout are cold-blooded, their entire systems slow down in cold water and that includes their digestive tract, the trigger that tells a trout when to eat. The fewer times that trigger is pulled, the fewer times you're going to get bit.

There is nothing about springtime fishing that involves speed. Nothing. Trout move slowly, feed slowly, digest slowly, and their prey, insect or fish, also move in slow motion.

If you're going to be consistent with the slower pace of spring time, you're going to have to force yourself to slow everything. In my stillwater fly fishing schools, I tell my students that when they believe they are fishing slowly they're probably about half-way to where they should be. The longer you leave your fly in front of a cold fish, the better the odds are that a fish will open it's mouth and. . .

The author hooked this 12-pound rainbow in early April in just one foot of water. [Ray Beadle Photo]

As a rule, spring fish don't chase their food. If it's moving fast, they usually let it go. Something easier will be along shortly.

There's no doubt in my mind, after watching thousands of anglers, that the most common mistake of early spring fly-fishing is to retrieve the fly too fast.

And that's natural.

We haven't touched fish lips for months. We haven't heard a line sing, a reel chatter, or danced a fly for so long we're afraid we may have forgotten. We're up. We're eager. We're full of energy. We're fishing way, way too fast.

Spring fishing demands even more patience than normal and it's hard to go slow with spring fever lighting small fires everywhere in your body. It's part of the discipline and without it you'll just be another rod on the water.

Like all rules, the go slow rule can occasionally be broken, and when the rule is violated in the spring, it will probably be broken by minnows.

On occasion, I've watched trout trap a school of minnows, usually in shallow water, and feed with a slashing abandon that literally churns the water. This happens mostly in the latter days of spring, but can happen anytime. When you get lucky and spot a school of bait fish in full panic splattering on the surface, pull out the streamer box and cast. When I work a bait ball, even in early spring, I retrieve the streamer with a semi-rapid pull, hopefully matching the wounded panic of the school.

Sometimes it takes a few casts to isolate the proper stuttering pace of the pull-pause-pull retrieve. Don't be afraid to experiment. I've had trout engulf streamers as they sink, as they dart away, as they flutter, as they leave the water. Mix up your retrieve and keep track of what you were doing and how you were doing it when that first big trout of the spring unloads on your streamer. Then do it again!

Fly-Fishing Through The Seasons

As the long days of June warm air and water temperatures, metabolism rates go up. Trout and everything they eat pick up the pace.

And so will you.

SUMMER
Mid-June through Mid-September

For Western fly-fishermen, summer fishing techniques and requirements apply pretty much from mid-June through mid-September. This is the period when big trout are most active, hatches most intense, weather patterns stabilize, lakes are fishable, and fly-fishing can be both rewarding and frustrating.

Part of the frustration can be blamed on the seemingly endless options that come with summer's generosity. For some anglers, working through the maze of summer fishing possibilities is a horror. For others, summer is a trough overflowing with possibilities and the only concern is that we will wear ourselves out running from adventure to adventure, gorging on the seasonal smorgasbord of opportunities.

Denny's callibaetis nymph was the downfall of this 5½ pound rainbow taken during a callibaetis hatch.

FLY-FISHING STILLWATERS

Fly-Fishing Through The Seasons

Depending on where you fish, or where you want to fish, these options can range from high elevation lakes just slipping out from beneath 8 months of ice, to deep lakes in the throes of stratifying, or rich desert lakes bulging with food and fast-growing fish. Summer is also the season of natural extremes: temperatures, drought and the like.

These extremes are important for big trout specialists because these are the conditions that will move big trout into predictable habitat corners. For a fisherman who has learned to read the signs, the trail leading to these fish is as clear as if it were painted with directional arrows.

When you know where the fish are, then summer success becomes a matter of selecting tackle, patterns, timing and presentation.

Summer Tackle

Tackle selected for summer fishing differs slightly from the rod, reel, lines, and leaders wielded so successfully in spring.

Because flies are smaller 10s to 16s (See, Summer Pattern Selection), tippet diameters downsize as well. I typically use a 4X or 5X during this period.

Lighter end tippets require a moderately slow rod tip action. The faster tips that produced positive sets with big hooks on lethargic early spring trout will snap a light tippet when set against an energized summer fish.

Do yourself a favor for summer fly fishing, select a trout rod with good backbone but a bit of forgiveness in the tip.

My rod of preference for summer is a 9-foot custom graphite rod for 5/6 line. This rod, and those I sell, are designed and built to my specifications for a balanced marriage between a fast butt-section and a soft tip.

For summer fly lines, 90 percent of the time I expect to find trout feeding shallow, and in perfect range for an intermediate slow sinking line. If the day is unusually calm and the water outrageously clear, then I go a step further and change over to the nearly invisible, translucent Stillwater full sinking line. When you make the switch, adjust your presentation to account for the quicker sink rate of the Stillwater line--about twice as fast as the intermediate line.

For picking those to hard-to reach pockets deep in weed mass, or fishing emergers near the surface, a weight-forward intermediate or floating line might be a good choice.

Summer Patterns

Repetition dictates choice, which is why we tend to establish our favorite patterns and then stick with them come drought or high water. I call these Go-To Patterns. We go to them because we like how they fish and because we have confidence: we catch fish with them.

I'm no different.

I rarely use anything other than five patterns which I've designed or refined to fit my likes and avoid my dislikes. I make my seasonal adjustments, not by changing patterns, but by changing fly sizes and color dressings.

Patterns of choice are my Seal Bugger, Stillwater, Callibaetis, and Black Diamond nymphs, and my All Purpose (AP) Emerger Nymph.

[For specifics patterns, materials refer to Chapter 4]

The exceptions to these five flies are when specific feeding patterns require a big target. That's when I go with my shiner minnow or chub minnow pattern, Hal Janssen's marabou leech, or Dan Byford's Zonker.

My five flies, however, when tied in various sizes and colors, are the deadliest patterns I've ever used on lakes all over the world. I use them 99 percent of the time, year-round, because they are so consistent. I'm not making this statement to blow my own horn, but because it's true.

If I were to use conventional ties, and for years I did, there are a lot of very good, very effec-

FOR TROPHY TROUT

tive patterns to use. It would be difficult to go wrong with a fly box holding a selection of Hare's Ear, Pheasant Tail, Prince and Zug Bug nymphs.

My bottom line is, fish with a fly you can trust.

Summer Casting

This is a time of year when lakes are often windless for long periods of the day. It's also a time when big trout are most cautious, under flat water and a cloudless sky. You know you will need long casts unless you are fishing in nutrient clouded water or some other form of cover. Otherwise, productive hours will be limited.

Locating Summer Fish

Beginning in mid-June, trout begin to gravitate toward those areas of the lake with the coolest water temperatures and highest oxygen content. Food is still a consideration, however food is plentiful and comfortable habitat isn't.

When you're looking for summer concentration points, look first to areas of cool, highly oxygenated water, and then narrow the hunt to qualified areas that also have nearby feeding zones. Summer trout prefer to feed along shorelines, shoals, vegetation, springs, flooded river channels, and inlets.

On large lakes, prime feeding areas may be some distance from prime habitat areas. On smaller lakes, the habitat/feeding areas are more concentrated, and easier to identify, if for no other reason than the diminished scale.

During normal summer feeding hours, I've found that I can almost always depend on weed beds, shoals, channels, and inlets to hold aggressive feeding trout.

Best Time To Fish

Low light periods are some of the most productive times for big fish during summer, especially low light periods with other forms of cover such as wind chop or light algae. When the sun is low to the horizon during those magical hours of early morning and late evening, fishing is usually as good as it will be for the rest of the day. On most lakes, these are peak summer feeding periods.

On Upper Klamath Lake, I often fish areas of the lake where I know that water temperatures are prime for early feeding, but becomes too warm by late morning for consistent action. When this occurs, I relocate to cool areas, water that in the early morning was too cold for a good bite, but at midday is warm enough to develop a hatch and trigger a bite.

The trout in every lake develop specific, yet slightly different, time tables for activity, and these tables can vary hour to hour and day to day. The only solution to this vexation is experience and familiarization. The more you fish the water, the better you understand it, the more predictable it becomes. If you lack the time to fish often, then question those who do.

Summer Presentation

Summers are usually blessed with long periods of fair weather. From your standpoint as a trophy trout seeker, stabilized weather patterns reduce the options and that makes success a bit easier for most of us to isolate.

As always, presentation is the key, and the guide to establishing an effective presentation is to be able to identify the food forms you'll be imitating. Pattern selection, remember, dictates line choice and retrieve style.

By varying retrieve styles or line selection, it's possible to use just one fly that will imitate multiple life stages of several insects.

Fly-Fishing Through The Seasons

For example, when imitating the restricted movements of most small insects that can be matched with flies ranging from No. 10 down to 16s, I favor a short, slow pull, sometimes waiting several seconds between pulls.

When using bigger flies in these same patterns, I usually increase the speed and length of each pull. Because summer waters are often literally crammed with several sizes and types of insects, varying the speed and length of the retrieve will usually unlock the mysteries of a trout's feeding preferences.

In my experience, behind a big trout's reputation as a finicky, unreasonably selective connoisseur lurks a greedy opportunist that has a tough time passing up any morsel.

To match this type of feeding mood, use impressionistic flies that imitate nothing, but resemble many things.

Flexibility and variety are major factors. Because trout feed opportunistically most of the time, despite selective feeding patterns, not one, but many fly patterns will work, if manipulated in a manner that imitates the natural movements of aquatic insects.

If a slow retrieve comes up empty, switch to a short, fast style. One of my favorite retrieves, especially when slow isn't working, is a very rapid two-inch pull that I believe simulates an emerging or escaping insect.

This highly agitated, stop-start-stop action works extremely well during the summer when all other retrieves fail, but only near the surface. I've never done well with it when fishing deep.

FALL
Mid-September through Mid-November

Feeding periods shorten, hatches dwindle and there is an urgency on the water that causes big trout to feed with an abandon that makes them unusually vulnerable to predators.

This devil-may-care urgency affects all trout, but none as blatantly as brown trout. Like all big trout, giant browns that are, with only a few exceptions, unreachable if not uncatchable all summer, are driven by pre-spawn requirements for food and lots of it, into areas of vulnerability.

Fall becomes the season of choice for dedicated, big trout fishermen. If you're going to catch a huge trout, and that's a fish it takes two hands to support before release, late fall is when the gremlins of good luck, untrustworthy scamps though they may be, are most likely to show some compassion.

(This is true of all fall spawners, especially the chars, including brook trout, and extends to those few waters with fall-spawning rainbows.)

Fall spawning brookies are as brightly colored as the foliage.

Fly-Fishing Through The Seasons

Several years ago in late summer I was fishing Duck Lake, a renowned big trout water in northwestern Montana. Brown trout, so numerous I couldn't begin to estimate their numbers, were cruising just off shore or powering through the surface in showy frolics that would stop your pulse.

Many of these fish weighed 10 pounds plus, and some were giants. Without a river to ascend to spawn, these fish were following their instincts into the shoreline shallows where there was a good gravel bottom and wave action. At no other time of the year were these giant fish likely to be caught, and if you hit a similar situation, I ask that you use restraint.

I'm not sure why trout feed heavily in the fall, and it may simply be that they, like other animals, are stocking up enough protein to see them through the winter.

Whatever the reason, big trout definitely increase feeding periods from mid-September to ice-in, and even better, the number of anglers competing with you for their favors is down to the hard cores.

Fall Tackle

I pretty much stay with the same rod and lines that I use for summer fishing. Leaders often need to be lengthened and the diameters reduced in size as a concession to low clear water.

Frequently check your line for weak knots or leader frays, especially during fall when you stand your best chance of hooking that lifetime fish.

Fall Fly Patterns

As the season progresses from spring to summer and into fall there will be a series of changes. The obvious are that hatches become fewer and insects more sparse. What most anglers don't notice, however, is that the size of the average insect also decreases as the season progresses.

Fall bugs are smaller than summer bugs. Exceptions to this rule are terrestrials--'hoppers, ants, and the like.

Pattern sizes that worked in the spring are likely to spook trout in the fall. As an example, in the spring I often use a No. 10 Stillwater Nymph. In the summer I drop down to a No. 12, and by fall I'm mostly using a No. 14s.

Spring patterns will also produce well for fall fish, but I tend to use more streamer patterns in the fall than in summer. Fall feeders, especially browns and brookies, will often go out of their way to hammer minnow-imitating streamers when they invade their territory.

Fall Casting

Many lakes, especially reservoirs, will be at their lowest levels and water clarity is as clear as it will be all year. Consequently, this will be a demanding time for anglers as well.

There is very little room for casting mistakes. If you want to land a trophy fish, longer casts, perhaps the best effort you have, will be necessary. Consider the conditions and let 'er rip.

Locating Fall Trout

There's no big mystery here. Look for fall spawners to start concentrating near the mouths of inlets or cruising shoals and shorelines, weed beds, and drop-offs in deep lakes.

Weather is often a part of fall fishing which bring trout to the surface on overcast days. Trout move around more in the fall than during summer as the areas of tolerably cool water increases. I've enjoyed some absolutely explosive fall fishing just by prowling shallow bays and shorelines on foot.

Fly-Fishing Through The Seasons

Best Time To Fish

At this time of year, there are no bad hours to be fishing. Weather, especially early winter conditions, can be a factor, but if you can stand it, the fish will be feeding in it

I still get out at the crack of dawn in the fall, more because I enjoy this time of day than for any other reason. Expect trout to feed throughout the day, with few pauses as long as weather patterns are consistent.

Fall is an excellent time to stalk big trout in the shallows.

Fall Presentation

Fall water is usually the clearest water of the year, and despite the increased feeding activity of the trout, this water demands careful presentations. Splatter a bad cast or drape a line shadow over a fish in this gin-like water and that fish is gone just as quickly as if it were June.

Long, light leaders and careful casting are critical to low, stillwater presentations. Never assume you need heavier tippets to land these big fish. In fact, conditions will probably require just the opposite logic. A little wind chop, dark skies, or other cover may cut you some slack, but don't count on it. Because of the colder water, retrieves should be slower than our favorite summer pulls. Like always, consider pattern size and conditions present.

Fall can deliver the biggest fish of the year and more of them, but it also demands your best presentations. You're the predator and your success hinges on your presentation skills.

WINTER
Mid-November through March

Fly fishing lakes during winter is primarily a matter of slowing down.

The water is colder, and cold blooded trout move slowly and not very often. The same can be said for most of what trout eat.

FOR TROPHY TROUT

Fly-Fishing Through The Seasons

If you could take the pulse of a lake and everything that lives in it during winter, it would be moving at a minimum of 50 percent of a summer count. Trout often go several days without feeding and when they do feed, it is out of necessity, mostly opportunistic and definitely lacks enthusiasm.

On the upside, there are fewer food forms to imitate, fewer habitat options to evaluate, and fewer anglers to share the water with.

Winter Tackle

Almost any rod action and weight will work for winter fishing. Rod selection is more often made in the winter on the basis of personal choice and weather conditions.

I use a 6 weight most of the winter, unless I'm using very large flies or I need a heavier rod for windy conditions. I stick with the uniform Sink II or intermediate style fly lines for most of my winter fishing. I rarely change leaders and stay with the same 12-foot leader setup that worked in summer and fall. Tippets should always be adjusted to match flies and water conditions.

Winter Fly Patterns

As with all seasons, the basic reason for selecting a specific pattern is to match or simulate the available food sources. I favor suggestive or impressionistic patterns over imitative.

The patterns that work in fall will also work in winter, with the exception of dry flies. Occasionally, you will find a good winter midge hatch. Some call these tiny dries snow flies, and often these midge look-alikes are the only game in town. I would recommend that you come prepared to fish wet patterns, but I'd also suggest you tuck a few midges into the dry-side of the fly box just in case.

Locating Winter Trout

Most of us have very few options when it comes to stillwater fishing during winter. I've always found that trout, all sizes, are fairly well scattered during winter. Expect to find some concentrations in areas with temperatures slightly above the mean and with abundant food sources. Trout usually leave their cold-water sanctuaries in deep water to hunt for food along the shallow shoreline areas by early November, after frosty night temperatures cool these regions.

If I could pick one area to fish in the winter it would be where the waters are warmest. This includes shoreline areas, a spring hole, spring creek, or an artificial source. Some of the hottest, big trout success has been during the winter in lakes with warm-water discharges.

Laying your fly on a perfect cast into the swirl of a feeding frenzy may be the most rewarding fishing you will encounter all winter. It can however, be brief.

Best Times To Fish

In winter, with its short days, and a low, weak sun, the best fishing is generally in the center of the day--from mid-morning until mid-afternoon. Each lake is different, of course, but I would be willing to bet that there is not a big trout lake in the West that won't give up fish during the center of a winter's day--if it's going to give up fish at all.

Unlike the other three seasons, winter bites usually go off well before dark, rarely holding up later than 4 p.m. You can expect winter trout to husband their energies and move and feed as little as possible. The elevation of the lake will influence this time factor, with lower elevation lakes being much more productive than those found above 4,000 feet.

Winter Presentation

The key word here is S-L-O-W. Cold, uninterested, non-feeding winter fish will not chase anything more than a few inches. If you're going to draw a strike out of this lethargic bum, you're going to have to put your fly in front of that fish's nose and keep it there--teasingly--for as long as possible. The tease factor is one of the reasons that some tiers use marabou, with its propensity for flaring with the slightest motion, extensively on winter patterns.

Retrieves should always be on the slow side, regardless of the pattern used. Feeding periods will be brief, and for many trout, nonexistent for several days. If you move the fly faster than trout expect it, you will earn a refusal. That's the way it is in winter.

Trout will frequent shallow shoreline areas just before and right after ice-out.

I'm not as concerned during winter with the length of line I retrieve with each strip or twist, but pay extra attention to the length of the pause between each strip. The length of the pause can be critical, and I usually spend a lot of time experimenting before I find a rhythm trout will respond to.

I have found, however, that once you find the rhythm that works in the winter, stick with it. Don't change. What doesn't work, save for another day. That pace may never work again, but it's what the trout want right now, and there's very little that they do want during this masochistic challenge that we call winter fishing.

FOR TROPHY TROUT

A Wyoming snowstorm didn't deter float-tuber David Freel, or this beautiful rainbow.

Chapter 13

EXTERNAL FACTORS
Full Moons, Barometers, Storm Fronts, and Fish

We all know that big trout can be extremely moody and selective about what they eat. Their temperamental flings can be maddening frustrations for fishermen.

In order for us, the predators, to rationalize our lack of success during these dull periods, while keeping our fishing reputations intact, we usually dismiss it as simply an unalterable mystery of nature and go home.

The more I concentrate on catching big fish, the more convinced I am that these so-called mood swings are not the random fits of hyper selectivity that we prefer to blame, but nearly always the result of external environmental changes created by variable weather patterns.

In other words, when all other factors are in line (pattern selection, fly-line, location, presentation) and a trout refuses to eat, the cause is usually weather related. Simply put, when there's a change in the weather trout behavior is altered. To what extent is relative to the severity of the change. From a fishing perspective, this means trout often refuse to eat. Of course, not all fluctuations are disruptive to a trout's feeding behavior, but I suspect many are.

There are many common natural disruptions that can have major impacts on a trout bite, all relatively easy to recognize. The dominant and most obvious ones are approaching storm fronts, northerly winds, a quick drop in water levels, and periods near a full moon. Those not so obvious are falling or low barometric pressures and sudden changes in water temperatures.

I'm sure there are other bite-killing changes, so subtle we don't pick up on them. Occasionally, a bite will even develop in the face of one these external changes, but it's rare and not to be expected.

Being cold blooded creatures, trout are slow to react to and recover from changes to their environment, sometimes taking as long as several days to adjust. More likely, the down-time between feedings will be measured in hours.

Weather and environmental phenomena will always be a part of fishing and the more we understand them, the more consistent our successes will be.

Low Pressure Storm Fronts

Approaching storm fronts are synonymous with falling barometric pressures, and over the past decade I've tried to monitor trout behavior during these periods. Invariably, trout become almost dysfunctional. As the barometer falls, so does the level of activity. Fish tend to be sluggish, completely non-aggressive, have little if any interest in feeding, and, if given an opportunity, will slink off to deep water and hold up until the weather improves.

Most often, these periods of inactivity will coincide with a barometric pressure reading of under 30.

Fishermen can use a barometer to predict the level of fish activity as effectively as a television weatherman uses it to predict weather changes.

External Factors

Lakes in mountainous areas are more susceptible to sudden weather changes, like this brief, intense hail storm just below the Continental Divide at Henry's Lake, Idaho.

When the barometric pressure reading hits 29.7 or lower, I find that trout become sluggish and rarely respond to food. The lower the barometer falls, the more dramatic the impact. My advice is to stay home and tie flies. A twist, however, is while the barometer is skidding just before a summer thunderstorm, trout activity can approach frenzy levels. I've had some of my finest moments fishing as a storm front hovers on the horizon. But once the front hits and the barometer stabilizes on the low-side, fishing is usually poor until the barometer moves above 30.0.

I rarely concern myself with barometric pressure readings during periods of extended fair weather. When the barometer reading stabilizes around 30.2, trout feed fairly consistently. I rarely see the barometer get above 30.5, so it's a guess as to how trout behave when that happens.

Water Temperature Swings

Trout, trout food, and just about every other living aquatic organism in lakes are affected by changes in water temperatures. Often these changes are stunning, literally. A quick surge in water temperature normally has an impact on temperature-sensitive cold-blooded creatures, and the effects will take hours, sometimes days, to wear off.

Fortunately, temperatures in most of our lakes are slow to change and fluctuations can be traced to the angle of the sun, how long and how intense it is on the water, and occasionally to precipitation--snow, rain, hail.

If water temperatures are the key to trout behavior, and I'm convinced they are, then changes in those temperatures--no matter how subtle--are responsible for their level of aggressiveness.

Stormy periods don't necessarily mean the bite will be off, but low barometric pressure usually does.

I've found that hot and cold surges in water temperature have a lethargic effect on trout activity, movements, and how much effort they are willing to invest in feeding.

A lake's water temperature is heavily influenced by its physical characteristics: elevation, depth, nutrient level, feeder creeks, springs, location, as well as the time of year.

Fishing success or lack of it can be altered by as little as a degree or two swing in water temperature. The greater the change, the longer it takes cold-blooded fish to adjust. While the trout population is making this physical adjustment, fishing success will tail off and remain that way until both water temperature and trout behavior stabilize.

This impact of temperature change makes it difficult, if not impossible, to predict trout feeding and movement patterns.

This was never more in evidence to me than during the high-water year of 1995 on Upper Klamath Lake. The bottom of Pelican Bay is literally pocked with freshwater spring holes, which have a profound effect on water temperature in that area of the lake.

Because of the stabilized temperatures produced by the spring water, and because the bay is located adjacent to the Upper Klamath Wildlife Refuge, it is a summer sanctuary for big rainbows escaping the warmer waters in the main lake.

During the exceptionally high water period in 1995, the marsh water surrounding the bay was two-feet deep all summer. In a normal water year the marshes would be dry by late summer.

By mid afternoon, the hot summer sun would boost water temperatures in the shallow marsh into the high 70-degree range. When the daily afternoon winds came up, the warm water was pushed into the bay, mixing with the colder spring water that sent afternoon bay temperatures from the mid 50s soaring into the mid to high 60s. On some days, temperature extremes

External Factors

went into the low 70s

The effect on the trout was dramatic. Most fish went completely off the bite, largely abandoned their traditional weed bed feeding areas, and took refuge in the very deepest and coldest spring holes. At times, it was one of the most unpredictable fishing years on this big-fish lake that I can remember.

During the summer, when water temperatures reach normal highs, the highest daily extremes will be recorded around 4 p.m. Changes in temperature are most dramatic in desert lakes where oxygen depletion can also become a late summer mortality factor when hooked fish are played to exhaustion.

Full Moons

So far, no one has been able to unravel the mysterious reasons why a full moon has a negative impact on fishing success.

During the monthly full moon phase, and for several days especially after the full moon, trout fishing becomes incredibly tough. The fish seem to be lethargic, almost passive about feeding during daylight hours.

The most common explanation, an old fish tale if you will, is that fish feed all night when the moon is bright and rest during the day. I've put this theory to the test on many, many moon-bright nights and I haven't found any consistency to it, at least not enough to form an opinion.

As nearly as I've been able to tell, the bite goes off day and night during full moon periods. The effect is even worse for big trout specialists because my records indicate that while some big trout have been caught during full moons, most become inactive.

Monitoring moon cycles for 10 years, I've found the least successful fishing periods are a day before, during and two days after a full moon. During those four days, if there is any bite at all, it usually occurs during the first hour of daylight and the last hour before dark. On cloudy overcast nights, it is a toss up as to what kind of bite you will experience the next day.

A good example of the full-moon impact on success took place 12 years ago while I was fishing the Upper Klamath Lake on the day after a full moon. At that time, I had no idea of the impact of the moon on fishing and was baffled at my lack of success on water where the week before I had recorded incredible action.

Near the end of the full moon day, I was not only baffled but frustrated and confused. Questioning other fisherman, I found no one had done any better than a fish here and there.

As the sun rested on the horizon, I started prowling through my fly box and finally settled on a long black leech. Using an intermediate line, I cast the fly and retrieved it with a series of short, quick strips. The lake might as well have been barren.

The moon was well up and as bright as a spotlight when I made my last cast toward shore. For some reason that I can't remember, I changed my stuttering retrieve to a long, slow pull. The line came tight, but after a full day of empty casting, I didn't react. For just a second there was no indication of a fish--just a tight line. Then the line began to move, and a thick, 5-pound trout rolled on the surface. It was the first of six consecutive hook-ups and then the bite simply stopped.

It was a valuable lesson. Trout can be caught during a full moon, but only when it's right for them, not me. This month, I'll fish the full moon, but I'll concentrate on those 60 minutes of magic at dawn and dusk.

There are exceptions, sometimes trout will take a fly at noon, but these are just exceptions and not to be counted upon.

Wind

Wind is something stillwater fly fishermen learn to expect and adjust to. It can be a hindrance or a help, a negative or a positive, but whatever it is, it has to be dealt with.

External Factors

A north wind, which brought the new snow to these peaks, nearly always has a negative impact on big-trout success.

Wind dissipates heat and cold, distributes oxygen, aerates surface water, provides cover for trout and angler and usually triggers a bite.

That's the good wind.

The other wind, dumps back casts, buffets forward casts, curtails insect hatches, and makes it hard to spot fish. Personally, I don't pay much attention to wind direction unless it comes from the north. There's an old saying, "Wind from the North, don't go forth" and I've found that I catch far fewer fish in a north wind. North winds are associated with cold air and maybe it's the cold air and lack of hatches that puts trout off the bite.

Perhaps it is best to experience a day with a north wind and form your own opinion. Just don't be surprised if you don't do well. Usually, a north wind will blow out and change to a more favorable direction within a day or two.

Fluctuating Water Levels

Fluctuations in the level of water in a lake have predictable influences on fish behavior. The influence is more dramatic in small, shallow reservoirs than large natural lakes not tapped for agricultural irrigation or other supply-side drains.

Upper Klamath Lake is a natural lake, but has been dammed to increase storage capacity for irrigation demands and to help anadromous fish during low-water periods.

The lake is shallow, averaging less than 7 feet, and it fluctuates very little until July, when the local irrigation district taps in.

In 1994, a large school of rainbows took up residence in an area we called the Fish Banks. These fish were beautiful. They weighed between 4 and 15 pounds, and they were holding in an area where there were stable oxygen levels.

FOR TROPHY TROUT

External Factors

These huge fish had been funneled into this area by their natural requirements for high oxygen levels and low water temperatures-factors that were being eliminated in other parts of the lake as a slow, but steady draw-down during the height of summer heat, increased water temperatures and depleted oxygen reserves.

There were just a few of us who knew about this concentration of wall hangers. The holding water was only five feet deep, and for more than a month I experienced action unparalleled in 23 years of fishing on this lake.

Ten pound fish were landed almost daily. This particular slice of fly-fishing heaven ended in August when the lake level was dropped suddenly, and within a few days the fish had scattered to other, smaller holding zones.

Dropping water levels, especially in reservoirs, will force fish from their preferred habitat. Trout can and will adjust as long as there are ample food, oxygen, and shelter. Find an area that offers these three requirements and you'll find where the trout have holed up to ride out the draw down crisis.

Let's not lose sight of the fact that any time spent on the water is a time to hone our skills, usually a pleasure, and always a learning experience.

Negative factors are a part of fishing, but what can be learned from these influences could make the next outing more enjoyable.

So go fishing, learn, enjoy!

FOR TROPHY TROUT

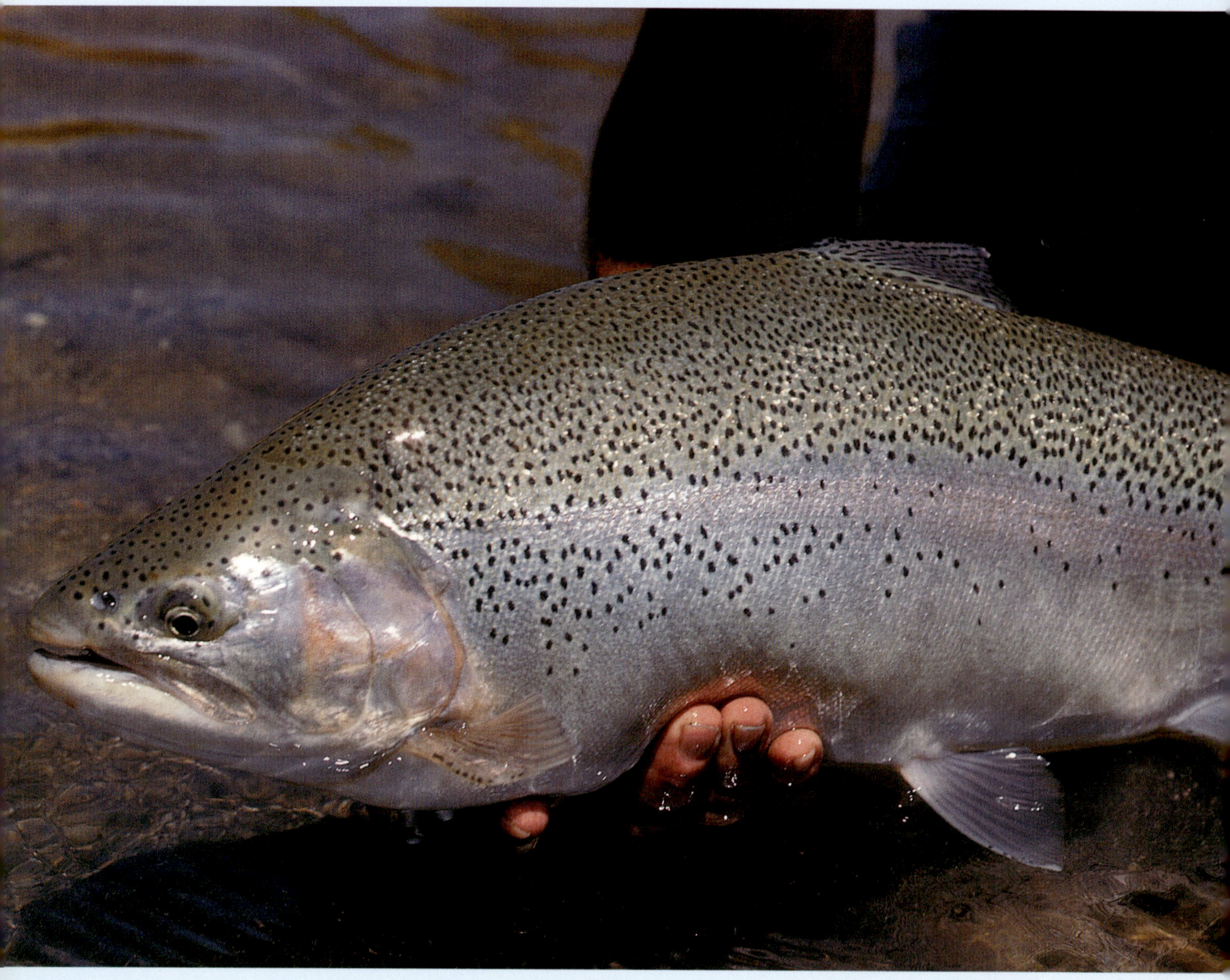

Chapter 14

100 TIPS FOR FLY-FISHING STILLWATERS
The Results of 20 Years and 300 Lakes

Catching big trout in lakes is directly relative to how much time you invest. The more often you fish, the better the odds become that you will catch a truly trophy-size trout, a fish so big you find it pointless to brag, and so powerful that even years later the memory of that fight will bring a smile.

There is no substitution for practice and experience, and no experience that can't be polished by repetitive practice. The more you fish, the more you learn. Consequently, the more consistent you become, and the bigger your trout. As we learn, the more proficient we become and the more confidence we gain in our ability to make the right choices.

Success has that annoying habit of continually redefining itself. As goals are reshaped, expectations will grow with each victory until finally success becomes defined as not how big a fish you caught, but how consistently you can catch big fish.

As I stated in Chapter 4, there are six key functions to master en route to success on stillwaters, but it is the options incorporated with those functions that make selective fly-fishing so wonderfully difficult.

To recap, the six are:
1) Tackle selection
2) Fly pattern choice
3) Casting ability
4) Locating fish
5) Recognizing when to fish
6) Presentation

Master these key points and success will become routine. Please remember, there are no short-cuts to experience, only practice and education. Here are 100 tips that I have learned in 20 years of fishing more than 300 lakes for big trout that have helped me become a more consistently successful angler.

Take what you need, and file the others for later use.

1. To catch big trout, fish lakes that can support big fish. Concentrate on alkaline, high desert-type lakes and ignore high elevation lakes with short growing seasons.

2. Fish by the three Ps; **P**erseverance, **P**ersistence, **P**atience. Trophy trout are demanding. Success is so sweet it's worth waiting out.

3. Large trout are often territorial, and consistently found in a specific holding area. Don't challenge a big fish until conditions are in your favor. A presentation bungled by tough wind, weather, or water conditions will only help educate the trophy and it will only be that much harder to catch when conditions improve.

4. Little fish may feed all day, but not big fish. Trophy-size trout have selective feeding periods, times that offer maximum protection from predators. Concentrate on these major feeding periods and you'll find selective trout more responsive.

5. Use streamers that imitate specific bait fish. Trophy trout, except for some strains of Kamloops feed on minnows and forage fish. Patterns should imitate the dominant bait fish in each lake.

6. The presence of small bait fish usually indicates that resident big trout are either absent or non-feeding.

7. Avoid false casting on the water to gain distance. Stillwater fish are exceptionally spooky and I've seen them leave an area at the impact of a noisy cast yards away from their lair.

8. Wade, tube, or row slowly and watch carefully. A spooked trout is impossible to catch.

9. When external changes become a factor, be ready to change techniques. Big trout are unpredictable and behavioral changes demand presentation and fly changes.

10. Big trout are rarely leader shy when aggressively feeding. Be sure to use a tippet strong enough to hold big trout.

11. Fly patterns are not as important as knowing how to fish them. Never confuse creativity at the tying bench with proper fishing technique on the water.

12. Big trout feed on the move. Don't waste time fishing vacated water. Move often if you are not getting hits.

13. Never challenge a big fish when you first hook it. Give these fish their head and keep your hand off the drag rim. Most fish are lost on the take or while being landed.

14. Always land big trout head first. Fish have one gear and it's not reverse.

15. When you hook a big trout, it's not what the fish does but what you do that determines the outcome.

16. Enticing a big fish to strike is a much more difficult task than landing it.

17. Be prepared for trout to make a run when they come near the boat, are shown the net, or enter shallow water.

18. Avoid pastel or fluorescent-colored fly lines on flat clear water or during high sun. Forget contrary arguments, brightly colored lines spook trophy trout. Under these conditions, use transparent stillwater lines.

19. If the leader knot is cocked off-center at the eye, the fly will swim unnaturally. Check the knot often, especially if you are not getting hits.

20. Wind knots weaken leaders by 50 percent. Don't take a chance, re-tie.

21. A territorial fish will often take the first cast if the presentation is well executed. If it doesn't want it then, it won't want it on repeated casts.

22. Mobility is critical to locating trophy fish on large bodies of water. Boats are more efficient than wading or tubing, or when fishing big unknown lakes.

A 6-pound high-desert rainbow, from Clark Canyon Reservoir, Montana. (Sheely Photo)

23. Fish are visual feeders. Flies constructed of materials that breathe and move naturally will trigger a trout's feeding instincts.

24. One of the greatest skills we possess, is learning to use our eyesight to spot cruising fish, feeding directions and rise types. It's a key indicator of the presentation technique and pattern required.

25. From an angling perspective, big trout are most vulnerable when protected by cover. Learn to stalk them when there is a ruffled surface, slanted sun, semi-darkness, algae, or around weeds, logs, and rocks.

26. Learn to spot nervous water, slight surface disturbances caused by feeding trout.

27. If trout appear to not be feeding or refuse a good presentation, the problem is probably external and not correctable. If trout are feeding and refuse your offering, change. The problem is with you.

28. Always fish with polarized glasses. To see cruising fish requires rapt attention and clear vision.

29. Certain trout foods are available year-round, some seasonally. Learn the timetables and fish with patterns that simulate those food sources most available.

Early morning on Upper Klamath Lake, a prime time for hooking big rainbows.

30. When trout are not selectively feeding, use the most suggestive pattern in your box and fish it slowly.

31. Over 90 percent of what big trout eat lives under the water, not on the surface.

32 Dry fly fishing, while great fun, is an inefficient technique for trophy trout.

33. Trout are creatures of habit. Whenever you catch an outsize trout, note the habitat, time of day, weather conditions, fly pattern, line type, and retrieve. If it worked once, it'll work again.

34. Large patterns that work well in spring, usually scare fall fish. In autumn, reduce your fly by a size or two.

A big trout cruising under flat water is a test of all your skills.

35. Big trout are masters of their living space. They know when hatches begin, what insects are available, how those insects behave. Keep that in mind when you choose your fly, line, and retrieve.

36. Low water concentrates fish, both the giant trophies we want, and the smaller bait fish they want.

37. Trout are easier to locate when water temperatures hit 68 degrees or more. Concentrate on working cooler areas, inlets, springs, and well oxygenated areas.

38. Rule of fishing thumb: warm or low water concentrates trout, cold or high water spreads them out.

39. Summer low water levels coupled with higher temperatures reduce oxygen and force trout to migrate to areas more acceptable.

40. On lakes you fish regularly, learn them well enough to predict seasonal movements.

41. Limited presentation skills limit the chance for success. Fish often to hone those skills.

42. Anglers who have difficulty casting more than 40 feet will catch fewer fish than those who can cast 50 feet or more.

43. When a trout really wants your fly, it seldom misses. If it does miss, they never really wanted it to begin with. Change flies and use different sizes and colors.

44. Console yourself with the fact that the best pattern ever tied is worthless if fish don't see it or want it.

45. When blind casting, space casts 10 feet apart to effectively cover the water. Never cast in the same place unless you are getting hit.

46. Weather affects trout behavior. A change overhead will usually trigger a change underwater.

47. Small trout eat bugs. Trophy trout eat fish or any animal that will fit between their jaws.

48. You can't catch a fish that doesn't want to be caught.

49. The best leaders are inexpensive. Don't cut corners here. The leader and tippet are usually the most overlooked part of our tackle. For a big fish predator, they are often the difference between success and failure.

50. The exclusive use of any fly, line or retrieve can severely limit your knowledge and success.

51. Leaders less than 9-feet are difficult to lay softly on the water. More often than not, they crash the surface and spook fish.

52. If you are right handed and the wind is blowing right to left, turn your wrist so the rod tip is over your left shoulder and extend your arm above your head to avoid being hit by the fly. If you are left handed, reverse the process.

This big rainbow was hooked while stalking minnows in shallow water.

53. Trout feed selectively less than 10 percent of the time. On the other hand, opportunistic feeding occurs about 90 percent of the time.

54. A drifting boat spooks fish and makes a proper presentation impossible. Put your anchor down.

55. Selective feeding not only means matching the size, shape, and color of an insect, but the form of that insect, such as pupa, larva, emerger, or dun.

56. Selecting the right fly line means determining what depth the fish are feeding at, and which line will hold your fly in that zone the longest.

57. To intercept cruising feeders, count the seconds between rises, determine direction and cast to the spot where the fish will rise next.

58. The keys to stillwater success include, fly selection, line selection, retrieve, and casting.

59. When fishing nymphs in lakes, never assume your pattern is being eaten because of what you think it imitates. If it is suggestive, it may be attracting strikes because of the way you retrieve it or the depth and angle you are fishing it.

60. Flies are divided into two categories imitators and suggestive. Direct imitations are designed to imitate one food source. Suggestive patterns are almost always more productive because they loosely imitate many foods.

61. Selective feeding not only means that trout want a specific food, but want it in a specific zone or depth where they normally expect to find it.

62. Pattern selection is relative to the retrieve and both are dictated by line choice. We can't be sure what a trout will eat, but we can be sure of the depth he wants it.

63. Except for spawning, food and oxygen/temperature is the primary reason trout migrate within a lake.

100 Tips For Fly-Fishing Stillwaters

64. Before changing flies, never assume that your fly is being rejected. Many casts are made into barren waters and never seen by fish. Change patterns when you are confident trout have seen it but refused.

65. The shoals or shallows are the greatest food-producing areas in any stillwater fishery.

66. More than 70 percent of strikes occur in the first 10 feet of a retrieve, 20 percent in the next 10 feet, and less than 10 percent during the remainder of the retrieve regardless of the distance you cast.

67. Trout always look up for food, never down, unless rooting on the bottom.

68. Most of the limitations we face on stillwaters are self-imposed.

69. Find areas in a lake with the three essentials--food, cover and an comfortable oxygen-water temperature level and you will find fish.

70. Weed beds are prime areas for locating trout because they contain the three essentials for trout to survive.

71. Floating lines will catch more fish if left motionless on the water or retrieved with a very slow hand twist. Retrieving a floating line fast creates surface disturbance that puts fish down.

72. Big trout specialists always anticipate a strike, others hope for one.

73. Even selective trout are opportunists and sometimes it is better to throw a big juicy whatever, than to compete for attention with thousands of look alike insects.

74. When fishing from a boat, never drift when fishing downwind. Otherwise, you may be retrieving slack instead of your fly.

75. Trout become selective feeders when large numbers of a specific insect appear on the water.

76. Whenever sight fishing a rise, cast to the closest fish first to avoid lining unseen targets.

Late evening is prime time for stalking big trout

Careful wading is critical when stalking big trout in shallow water. Note fish, and current break line.

77. Many strikes are missed when you allow slack to enter your retrieve. Keep a tight line by sticking the top few inches of your rod underwater.

78. If you plan to fish a lake from shore early in the morning, the trout will already be there waiting for you.

79. When wading, never be moving while retrieving your fly. Remember, sounds travel faster and further underwater than above.

80. Few anglers realize line selection (which determines depth) and speed of retrieve are more important than pattern selection.

81. A trout's food preference is largely influenced by availability and nutritional (protein) value.

82. In stillwater, scuds, dragon flies, damselfly nymphs, and leeches are usually favored over caddis and mayflies by big trout.

83. When something works, don't change it, just refine it for consistency.

84. Intermediate fly lines offer stillwater anglers more retrieve options than other lines because of the very slow sink rates.

85. Most big trout are never caught because they begin to feed after we leave the water at night.

86. Leaders should be 12 to 18 feet with floating lines, 9 to 15 feet with intermediates, and 6 to 9 feet with fast sinking lines unless conditions dictate otherwise.

100 Tips For Fly-Fishing Stillwaters

Wendy Hudson with a Upper Klamath Lake rainbow taken on a black leech pattern.

87. Lakes have their highest oxygen content immediately after ice-out. Look for big trout to cruise the shallows near shore during these periods.

88. Regardless of how far you can cast, most casts don't come down in a straight line. Presentation suffers unless you immediately pull out slack, otherwise you fail to move the fly, resulting in missed strikes.

Killing a trout of this size is a waste. If you must kill a trout to eat, kill a smaller fish. (Gordon Honey photo)

180

FLY-FISHING STILLWATERS

89. It's not the amount of weight you put on a fly that's important, but where you place it. Position weight at the head to create an undulating motion when the fly is retrieved.

90. Don't kill trout to check stomach contents, just pay attention, or use suggestive nymph patterns.

91. The fastest way to learn fly-fishing is to do it.

92. Trout fishing is most productive when external factors are consistent. Inconsistent weather patterns produce inconsistent trout bites.

93. Don't be fooled thinking that long tails on flies result in short strikes. Long tails create motion, a key to suggestiveness. Short strikes indicate a problem with your presentation or the wrong hook size.

94. Trolling a fly from a float tube is effective and fun but doesn't teach us how to retrieve the fly, or improve our casting and presentation techniques.

95. A fly line's main purpose is to deliver the fly to the fish, but it also allows us to fish flies in a manner that matches natural movements of the insect which we are striving to imitate.

96. When using a fly pattern that matches a food source traveling parallel in the water, you don't want to use a floating or sink-tip line that will move the fly up through the water column.

97. The forgiveness of a flexible soft tip rod is critical when using small tippets against big fish.

98. Match the weight of the rod to the size of the fly and tippet you use, not the size of the fish.

99. Sight fishing requires extra patience, refined presentations, and a high threshold for excitement.

100. It's not the distance you pull the fly on the retrieve, but the speed that determines success. Most insects move slowly. The smaller the fly, the slower the retrieve.

And when you get frustrated remember, there's always tomorrow!

CONCLUSION

Fly-fishing in stillwater over the past 25 years has expanded my definitions of patience, frustration, jubilation, and disappointment.

The more we fish lakes, the more it exposes how little we really know or understand about trout and how they behave.

Because stillwater fly fishermen specializing in trophy trout are constantly learning and pushing into new areas, there are no real experts in this arena, only good fishermen who have learned more than most.

I'd like to think that this book will provide enough clues to solve some of the mysteries and eliminate many of the intimidation factors that stand between us, open water, and the biggest trout of our life.

There is, however, simply no substitute for fishing. As we gain experience, we begin to identify with all of the pieces of the puzzle. And when we understand where all of the pieces of the stillwater puzzle are located, then we can consistently complete the puzzle.

Fishing on lakes with a fly is, I believe, the fastest growing segment of fly-fishing in the past 15 years. There are reasons for this growth; the solitude it affords, increasingly limited stream access, proliferation of float tubes, kick boats and the like, and the realization that lakes, more than flowing water, simply have the ingredients to grow truly trophy-size trout.

Whatever the reason, there is no doubt that stillwater fly-fishing is having an impact and making inroads in the fly-fishing fraternity at a time when fly-fishing popularity is rocketing. The intensity of this interest is pushing manufacturers to develop tackle specific to solving stillwater problems, which in turn will permit more breakthroughs in our sport.

If you are exploring stillwater fly-fishing for the first time, remember that you are in an alien environment with natural rules that separate it from those governing fishing in moving water.

The point of this book is to give you the educational edge that will allow you to learn how to catch trophy trout in stillwaters. Once gained, I trust that you will use this knowledge responsibly with a full measure of catch-and-release ethics.

This way you may catch that fish of a lifetime, perhaps several times in the same lifetime. And wouldn't that be something!

---Denny Rickards,
Stillwater Fly Fisherman

EPILOGUE

With this project now completed, I think tomorrow I'll go fish a lake somewhere.

I'll take my soft-tip 9-foot rod for a 5/6 line, and two fly lines: an intermediate and a translucent Stillwater line, and rig both with 12-foot leaders and 5X tippets.

I'll start with a Seal Bugger, but if I'm not getting hits or if conditions warrant, I won't hesitate to change to a Stillwater Callibaetis or AP Emerger Nymph.

Most of my casts will be 60 to 70 feet, and if there is any wind I'll throw across it.

I'll work the shoreline areas first, then look for weed beds and springs, if there are any.

I'll start at first light and take advantage of windy periods when they occur. If there is any algae, I'll take my time, anticipating takes near the end of the retrieve.

I'll check the water temperature, but will use a long slow pull with my seal bugger, and if I switch to one of the smaller nymphs I'll employ a short, slow or rapid one-inch pull depending on the conditions present.

And I'll learn something tomorrow because this is what I do.

This is what works.

--Denny Rickards
Stillwater Fly Fisherman,
Trophy Trout Specialist

Bibliography

BORGER, Gary A., *Presentation*, Tomorrow River Press, Harrisburg, PA, 1995.

BORGER, Gary A. *Naturals*, Stackpole Books, Harrisburg, PA, 1980.

CORDES, Ron and Randall Kaufmann, *Lake Fishing With A Fly*, Frank Amato Publications, Inc., Portland, OR, 1984.

DAVY, Alfred G., *The Gilly: A Fly-Fisher's Guide*, Alf Davy, Kelowna, B.C. Canada,1985.

HAFELE, Rick and Dave Hughes, *The Complete Book of Western Hatches*, Frank Amato Publications, Inc. Portland, OR, 1981.

HUGHES, Dave, *Strategies For Stillwater*, Stackpole Books, Harrisburg, PA, 1991.

McCLANE, A. J., *McClane's New Standard Fishing Encyclopedia*, Holt Rinehart and Winston, New York, NY, 1974.

MERWIN, John, *Stillwater Trout*, Nick Lyons Books, New York, NY,1980.

RAYMOND, Steve, *Kamloops*, Frank Amato Publications, Inc., Portland, OR,1980, 1994.

ROBERTS, Donald V., *Fly Fishing Still Waters*, Frank Amato Publications, Inc., Portland, OR, 1984.

SHAW, Jack, *Fly Fishing The Trout Lakes*, Mitchell Press Ltd., Canada, 1976.

Get The Complete Stillwater Fly System: Custom Rod, Lines, Flies

*ORDER YOUR AUTOGRAPHED
GIFT COPY TODAY!*

FLY-FISHING STILLWATERS FOR TROPHY TROUT

P.O. Box 470 • Fort Klamath, Oregon 97626

SEND TO:

Name _____

Address _____

City _____

State_____ Zip _____

☐ **$34.95** Autographed Copy of *Fly-Fishing Stillwaters For Trophy Trout*

☐ **$100** Gold Embossed, Leather Bound, Limited Edition.
   Only 100 Copies Printed. Includes A Personalized Autograph plus A Custom Set Of Denny's Top 6 Stillwater Nymph Patterns, Personally Tied By The Author.
   • *A Beautiful Collector's Classic* •

☐ **$29.95** 55-Minute VHS Video, *Fly-Fishing Stillwaters For Trophy Trout*

☐ **$29.95** 55-Minute VHS Video, *Tying Stillwater Patterns For Trophy Trout*

☐ **And, YES, Please contact me, I'm seriously interested in ordering:**

  ☐ Denny Rickards' Stillwater Fly Patterns (See, Denny's Deadly Dozen, Chapter 6)

  ☐ Denny Rickards' Stillwater Custom Fly Rod

  ☐ Scientific Angler's Fly Lines ☐ *Intermediate* ☐ *Stillwater*

Please add $5.00 shipping & handling for each item *(Books are shipped separately)*. Total $_____

☐ Paid with order   ☐ Ship C.O.D.   ☐ Notify When Available

☐ VISA   ☐ M/C   Account #_____ Expiraton Date_____

_____   _____
Authorized Signature   Print Authorized Signature